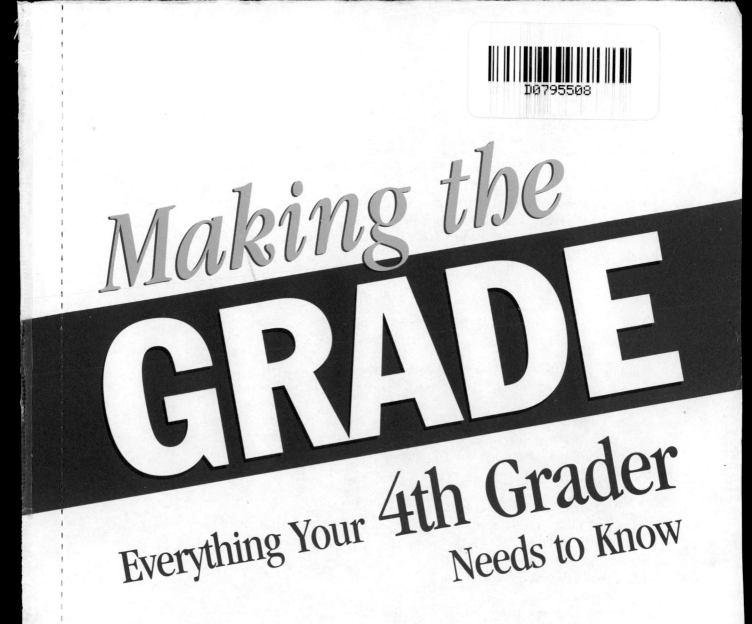

Making the GRADE

Everything Your 4th Grader Needs to Know

by
Robert R. Roth

BARRON'S

About the Author

Robert R. Roth has been teaching for more than 30 years in Illinois. He is a member of numerous educational organizations and a National Endowment for the Humanities grant recipient. Robert graduated cum laude from West Virginia Wesleyan College with a B.A., and he holds an M.A. from Teachers College, Columbia University in New York City. He is currently working toward completion of a certificate in education administration and supervision at National-Louis University.

All inquiries should be addressed to:
Barron's Educational Series, Inc.
250 Wireless Boulevard
Hauppauge, New York 11788
http://www.barronseduc.com

Library of Congress Catalog Card No. 2003045107

International Standard Book No. 0-7641-2480-3

Library of Congress Cataloging-in-Publication Data
Roth, Robert R.
    Everything your 4th grader needs to know / Robert R. Roth.
        p. cm.— (Making the grade)
    Includes bibliographical references (p.) and index.
    ISBN 0-7641-2480-3 (alk. paper)
        1. Fourth grade (Education)—Curricula—United States. I. Title. II. Making the grade (Hauppauge, N.Y.)

    LB15714th .R68 2004
    372.24'1—dc21   2003045107

Printed in China
9 8 7 6 5 4 3 2

Table of Contents

PROMOTING LITERACY

MATH

SCIENCE

SOCIAL STUDIES

How to Use This Book

Welcome to the *Making the Grade* series! These seven books offer tools and strategies for hands-on, active learning at the kindergarten through sixth-grade levels. Each book presents real-world, engaging learning experiences in the core areas of language arts, math, science, and social studies at age-appropriate levels.

Who should use this book?

Whether you're a stay-at-home or working parent with children in school, a homeschooler who's guiding your children's education, or a teacher who's looking for additional ideas to supplement classroom learning experiences, this book is for you.

- If you have children in school, *Making the Grade* can be used in conjunction with your child's curriculum because it offers real-world, hands-on activities that exercise the concepts and topics he or she is being taught in school.
- If you're a homeschooler who's guiding your children's education, this series presents you with easy-to-access, engaging ways to interact with your child.
- If you're a teacher, this book also can be a source for additional activities.

This book is your passport to a whole new world, one that gives you enough support to be a successful educator while encouraging independent learning with one child or shared learning among your children.

What is *Making the Grade*?

We're glad you asked! First, we'd like to tell you what it's not. It's not a textbook series. Rather, each book in the series delivers age-appropriate content in language arts, math, science, and social studies in an open-ended, flexible manner that incorporates the "real" world. You can use this book as a supplement to your core learning instruction or use it to get a jump start on the fundamentals.

Each subject section presents lessons comprised of both "teaching" pages and "student" pages. And each book in the *Making the Grade* series is perforated for flexible learning so that both you and your child can tear out the pages that you're working on and use one book together.

How do the lessons work?

The teaching and student pages work together. The lesson instruction and teaching ideas for each specific lesson appear first. Activities that offer opportunities for your child to practice the specific skills and review the concepts being taught follow. Throughout each lesson, hands-on activities are incorporated using concepts that are meaningful and relevant to kids' daily lives. Each lesson also reveals how to enrich the learning experience through field trips, online research, excursions to the library, and more. Creativity and imagination abound! The activities account for all kinds of learners—that is, visual, auditory, and kinesthetic. (For more information on learning styles, see the Glossary on page 353.) Be encouraged to allow ample time for discovery of the concepts in each lesson— whether that be a few hours or a few days—and ample time for unstructured independent exploration. Your student can help guide the pace. Follow your child's interests, as it will make learning fun and valuable.

Objective and Background

Each lesson opens with an objective that tells you exactly what the lesson is about. The background of the lesson follows, giving you the rationale behind the importance of the material being addressed. Each lesson is broken down for you so that you and your student can see how the skills and concepts taught are useful in everyday situations.

Materials and Vocabulary

Have you ever done a project and found out you're missing something when you get to the end? A list of materials is given up front so you'll know what you need before you begin. The lessons take into account that you have access to your local library, a computer and the Internet, writing instruments, a calculator, and a notebook and loose paper, so you won't find these listed. The materials are household items when possible so that even the most technical of science experiments can be done easily. The *Making the Grade* series paves the way for your learning experience whether you and your student are sitting side by side on the couch or in a classroom, at the library, or even on vacation!

Following the materials list, vocabulary words may be given offering clear, easy-to-understand definitions.

Let's Begin

Let's Begin is just that, "Let's Begin!" The instructional portion of the lesson opens with easy, user-friendly, numbered steps that guide you through the teaching of a particular lesson. Here you'll find opportunities to interact with your student and engage in discussions about what he or she is learning. There also are opportunities for your student to practice his or her critical-thinking skills to make the learning experience richer.

In the margins are interesting facts about what you're studying, time-savers, or helpful ideas.

Ways to Extend the Lesson

Every lesson concludes with ways to extend the lesson—teaching tips, such as hints, suggestions, or ideas, for you to use in teaching the lesson or a section of the lesson. Each lesson also ends with an opportunity for you to "check in" and assess how well your student has mastered the skill or grasped the concepts being taught in the lesson. The For Further Reading section lists books that you can use as additional references and support in teaching the lesson. It also offers your student more opportunities to practice a skill or a chance to look deeper into the content.

Student Learning Pages

Student Learning Pages immediately follow the teaching pages in each lesson. These pages offer fun opportunities to practice the skills and concepts being taught. And there are places where your student gets to choose what to do next and take ownership of his or her learning.

Visual Aids

Throughout the book you'll see references to the Venn Diagram, Comparison Chart, Web, Sequence Chain, and Writing Lines found in the back of the book. Many lessons incorporate these graphic organizers, or visual methods of organizing information, into the learning. If one is used in a lesson, it will be listed in the materials so that prior to the lesson you or your student can make a photocopy of it from the back of the book or you can have your student copy it into his or her notebook. See the Glossary for more information on graphic organizers.

What about field trips or learning outside the classroom?

One very unique feature of the *Making the Grade* series are the In Your Community activities at the end of each subject section. These activities describe ways to explore your community, taking advantage of your local or regional culture, industry, and environment while incorporating the skills learned in the lessons. For example, you can have your student help out at a farmer's market or with a local environmental group. These unique activities can supplement your ability to provide support for subjects. The activities give your student life experiences upon which he or she can build and expand the canvas upon which he or she learns.

These pages are identified in the Table of Contents so that you can read them first as a way to frame your student's learning.

How do I know if my student is learning the necessary skills?

Although each lesson offers an opportunity for on-the-spot assessment, a formalized assessment section is located in the back of this book. You'll find a combination of multiple-choice and open-ended questions testing your student on the skills, concepts, and topics covered.

Also, at the end of every subject section is a We Have Learned checklist. This checklist provides a way for you and your student to summarize what you've accomplished. It lists specific concepts, and there is additional space for you and your student to write in other topics you've covered.

Does this book come with answers?

Yes. Answers are provided in the back of the book for both the lessons and assessment.

What if this book uses a homeschooling or educational term I'm not familiar with?

In addition to the vocabulary words listed in the lessons, a two-page Glossary is provided in the back of the book. Occasionally terms will surface that may need further explanation in order for the learning experience to flourish. In the Glossary, you'll find terms explained simply to help you give your student a rewarding learning experience free from confusion.

Will this book help me find resources within the schools for homeschoolers?

In Communicating Between Home and School, there are suggestions for how to take advantage of the opportunities and resources offered by your local schools and how these benefits can enhance your homeschooling learning experiences.

I'm new to homeschooling. How can I find out about state regulations, curriculum, and other resources?

In For Homeschoolers at the beginning of the book, you'll find information about national and state legislation, resources for curriculum and materials, and other references. Also included is a comprehensive list of online resources for everything from homeschooling organizations to military homeschooling to homeschooling supplies.

How can I use this book if my student attends a public or private school?

Making the Grade fits into any child's educational experience—whether he or she is being taught at home or in a traditional school setting.

For Homeschoolers

Teaching children at home isn't a new phenomenon. But it's gaining in popularity as caregivers decide to take a more active role in the education of their children. More people are learning what homeschoolers have already known, that children who are homeschooled succeed in college, the workplace, and society.

Whether you're new to homeschooling or have been educating your children at home for quite some time, you may have found the homeschooling path to have occasional detours in finding resources. This book hopes to minimize those detours by offering information on state regulations, homeschooling approaches and curriculum, and other resources to keep you on the path toward a rewarding learning experience.

Regulations

There never has been a federal law prohibiting parents from homeschooling their children. A homeschooler isn't required to have a teaching degree, nor is he or she required to teach children in a specific location. Each state has its own compulsory attendance laws for educational programs as well as its own set of regulations, educational requirements, and guidelines for those who homeschool.

Regardless of the level of regulation your state has, there are ways to operate your homeschool with success. Here are a few tips as you negotiate the homeschooling waters:

- Be aware of your district's and state's requirements.
- The rules and regulations may seem like more trouble than they're worth. The National Home Education Network (NHEN) may be able to help. Go to the association's Web site at *http://www.nhen.org*. For even more information on your state's laws and related references, see Homeschooling Online Resources that follow. They can help you find information on your specific state and may be able to direct you to local homeschooling groups.
- Veteran homeschoolers in your area can be a fountain of practical knowledge about the laws. Consult a variety of homeschoolers for a clear perspective, as each family has an educational philosophy and approach that best suits it.

Homeschooling Military Families

Frequently moving from location to location can be exhausting for families with one or more parent in the military. If you have school-age children, it can be even more complicated. Schools across states and U.S. schools in other countries often don't follow the same curriculum, and states often can have varying curriculum requirements for each grade.

The Department of Defense Dependent Schools (DoDDS) is responsible for the military educational system. There are three options for military families in which they can educate their children:

1. attend school with other military children
2. if in a foreign country, attend the local school in which the native language is spoken, although this option may require approval
3. homeschool

Homeschooling can provide consistency for families that have to relocate often. The move itself, along with the new culture your family will be exposed to, is a learning experience that can be incorporated into the curriculum. Note that military families that homeschool must abide by the laws of the area in which they reside, which may be different from where they claim residency for tax purposes. If your relocation takes your family abroad, one downside is the lack of curriculum resources available on short notice. Nonetheless, military homeschoolers may be able to use resources offered at base schools.

Approaches and Curriculum

If you're reading this book you've probably already heard of many different approaches to and methods of homeschooling, which some homeschoolers refer to as *unschooling* (see the Glossary for more information). Unschooling is not synonymous with homeschooling; it's a philosophy and style of education followed by some homeschoolers. It's important that you choose one approach or method that works best for you—there's no right or wrong way to homeschool!

The curriculum and materials that are used vary from person to person, but there are organizations that offer books, support, and materials to homeschoolers. Many homeschoolers find that a combination of methods works best. That's why *Making the Grade* was created!

Support Groups and Organizations

Homeschooling has become more popular, and the United States boasts a number of nationally recognized homeschooling organizations. Also, nearly every state has its own homeschooling organization to provide information on regulations in addition to other support. Many religious and ethnic affiliations also have their own homeschooling organizations too, in addition to counties and other groups.

Homeschooling Online Resources

Beginning on the next page are some of the online resources available for homeschoolers. You also can check your phone book for local organizations and resources.

National Organizations

Alliance for Parental Involvement in Education
http://www.croton.com/allpie/

Alternative Education Resource Organization (AERO)
http://www.edrev.org/links.htm

American Homeschool Association (AHA)
http://www.americanhomeschoolassociation.org/

Home School Foundation
http://www.homeschoolfoundation.org

National Coalition of Alternative Community Schools
http://www.ncacs.org/

National Home Education Network (NHEN)
http://www.nhen.org/

National Home Education Research Institute (NHERI)
http://www.nheri.org

National Homeschooling Association (NHA)
http://www.n-h-a.org

Homeschooling and the Law

Advocates for the Rights of Homeschoolers (ARH)
http://www.geocities.com/arhfriends/

American Bar Association
http://www.abanet.org

Children with Special Needs

Children with Disabilities
http://www.childrenwithdisabilities.ncjrs.org/

Institutes for the Achievement of Human Potential (IAHP)
http://www.iahp.org/

National Challenged Homeschoolers Associated Network (NATHHAN)
http://www.nathhan.com/

Military Homeschooling

Department of Defense Dependent Schools/Education Activity (DoDDS)
http://www.odedodea.edu/

Books, Supplies, Curriculum

Federal Resources for Educational Excellence
http://www.ed.gov/free/

Home Schooling Homework
http://www.dailyhomework.org/

Home School Products
http://www.homeschooldiscount.com/

Homeschooler's Curriculum Swap
http://theswap.com/

HomeSchoolingSupply.com
http://www.homeschoolingsupply.com/

General Homeschooling Resources

A to Z Home's Cool
http://www.gomilpitas.com/

Family Unschoolers Network
http://www.unschooling.org

Home Education Magazine
http://www.home-ed-magazine.com/

Home School Legal Defense Association (HSLDA)
http://www.hslda.org

Homeschool Central
http://www.homeschoolcentral.com

Homeschool Internet Yellow Pages
http://www.homeschoolyellowpages.com/

Homeschool Social Registry at Homeschool Media Network
http://www.homeschoolmedia.net

Homeschool World
http://www.home-school.com/

Homeschool.com
http://www.homeschool.com/

HSAdvisor.com
http://www.hsadvisor.com/

Unschooling.com
http://www.unschooling.com/

Waldorf Without Walls
http://www.waldorfwithoutwalls.com/

Communicating Between Home and School

For homeschoolers, often there is limited contact with the schools beyond that which is required by the state. Yet a quick glance at your local schools will reveal opportunities, resources, and benefits that can offer you flexibility and that can supplement your child's total learning experience.

Special Needs

If you have a child with special needs, such as dyslexia or ADHD (attention deficit hyperactivity disorder), taking advantage of the programs and services your public school provides can expand your support system and give you some relief in working with your child. In many instances, the easy access and little or no cost of these services makes this a viable option for homeschoolers.

Depending on your child's diagnosed needs, some school districts may offer full services and programs, while some may only provide consultations. Some school districts' special education departments have established parent support networks that you may be able to participate in as a homeschooler. States and school districts vary in terms of what homeschoolers are allowed to participate in, so check with your local school administrator and then check with your state's regulations to verify your eligibility.

Two organizations, the Home School Legal Defense Association (HSLDA) and the National Challenged Homeschoolers Association Network (NATHHAN), offer a wide range of information and assistance on services and programs available for special needs children. Check them out on the Internet at *http://www.hslda.org* and *http://www.nathhan.com*. Your local homeschooling group—especially veteran homeschoolers—will have practical information you can use.

Additionally, some homeschooling parents combine the resources of a school with those offered by a private organization to maximize support.

Gifted Children

If your child is considered gifted, your local public school may have programs available for students who require additional intellectual attention. Check with your local school administrator and your state's regulations first. In addition to providing information on special needs children, HSLDA and NATHHAN offer resources for parents of gifted children.

Don't be afraid to check out the colleges in your area, too. Many times colleges, especially community colleges, offer classes or onetime workshops that might be of interest to your child. Check with your local schools to see how you can take advantage of these opportunities.

Extracurricular Activities

Opportunities abound for homeschoolers to get involved with extracurricular activities. Clubs and interest groups allow children and parents to interact and share ideas with other homeschoolers. Extracurricular activities not only enrich the learning experience, they can also provide opportunities for friendship.

You might want to meet regularly for planned activities focusing on a particular subject matter, such as math. You could meet at someone's home or perhaps at a community or religious center. A parent can lead the discussions on a particular topic, but sometimes other knowledgeable individuals can be invited to teach, either for a fee or on a volunteer basis. Another enriching idea is to form a theme group, such as a science-experiment club, an adventure book club, or a nature club. Or just get together to simply share ideas or plan group activities, such as a craft project or a book discussion. Parents and children can work together to plan activities and events.

If you can't find a meeting on a particular subject area or theme in your region, don't hesitate to form one in your community. One way to begin might be to check out the Homeschool Social Register at *http://www.homeschoolmedia.net*. Here you can find other homeschoolers in your area and homeschoolers who share your educational philosophy and interests.

Other extracurricular activities, such as 4-H, Girl Scouts, Boy Scouts, religious youth groups, arts and crafts, athletics, music, and language or debate clubs, may be offered in your community. They can provide additional opportunities for your homeschooler to interact with his or her peers and have a valuable learning experience at the same time. Extracurricular activities offered at local schools also may prove worthwhile to investigate.

Returning to School

If you plan on having your child return to school, taking advantage of the programs and opportunities offered can help ease the transition back into the classroom. Your child will already experience a sense of familiarity with his or her surroundings and peers, which can help smooth the transition to a different structure of learning.

Meet Your Fourth Grader

No matter what age, every child is one of a kind with distinct influences shaping his or her development. However, in the fourth-grade year the spark of individuality begins to manifest itself in a child's behavior, preferences, and talents at a deeper level. Differences between children begin to grow more apparent, as does the unpredictability of the same child's behavior from day to day. Nonetheless, there are a number of characteristics that many nine to ten and a half year olds share. Having an understanding about the common tendencies of this growth stage can be helpful as you strive to understand your nine to ten and a half year old and promote his or her well-being.

Take Note of Internal Discoveries

Your fourth grader is on a path of discovery that takes him or her inward. The feelings, talents, interests, personal traits, and learning style that emerge at this time are coming from a very authentic and personal place. This is so much so that some savvy career counselors will ask their 30-year-old clients who are examining their professional direction, "What is it that you enjoyed doing when you were nine years old?"

It may seem as though the child who was so recently eager to share every private feeling has now withdrawn. Although your child may have experienced introverted stages before, this introversion may be more profound and closer to home. Similarly, children who have remained extroverted throughout their development may, for the first time, display introverted tendencies. Instead of trying to reclaim the position of emotional confidant with your child, be supportive by taking an interest in your child's talents. Develop a facility for naming them and pointing them out. You may even want to take some notes in a journal about the ideas and activities your child is excited about or excelling in. When the doubts and challenges of adolescence kick in and your child insists he or she is completely awkward and can't do anything right, these notes about your child's strengths and interests will help you keep it all in perspective.

Recognize Needs for Choice and Time

Learning from the prescribed methods of others is unstimulating and even insulting to a fourth grader. A fourth-grade child can be best served when allowed to learn from his or her own mistakes, provided he or she feels safe enough from criticism and humiliation to make them. Your fourth grader will appreciate being allowed to discover unique methods of solving problems. Your child may also want time to review each step to learn from mistakes.

It's important to a fourth grader that he or she feel satiated and satisfied with the completion of a task before moving on to something new. A fourth-grade child has a keen eye for the details and a natural sense of the rhythm in his or her own learning process. He or she needs time to plan, think, warm up, practice, become engrossed in the work, experiment, and slowly wind down before changing focus.

When hurried, a fourth-grade child can become discouraged and anxious and may even choose to give up the project altogether. Your assistance in creating a realistic schedule for your time-challenged fourth grader and gently reminding him or her of halfway points and approaching end points in work time can be helpful.

Acknowledge Skill Seeking and Perfectionism

Fourth graders are ready and eager to soak up new skills. A fourth grader's persistence makes him or her an excellent learner when a safe and caring environment is provided. Activities involving hand-eye coordination and fine motor skills are especially satisfying for children at this age. From technical drawing and fine arts to handiwork, a fourth-grade child wants to increase his or her repertoire of skills. He or she may develop an interest in learning calligraphy, sewing, knitting, and other types of needlework. Sports expertise such as hitting a baseball or learning specific soccer skills also serve your fourth grader's desire to gain new talents. Some fourth graders will be inclined to begin music lessons. When given the time to practice, children at this age can become proficient at their chosen activities.

Complicating the drive to expand his or her skills is a fourth grader's obsession with being perfect. Your child may show an apprehension to taking risks and a fear of looking bad or being embarrassed in front of others. In order to take the chances necessary to try new things and explore new talents, fourth graders need to feel cared for and respected. However, once your fourth grader finds a sense of competence in his or her talent, he or she will work at it persistently, openly, and joyfully.

Identify and Address Anxiety

Fourth graders tend to feel things deeply and can be moody. A fourth-grade child may be a worrier, make mountains out of molehills, and experience anxiety about things that are unknown or of which he or she is unsure. Often the insecurities, troubles, or resistance of a fourth-grade child are clearly evident in his or her physical complaints. Your fourth grader may suddenly come down with a case of acute sore arms when it's time to tidy up his or her bedroom. If there's an event he or she has anxiety about attending, an upset stomach may be the affliction. If the pattern of symptoms begins to focus around a certain activity or issue, you may try getting to the source of the discomfort by gently probing beyond the physical malaise to the real issue.

Today's children are subject to media pressure at younger ages. Although still childlike in most ways, your fourth grader may become concerned with seemingly teenage issues such as body image, weight, and opposite-sex relationships. Keep an open mind and an open ear to these concerns and resist the urge to discount your fourth grader as "too young" for these troubles. Playing a visualization game with your child can help boost self-esteem and confidence and can help diminish anxiety. Have your child visualize, or draw on paper, a picture or representation of the issue he or she is struggling with. Then have your child draw or visualize himself or herself next to the first image. Work with your child until his or her own image is at least twice as big as the fear, concern, or anxiety.

Encourage Group Participation

Fourth graders often naturally seek out groups of friends who are interested in doing the same things they are. Fourth-grade relationships are built on common interests, such as athletics, theater, arts, band, scouting, or camp groups. Being highly self-critical and often critical of others, fourth graders can have a great fear of being criticized by peers or adults. It's the feeling of competence that will make your fourth grader's highest self come forward. Performing successfully and using skills well in front of a group can be great confidence builders for a fourth grader.

A growing emphasis is placed on friendship at this age, and a fourth grader may begin picking up ideas about how to dress, talk, and act from his or her peer group. Although usually loyal to friends, fourth graders can become competitive in groups when moodiness and insecurity are present. Teasing, mocking, and fighting can occur, but group interaction is likely to be a positive experience if the values of compassion and respect are emphasized by supervising adults.

Embrace Independence and Values

A fourth grader's focus is beginning to move away from the family and toward the individual self and friends. This budding independence leads to an increasing desire and ability to care for others. Fourth graders are also known to be champions of fairness. At this age, a child develops a sense of the injustices that exist between people and won't hesitate to point them out. Ethics, truth, and responsibility are often found at the top of a fourth grader's list of values. To set a solid example and prove your fourth grader's faith in your actions, be conscientious about your judgments and disciplinary actions. If they are consistent and fair, you will find that your fourth grader responds much more favorably.

Impart Lessons of Consequence

Along with an acute attention to fairness, a fourth grader also seeks a sense of order and predictability in his or her world. Your child is more aware, responsible for himself or herself, and open to reason and logic. Fourth graders are comfortable living by clearly defined rules and having others live by them as well. A fourth grader needs you to acknowledge and respect his or her maturity level when making decisions and offering discipline. Your child may demonstrate new negotiating skills and want to use them when discussing household responsibilities, lesson work, and so on. This is normal developmental behavior; however, be aware of when your child is using manipulation and hold firm.

This is also an important stage for learning that every choice, positive as well as negative, has a corresponding consequence. A fourth grader is ripe for this lesson and is relying on the wise adults in his or her life to help administer it. Be careful not to shortchange your fourth grader of these timely lessons under the guise of protection. Demonstrate fairly that there are negative consequences of negative actions, such as destroying property or missing curfew, whether intentional or accidental. Conversely, the positive consequences of positive actions, such as helping a neighbor or cleaning up before being asked to, should also be pointed out.

Facilitate Learning

A fourth-grade child has the ability to concentrate for long periods of time and is drawn to in-depth learning. Fourth graders want to focus on a single topic and will investigate it at length. When given brief overviews of too many subjects at once, a fourth grader may become disinterested in your teaching. *Making the Grade* allows your child to choose his or her own pace and depth of learning. Each lesson includes hands-on activities that can extend the subject or topic being taught. The In Your Community activities provide ideas for expanding each subject area outside the home.

Many children also become visual learners at this age and are more comfortable when a topic they are exploring for the first time is presented visually, such as with a map, a diagram, or a picture. In their fondness for detail, fourth graders take a greater interest in the dictionary and thesaurus. Similarly, a fourth grader's artwork becomes more precision oriented. Fourth graders begin to move away from crayons and wide markers to finer tools such as colored pencils and ink pens. Your child may also be interested in expanding his or her skills with new media such as pastels or oil crayons.

Some fourth-grade children are, for the first time, reading for pleasure. Many children at this age become avid readers. Encourage your fourth grader to maintain a regular, or even daily, practice of silent reading. Although your child now reads well on his or her own, a fourth grader still benefits from your attention and participation in reading. Taking time to join your fourth grader in silent reading with a book of your own and maintaining a practice of reading to your child aloud are supportive ways to stay involved.

Enjoy Your Fourth Grader

Once the fear of embarrassment has been surpassed, the drive and enthusiasm for learning new skills will take your eager fourth grader far. This is a special time in your child's life, with many new ways of self-expression being developed. By showing interest in your child's chosen activities, friends, needs, and accomplishments, you are sure to share in your child's joys as well.

Promoting Literacy

Promoting Literacy

Key Topics

Fiction and Fables
Pages 3–16

Nouns and Pronouns
Pages 17–24

Adjectives and Adverbs
Pages 25–28

Biographies, Drama, and Poetry
Pages 29–46

Subjects and Predicates
Pages 47–50

Nonfiction and News Articles
Pages 51–62

Conjunctions, Prepositions, and Interjections
Pages 63–70

Irregular Verbs
Pages 71–74

Compare/Contrast, and Problem/Solution Writings
Pages 75–82

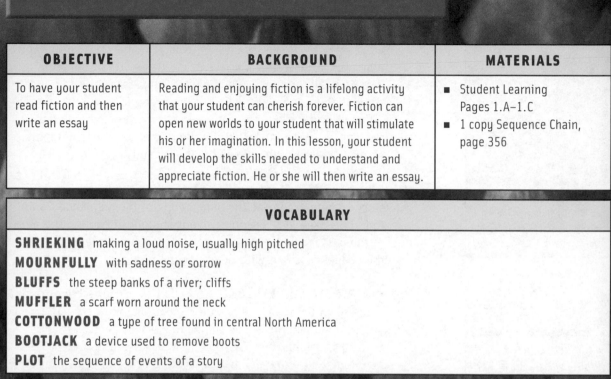

Reading and Writing

*Reading books can take you into unknown worlds
and set your imagination spinning.*

OBJECTIVE	BACKGROUND	MATERIALS
To have your student read fiction and then write an essay	Reading and enjoying fiction is a lifelong activity that your student can cherish forever. Fiction can open new worlds to your student that will stimulate his or her imagination. In this lesson, your student will develop the skills needed to understand and appreciate fiction. He or she will then write an essay.	<ul><li>Student Learning Pages 1.A–1.C</li><li>1 copy Sequence Chain, page 356</li></ul>

VOCABULARY

SHRIEKING making a loud noise, usually high pitched

MOURNFULLY with sadness or sorrow

BLUFFS the steep banks of a river; cliffs

MUFFLER a scarf worn around the neck

COTTONWOOD a type of tree found in central North America

BOOTJACK a device used to remove boots

PLOT the sequence of events of a story

Let's Begin

1 **INTRODUCE** Reveal that your student will read a section from *Little House on the Prairie* by Laura Ingalls Wilder. Explain that this book is fictional and is the second in a series of novels by Wilder. The series of books is about life on the American frontier in the 1800s. Discuss with your student what he or she knows about frontier life.

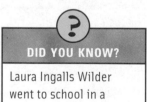

DID YOU KNOW?

Laura Ingalls Wilder went to school in a one-room schoolhouse.

2 **DISTRIBUTE AND BUILD** Distribute Student Learning Page 1.A. Review the vocabulary words (except *plot*). Give your student the meaning of each word and use it in a sentence. Explain that these are words he or she will encounter in the passage he or she is about to read. Then, for greater comprehension, ask your student to use each word in a sentence.

3 **READ** Now have your student read the story aloud. You could also allow time for your student to read silently. If he or she

Laura Ingalls Wilder's first book, Little House in the Big Woods, *was published when she was 65 years old.*

DID YOU KNOW?

Little House on the Prairie was a long-running series on television.

FOR FURTHER READING

In the Eye of the Storm, by Elizabeth Cody Kimmel and Scott Snow, ill. (HarperCollins Publishers, 2003).

Laura's Early Years Collection: Little House in the Big Woods, Little House on the Prairie, On the Banks of Plum Creek (*Little House Series: Classic Stories*), by Laura Ingalls Wilder and Garth Williams, ill. (HarperCollins Children's Books, 1999).

comes across a word he or she doesn't know, encourage him or her to figure out the meaning in the context of the sentence.

4   EXPLORE Talk to your student about the background of the story. Life on the western frontier was often harsh. With your student check out books or search the Internet for information about frontier life. If you'd like, go to http://www.pbs.org and search for frontier life. Together you and your student can look at how three modern-day families lived in rural Montana as though it were the 1880s. You can read about what life was like, what school was like, what food was available, and so on. You may even want to rent the videocassettes or DVDs showing how these families survived. Then have a conversation with your student about which time period he or she feels would be more difficult to live in—then or now—and why. Encourage your student to keep a journal and write down his or her thoughts about the stories and poems he or she reads.

5   ANALYZE PLOT Point out that **plot** is the sequence of events a story is composed of. Distribute a copy of the Sequence Chain found on page 356. Encourage your student to explain the plot of the passage he or she just read. Have your student complete the Sequence Chain with details of the plot.

6   DISTRIBUTE AND EXPLORE Now discuss if your student thinks Laura liked living on the frontier. Encourage your student to give you reasons why he or she thinks this way. Then distribute Student Learning Page 1.B to your student. Tell him or her that he or she will write an essay answering this question. Guide your student through the essay as necessary.

7   EXPAND If your student shows interest, you may wish to have him or her read the entire book, or even the entire series. If your library has two copies available of the book, you may wish to read them together.

Branching Out

TEACHING TIP

When your student is reading the passage, you might want to try different reading techniques. For example, your student can read the entire passage silently or aloud. You might also take turns reading.

CHECKING IN

To assess your student's understanding of how to read fiction, have him or her choose a story to read to you. When he or she is finished, ask your student to tell you the plot of the story and what makes that particular story enjoyable to read. You may be surprised at the answer!

Explore Fiction

Little House on the Prairie
by Laura Ingalls Wilder

All the time the wind blew, **shrieking,** howling, wailing, screaming, and **mournfully** sobbing. They were used to hearing the wind. All day they heard it, and at night in their sleep they knew it was blowing. But one night they heard such a terrible scream that they all woke up.

Pa jumped out of bed, and Ma said: "Charles! What was it?"

"It's a woman screaming," Pa said. He was dressing as fast as he could. "Sounded like it came from Scott's."

"Oh, what can be wrong!" Ma exclaimed.

Pa was putting on his boots. He put his foot in, and he put his fingers through the strap-ears at the top of the long boot leg. Then he gave a mighty pull, and he stamped hard on the floor, and that boot was on.

"Maybe Scott is sick," he said, pulling on the other boot.

"You don't suppose—?" Ma asked, low.

(CONTINUED) ▶

Student Learning Page 1.A: Explore Fiction

"No," said Pa. "I keep telling you they won't make any trouble. They're perfectly quiet and peaceable down in those camps among the **bluffs.**"

Laura began to climb out of bed, but Ma said, "Lie down and be still, Laura." So she lay down.

Pa put on his warm, bright plaid coat, and his fur cap, and his **muffler.** He lighted the candle in the lantern, took his gun, and hurried outdoors.

Before he shut the door behind him, Laura saw the night outside. It was black dark. Not one star was shining. Laura had never seen such solid darkness.

"Ma?" she said.

"What, Laura?"

"What makes it so dark?"

"It's going to storm," Ma answered. She pulled the latch-string in and put a stick of wood on the fire. Then she went back to bed. "Go to sleep, Mary and Laura," she said.

But Ma did not go to sleep, and neither did Mary and Laura. They lay wide awake and listened. They could not hear anything but the wind.

Mary put her head under the quilt and whispered to Laura, "I wish Pa'd come back."

Laura nodded her head on the pillow, but she couldn't say anything. She seemed to see Pa striding along the top of the bluff, on the path that went toward Mr. Scott's house. Tiny bright spots of candlelight darted here and there from the holes cut in the tin lantern. The little flickering lights seemed to be lost in the black dark.

After a long time Laura whispered, "It must be 'most morning." And Mary nodded. All that time they had been lying and listening to the wind, and Pa had not come back.

Then, high above the shrieking of the wind they heard again that terrible scream. It seemed quite close to the house.

Laura screamed, too, and leaped out of bed. Mary ducked under the covers. Ma got up and began to dress in a hurry. She put another stick of wood on the fire and told Laura to go back to bed. But Laura begged so hard that Ma said she could stay up. "Wrap yourself in the shawl," Ma said.

(CONTINUED) ➤

Making the Grade: Everything Your 4th Grader Needs to Know

Life on the prairie was sometimes dangerous for Laura Ingalls and her family.

They stood by the fire and listened. They couldn't hear anything but the wind. And they could not do anything. But at least they were not lying down in bed.

Suddenly fists pounded on the door and Pa shouted: "Let me in! Quick, Caroline!"

Ma opened the door and Pa slammed it quickly behind him. He was out of breath. He pushed back his cap and said: "Whew! I'm scared yet."

"What was it, Charles?" said Ma.

"A panther," Pa said.

He had hurried as fast as he could go to Mr. Scott's. When he got there, the house was dark and everything was quiet. Pa went all around the house, listening, and looking with the lantern. He could not find a sign of anything wrong. So he felt like a fool, to think he had got up and dressed in the middle of the night and walked two miles, all because he heard the wind howl.

(CONTINUED) ▶

Student Learning Page 1.A: Explore Fiction   7

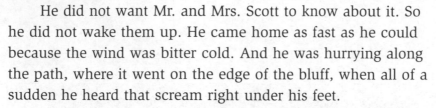

He did not want Mr. and Mrs. Scott to know about it. So he did not wake them up. He came home as fast as he could because the wind was bitter cold. And he was hurrying along the path, where it went on the edge of the bluff, when all of a sudden he heard that scream right under his feet.

"I tell you my hair stood up till it lifted my cap," he told Laura. "I lit out for home like a scared rabbit."

"Where was the panther, Pa?" she asked him.

"In a tree-top," said Pa. "In the top of that big **cottonwood** that grows against the bluffs there."

"Pa, did it come after you?" Laura asked, and he said, "I don't know, Laura."

"Well, you're safe now, Charles," said Ma.

"Yes, and I'm glad of it. This is too dark a night to be out with panthers," Pa said. "Now, Laura, where's my **bootjack?**"

Laura brought it to him. The bootjack was a thin oak slab with a notch in one end and a cleat across the middle of it. Laura laid it on the floor with the cleat down, and the cleat lifted up the notched end. Then Pa stood on it with one foot, he put the other foot into the notch, and the notch held the boot by the heel while Pa pulled his foot out. Then he pulled off his other boot, the same way. The boots clung tightly, but they had to come off.

Making the Grade: Everything Your 4th Grader Needs to Know

Write an Essay

From what you've read of *Little House on the Prairie* in this lesson, do you think Laura liked living on the frontier? Write an essay answering this question. Before beginning your essay, follow the steps.

1. First, think about what you can tell about her opinion of living on the frontier. Do you think she likes living there? What do you think she likes about it? What do you think she doesn't like about it?

2. Organize your essay into three paragraphs. The first paragraph will be your introduction. Here you will state your main idea, which is whether or not Laura likes living on the frontier.

3. The middle paragraph will include details to support your idea. The middle paragraph will be the longest one.

4. The third paragraph will be your conclusion. Here you will sum up your main idea.

5. Now, on a separate sheet of paper write a rough draft of your essay. Be sure to proofread your essay and check for any errors in punctuation, grammar, or spelling. You may also need to reread the section of *Little House on the Prairie* to check for details. When you have finished proofreading, write a final draft of your essay.

6. Show your essay to another person. Did you convince the person of your idea? Why or why not?

_____

_____

_____

_____

_____

_____

_____

_____

_____

_____

_____

_____

What's Next? You Decide!

Now it's your turn to choose what to do next in the lesson.
Read the activities and decide which one you want to do—
you may want to try them both!

Cook on the Frontier

MATERIALS

❑ reference books about food available on the frontier
❑ assorted cooking ingredients (see below)

STEPS

❑ Get help from an adult and research information about what types of food were common on the frontier during the 1800s. For example, would you be more likely to eat biscuits or french fries?

❑ Choose one of the foods, such as a homemade apple pie, and find a present-day recipe for that food.

❑ Read the ingredients. How difficult would it be to get all the items in your recipe if you couldn't go to the store? What would you do?

❑ Ask an adult to help you get the ingredients for your recipe. Be careful to measure the correct amount of ingredients.

❑ With an adult's help, make your frontier food.

❑ When your food is ready, serve it to your family and friends. Before serving, though, talk about what you made, how you would've made it if it were the 1800s, and what other foods would've been served with it.

Become a Costume Designer

MATERIALS

❑ reference books about clothing styles in 1800s frontier
❑ colored pencils
❑ 4 sheets drawing paper

STEPS

People on the frontier didn't wear the same styles of clothes that you wear now. Suppose you're the costume designer for a movie, television show, or play that takes place on the frontier in the 1800s. What would you have the actors wear?

❑ Ask an adult to help search for pictures of clothing styles found on the frontier in the 1800s.

❑ Look for the types of shirts, coats, shoes, dresses, pants, and hats that people wore. Did children wear different styles of clothing than adults?

❑ Find a common outfit that a male adult, a female adult, a male child, and a female child would wear.

❑ Sketch these outfits on paper.

❑ Then choose one piece of clothing from your drawing and see if you can make it. Be sure to ask an adult for help before beginning.

PROMOTING
LITERACY

LESSON
1.2

Learning from Fables

Animals can teach us a lot about life. Read a fable and find out!

OBJECTIVE	BACKGROUND	MATERIALS
To have your student read and examine a fable	Fables are stories that teach a lesson. The characters in fables are often animals that talk and act like humans. Fables have been passed down from generation to generation through the oral tradition. In this lesson, your student will read and study the features of a fable. He or she will also write and retell a fable.	<ul><li>Student Learning Pages 2.A–2.C</li><li>1 copy Sequence Chain, page 356</li></ul>

VOCABULARY
HERON a wading bird with long legs, a long neck, and a long bill
CRANE a bird with long legs, a long neck, and a long pointed bill

Let's Begin

1 **INTRODUCE** Begin the lesson by telling your student that the selection he or she is about to read is a fable. Fables are short stories that teach a lesson. Explain that most fables aren't set in a specific time or geographical place. The setting of the selection is simply a marsh. The characters in most fables are animals that talk and act like humans. Point out that the main characters of the selection are a **heron** and a **crane.** Ask your student to name a story that includes an animal as one of the characters.

2 **READ** Distribute Student Learning Page 2.A. Invite your student to read "Heron Woos Crane" out loud. Ask your student to pause if he or she doesn't understand a word. Encourage him or her to break the word into smaller parts and sound them out. For example, the word *outrageous* can be broken down into the sounds: *out-rage-ous.* Then challenge your student to use context clues to guess the meaning of one to three words that he or she doesn't recognize.

3 **MAKE INFERENCES** Invite your student to guess information in the fable using context clues and his or her own knowledge. As your student reads, pause and ask him or her to guess what might happen next. Also pause to discuss other inferences your student makes while reading. For example, have your student

? DID YOU KNOW?

Aesop's Fables are a well
known and beloved col-
lection of tales that are
credited to a Greek slave
named Aesop. Aesop
lived around 600 B.C.
You can find *Aesop's
Fables* at http://www.
aesopfables.com.

guess information about the characters that the author doesn't
tell the reader. Explain that making these types of guesses is
called drawing conclusions. Ask, *What did you conclude about
Crane after she changed her mind?*

4 **REVIEW** Remind your student that the events or action of a
story make up its plot. Then give him or her a copy of the
Sequence Chain found on page 356. In each of the boxes, have
your student summarize the important events in the fable. When
your student completes the Sequence Chain, ask him or her to
use it to summarize the entire story. Challenge him or her to use
this exercise to identify the fable's theme. Ask, *What is this story
about? What is the lesson of the story?* [Possible answers: The
story is about a heron and a crane who can't make up their
minds about marrying each other. The lesson is that people
should be decisive when they want to do something. People
shouldn't be proud with each other.]

5 **EXPLORE CAUSE AND EFFECT** Ask questions that begin with
"What caused . . ." to help your student identify causes and
effects in the fable's plot. Ask, *What caused Heron to visit
Crane?* [he wanted to ask her to marry him] Ask, *What caused
Heron to turn back home?* [Crane refused Heron's proposal] Ask,
What caused Crane to follow Heron? [she changed her mind]
Ask, *What caused Heron and Crane to go back and forth across
the marsh?* [they kept changing their minds]

6 **PRACTICE** Distribute Student Learning Page 2.B. Read the
directions with your student and answer any questions he or she
has about the activity. If necessary, review how to form the past,
present, and future tenses to prepare your student for writing his
or her fables. When your student has finished writing, invite him
or her to tell the fables out loud to friends and family members.

FOR FURTHER READING

*The Classic Treasury of
Aesop's Fables,* by
Caroline E. Tiger, ed.
(Running Press, 1999).

*Frederick and His
Friends: Four Favorite
Fables,* by Leo Lionni
(Knopf, 2002).

*The Town Mouse and the
Country Mouse: An
Aesop Fable,* by
Bernadette Watts
(North South Books,
1998).

Branching Out

TEACHING TIP

Encourage your student to brainstorm story elements, such as
characters, setting, and plot, before writing the fable. You may want to
distribute a new copy of the Sequence Chain found on page 356 to help
your student organize the order of events in his or her story.

CHECKING IN

To assess your student's understanding of fables, have him or her
compare and contrast this genre with a different type of fiction, such as
realistic fiction. Explore differences in the genres, such as fantasy versus
reality. Then invite your student to tell how some of the genres' story
elements are similar.

Enjoy a Fable

Heron Woos Crane
by David Kherdian

Crane and Heron lived at opposite ends of a very large marsh.

One day Heron said to himself, while thinking out loud, "It is about time I got married. Why don't I go wading across the marsh and woo Miss Crane."

And that was what he did. When he reached Miss Crane's house at last, he called to her to see if she was at home.

"I am here," Crane called down, "what do you want?"

"Why, I want to marry you," Heron said.

"What an outrageous idea!" Crane said to Heron. "I won't even consider it. Your vest is short, your legs are long, and your flight is wobbly and weak."

So back the heron marched on his spindly legs through seven miles of marsh.

(CONTINUED)

Student Learning Page 2.A: Enjoy a Fable   13

But he was hardly out of Crane's sight when she began to think over his proposal. "Hmmmm," she murmured to herself. "Shouldn't I get married?" she reasoned with herself.

So she followed Heron across the marsh. "Mr. Heron," she called up. "Were you serious when you said you wanted to marry me?"

"No, I was not," Heron shouted down from his perch. The truth was he had simply changed his mind. Heron said, "Why, I wouldn't marry you for all the fish in this marsh."

She slowly turned around and walked all the way back across the long marsh.

But this time it was the heron who had second thoughts. "Perhaps I should go back and propose once again."

When Heron reached Crane's home, he called up to her, "Oh Miss Crane, I've changed my mind. I would like to marry you after all."

"I've also changed my mind," she called back. "I wouldn't marry you for anything."

Once more, Heron trudged back home. He was hardly out of Crane's sight when she changed her mind *again*. "Oh, I've been a fool," she squeaked. "I'll marry Mr. Heron."

A long time has passed, but nothing has changed. The crane and the heron are still going back and forth across the marsh, wooing each other and then changing their minds.

Write and Tell a Fable

Write a short fable. Read your story out loud to family and friends. Don't forget to read with feeling! Change the tone, volume, and mood of your voice to express different characters and events.

Animals are characters, too!

What's Next? You Decide!

Now it's your turn to choose what to do next in the lesson. Read the activities and decide which one you want to do— you may want to try them both!

Write a Play

MATERIALS

❑ construction paper (optional)

❑ markers or paint (optional)

STEPS

Many plays are based on different types of stories. Write and perform a play for "Heron Woos Crane."

❑ Write the dialogue for Heron's and Crane's speaking parts. Remember that dialogue is the exact words a character says. Refer to the selection for help.

❑ Write stage directions for your play. Stage directions give the actors instructions about how to speak and act.

❑ Look at other written plays for examples of how to organize the dialogue and stage directions.

❑ Next, practice your play. You can act out the part of Heron or Crane. Ask someone to act out the other part.

❑ If you'd like, make props out of construction paper or things around your home. Ask for permission to use things in your home.

❑ Perform your play for family and friends.

Become the Illustrator

MATERIALS

❑ 1 sheet construction paper

❑ paints

❑ 1 paintbrush

STEPS

An illustrator is someone who draws pictures to go along with a story. Now it's your turn to be an illustrator!

❑ Choose a scene from "Heron Woos Crane" that you would like to paint.

❑ Picture the scene in your mind to help you determine how you will paint it.

❑ Use a paintbrush and different colored paints to illustrate the scene on construction paper.

❑ You may want to paint several different scenes from the fable.

❑ Hang your illustrations where others can see them!

❑ Be prepared to tell others what the pictures are about.

Understanding Nouns

Nouns are the people, places, and things in our lives!

OBJECTIVE	BACKGROUND	MATERIALS
To help your student learn to use nouns properly in writing and in speech	Nouns are a critical part of speech and writing. It's important for students to understand the difference between various types of nouns in order to use them correctly. In this lesson, your student will explore the differences between common, proper, singular, and plural nouns.	■ Student Learning Pages 3.A–3.B ■ 2 different colored highlighters ■ 1 copy of a page from a favorite book ■ 1 map

VOCABULARY
COMMON NOUN a noun that names any person, place, or thing
PROPER NOUN a noun that names a particular person, place, or thing
SINGULAR NOUN a noun that names one person, place, or thing
PLURAL NOUN a noun that names more than one person, place, or thing

Let's Begin

1 **INTRODUCE** Tell your student that a noun is a word that names a person, place, or thing. Have your student make a three-column chart with the headings "Person," "Place," and "Thing." Invite your student to think of three examples of each type of noun and write them in the correct column. Then ask your student to form two sentences using one noun from each column. For example, from the nouns *Sam, Florida,* and *truck* the sentence "Sam drove his truck to Florida" can be formed.

2 **RELATE** Tell your student that there are two major types of nouns. A **common noun** names any person, place, or thing. Some examples are *girl, school,* and *month*. A **proper noun** names a particular person, place, or thing. Some examples are *Alexis, Georgetown University,* and *February*. Tell your student that all proper nouns are capitalized and that some may consist of more than one word. Give your student a few examples of proper nouns and invite him or her to think of the matching common noun (for example, *Texas* and *state*). Then reverse the exercise and invite your student to name proper nouns so you can name the matching common nouns.

FOR FURTHER READING

Comic Strip Grammar—Grades 4–6, by Dan Greenberg (Scholastic, Inc., 2000).

Fun with Grammar: 75 Quick Activities and Games That Help Kids Learn About Nouns, Verbs, Adjectives, Adverbs, and More, by Laura Sunley (Scholastic, Inc., 2002).

Merry-Go-Round: A Book About Nouns, by Ruth Heller (Putnam Publishing Group, 1998).

Mink, a Fink, a Skating Rink: What Is a Noun?, by Brian P. Cleary and Jenya Prosmitsky, ill. (Lerner Publishing Group, 2000).

3 **EXPLAIN** Next explain to your student the difference between **singular nouns** and **plural nouns.** While a singular noun names one person, place, or thing (such as *cup*), a plural noun names more than one person, place, or thing (such as *cups*). Invite your student to think about how plural nouns are formed. Help him or her conclude that most plural nouns are formed by adding *–s* to the end of the singular noun. However, give examples such as *box, bus,* and *lunch* to demonstrate that sometimes plurals are formed by adding *–es*. Explain that, generally speaking, if a singular noun ends with *s, x, ch,* or *sh,* the plural can be formed by adding *–es*. Invite your student to write 10 singular nouns naming things in the room. Then have him or her write the plural form of each word.

4 **PRACTICE** Explain to your student that using specific nouns will enhance his or her writing. Point out that it is easier to follow a story if the nouns used are exact. Distribute Student Learning Page 3.A. Read the directions with your student. Have your student rewrite the story replacing the singular nouns with proper nouns. For a story-starter, encourage your student to write a different story using the first line of the paragraph.

Branching Out

TEACHING TIP

When teaching plural nouns, it is important to remember that there are exceptions to the spelling rules. Point out plural nouns such as *children, geese,* and *oxen* that have plural forms that don't end in *–s* or *–es*. Invite your student to name any such nouns that he or she can think of. Remind your student of the importance of looking up words in the dictionary when he or she is unsure about correct spelling.

CHECKING IN

To assess your student's understanding of different types of nouns, copy a page from one of his or her favorite books. Ask your student to read the page and highlight all the common nouns in one color and all the proper nouns in another color. Then read through the page with your student, helping him or her understand any mistakes.

Use Exact Nouns

Read the story. It has too many common nouns, so it doesn't make much sense. A good writer is more specific, using proper nouns to be more exact. Rewrite the story on the lines at the bottom of the page. Replace the underlined common nouns with specific proper nouns. Try to make the story more interesting.

A boy woke up one morning and sat up in his bed. It was a holiday, and he was very excited. He knew that it was early, but that in the afternoon he would go to a building where a person lived. He got out of bed and walked into the room. He was hungry, so he ate some food. Then he watched a show on television and played with a toy. Finally, a person said it was time to go. They got into a vehicle and drove away.

_____

_____

_____

_____

_____

_____

_____

_____

_____

_____

_____

_____

_____

_____

_____

What's Next? You Decide!

Now it's your turn to choose what to do next in the lesson.
Read the activities and decide which one you want to do—
you may want to try them both!

Create a Noun Book

MATERIALS

- ❑ 5 sheets construction paper
- ❑ markers or colored pencils
- ❑ 1 stapler

STEPS

- ❑ Make a list of nine singular nouns that you can draw.
- ❑ Fold five sheets of construction paper in half to create a book. Staple the pages together in the fold.
- ❑ Draw a picture of one of your singular nouns on the first left-hand page on the inside of the book (leave the cover blank for now). Write the singular noun under the picture. For example, if you draw a cat, write "Cat" below it.
- ❑ On the opposite right-hand page, draw more than one of the same noun. Write the plural form of the noun below the drawing.
- ❑ Continue drawing singular nouns on left-hand pages and plural nouns on right-hand pages until the book is full.
- ❑ Create a title and cover for your book. Share your book with a friend or family member.

Play a Memory Game

MATERIALS

- ❑ 1 large sheet construction paper
- ❑ markers or colored pencils
- ❑ 1 pair scissors

STEPS

- ❑ Cut a large piece of construction paper into 32 equal parts. This will be easier if you fold the paper in half five times, then cut on the fold lines.
- ❑ On half of the sheets of paper, write a proper noun. For each proper noun you write, make a card with the common noun that goes with the proper noun.
- ❑ When all the cards are made, ask someone to play a memory game with you.
- ❑ Place all the cards facedown on a table. Take turns turning over two cards. If the cards go together, the player who turned them over takes them and goes again. If they do not go together, the cards should be turned facedown again, and it is the other player's turn.
- ❑ Continue playing until all cards have been won. The person with more pairs is the winner!

Examining Pronouns

*Following the conventions of grammar helps
everyone express themselves more clearly.*

OBJECTIVE	BACKGROUND	MATERIALS
To help your student understand subject and object pronouns and singular and plural possessive pronouns	Pronouns, which take the place of nouns, are used to avoid repeating the same nouns over and over again. In this lesson, your student will learn and apply the grammar concepts of subject and object pronouns and singular and plural possessive pronouns.	■ Student Learning Pages 4.A–4.B

VOCABULARY

PRONOUNS words that take the place of a noun
SUBJECT PRONOUN a pronoun used as the subject of a sentence
PREDICATE the verb of a sentence
OBJECT PRONOUN a pronoun used in the predicate of a sentence
POSSESSIVE PRONOUN a pronoun that shows ownership

Let's Begin

SUBJECT AND OBJECT PRONOUNS

1 **INTRODUCE** Tell your student to imagine that he or she is drawing with three friends. Invite your student to tell what each person is drawing. Tell your student that he or she can't use his or her friends' names. Have your student use **pronouns** instead of their names.

2 **REVEAL** Share with your student that pronouns can be used as subjects or objects. A pronoun used in the subject of a sentence is a **subject pronoun.** *He* in the sentence "He often walks his dog in the morning" is a subject pronoun. *I, you, she, he, it, we,* and *they* are subject pronouns. A pronoun used in the **predicate** of a sentence is an **object pronoun.** *Her* in the sentence "Soccer and basketball excite her" is an object pronoun. *Me, you, him, her, it, us,* and *them* are object pronouns. (Notice that *it* can be both a subject and object pronoun.) Tell your student to draw a line down the middle of a sheet of paper. Have your student write subject pronouns on one side and object pronouns on the other. Ask your student to list as many of each type of pronoun as he or she can.

ENRICH THE EXPERIENCE

Work with your student to design a board game based on the grammar concepts studied in this lesson. After making the game, invite others to play with you.

3 **PRACTICE** Have your student write each of the following sentences. Ask him or her to underline the pronoun in the sentence. Then, above the underlined pronoun, tell your student to write an S if it is a subject pronoun and an O if it is an object pronoun.

[O]
The girl enjoyed it very much.
[S]
He ran quickly around second base.

SINGULAR AND PLURAL POSSESSIVE PRONOUNS

1 **INTRODUCE** Share with your student that a **possessive pronoun** takes the place of a possessive noun. Possessive pronouns show ownership. Ask your student to name some things that he or she owns. Tell your student that *my, your, his, her, its, our,* and *their* are possessive pronouns. Explain that some possessive pronouns are singular, such as *his* and *her*, and others are plural, such as *our* and *their*. Invite your student to use each of these words in a sentence.

2 **PRACTICE** Have your student write each of the following sentences. Ask him or her to underline the possessive pronoun in each sentence. Then have your student share what is being owned in the sentence.

Our dinner tastes wonderful. [dinner]
Her yard is covered with leaves. [yard]

3 **DISTRIBUTE** Distribute Student Learning Page 4.A. Have your student read aloud the directions. Invite him or her to ask any questions he or she may have about the activity.

Branching Out

TEACHING TIP

Different students learn differently. Your student may learn best through hearing a concept explained aloud, reading it silently, or practicing repeatedly. Make sure you vary the ways in which you teach a concept to your student so he or she can practice acquiring information and skills in multiple ways.

FOR FURTHER READING

Behind the Mask: A Book About Prepositions, by Ruth Heller (Paper Star, 1998).

Up, Up, and Away: A Book About Adverbs, by Ruth Heller (Paper Star, 1998).

CHECKING IN

Ask your student to summarize what he or she has learned in this lesson in 25 words or less. This will help your student focus on the main ideas and will allow your student to practice his or her summarizing skills.

Use Possessive Pronouns

Sometimes babies think they own everything. They often say, "Mine!" The problems list some things that a baby might think belong to him or her. In the parentheses are the people who actually own each object. Write a sentence for each problem using a possessive pronoun to show who owns the object. The first problem is done for you.

PROMOTING LITERACY

4.A

Mine!

1. Ball (two girls')

   Sentence: That is their ball. _____

2. Cake (one boy's)

   Sentence: _____

3. Book (one girl's)

   Sentence: _____

4. Flowers (your and Tom's)

   Sentence: _____

5. Bicycles (two children's)

   Sentence: _____

6. Skateboard (one man's)

   Sentence: _____

7. Shoes (Pam and Joe's)

   Sentence: _____

8. Purse (one lady's)

   Sentence: _____

9. House (one family's)

   Sentence: _____

10. Food (many birds')

    Sentence: _____

What's Next? You Decide!

Now it's your turn to choose what to do next in the lesson.
Read the activities and decide which one you want to do—
you may want to try them both!

Make a Book of Favorite Things

MATERIALS

- ❏ several sheets construction paper
- ❏ markers or crayons
- ❏ 1 stapler

STEPS

Make a book of your family members' and friends' favorite things!

- ❏ Take a few sheets of construction paper and fold them in half to make a book. Staple the book together along the fold.
- ❏ Write "Favorite Things" on the cover of your book and decorate it.
- ❏ Ask several family members and friends to name a favorite thing they own.
- ❏ Give each person you talked with a page in your book. Write what each person's favorite thing is using subject pronouns and possessive pronouns. For example, if your friend Mark says that his favorite thing is his dog, then write "Mark" at the top of a page. Underneath his name write "He says his favorite thing is his dog."
- ❏ Draw pictures of everyone's favorite thing to make your book more fun.
- ❏ Be sure to include a page that shows your favorite thing!

Interview Someone

STEPS

- ❏ Choose someone you know, perhaps a family member, a friend, or a neighbor.
- ❏ Ask that person questions and write the answers. Did you learn anything new or unusual about the person you chose?
- ❏ Write sentences that describe the person and what he or she shared with you.
- ❏ Practice using subject pronouns to replace the person's name in some of your sentences. Also practice using object pronouns in the predicate of some of your sentences. If you want to show possession, then use possessive pronouns.
- ❏ Underline all the pronouns you use.
- ❏ Write an S above the subject pronouns, an O above the object pronouns, and a P above the possessive pronouns.
- ❏ Share your writing with that person and then also with family members or friends.

Using Adjectives and Adverbs

*Good use of adjectives and adverbs allows readers
to put themselves in someone else's shoes.*

OBJECTIVE	BACKGROUND	MATERIALS
To teach your student to use adjectives and adverbs to modify nouns and verbs	Although adjectives and adverbs are not necessary to form complete sentences, they are very important in writing and storytelling because they help create a vivid picture of objects and actions in a story. In this lesson, your student will learn why descriptive adjectives and adverbs are important. He or she will also practice using them to enhance writing.	■ Student Learning Pages 5.A–5.B ■ 20 index cards ■ 1 pair scissors ■ 1 sheet each red, yellow, and blue construction paper ■ 1 selection of your student's writing

VOCABULARY
ADJECTIVES words that modify nouns **ADVERBS** words that modify verbs

Let's Begin

1 **INTRODUCE** Explain to your student that he or she will be learning about two parts of speech in this lesson. To begin, invite your student to copy the following pairs of sentences into a notebook:

> The dog chased the cat.
> The large, aggressive dog loudly chased the frightened little cat.

> The woman walked down the street.
> The elderly woman peacefully walked down the quiet street.

Ask your student to read each pair of sentences and circle the words that appear only in the second sentence of each pair. Point out that these words are the kinds of words your student will be focusing on. Have a discussion with your student about the information that is gained through the additional words. Help him or her see that although the first sentence in each pair is complete, it doesn't provide much information. The second sentence gives a colorful picture of the event taking place.

ENRICH THE EXPERIENCE

A simple walk around the block can be a great way to practice using adjectives and adverbs. While walking with your student, comment descriptively on the people, objects, and actions you see. Engage your student in the conversation by asking him or her questions that encourage descriptive answers.

FOR FURTHER READING

Grammar Puzzles and Games Kids Can't Resist (Grades 3–6), by Karen Kellaher (Scholastic, Inc., 2000).

Hairy, Scary, Ordinary: What Is an Adjective?, by Brian P. Cleary and Jenya Prosmitsky, ill. (Lerner Publishing Group, 2001).

Hot Fudge Monday: Tasty Ways to Teach Parts of Speech to Students Who Have a Hard Time Swallowing Anything to Do with Grammar, by Randy Larson (Cottonwood Press, 1998).

2 **EXPAND** Invite your student to look closely at the words he or she circled. Explain that some of these words are **adjectives** and others are **adverbs.** Tell your student that an adjective modifies a noun and often (but not always) comes before the noun that it describes. An adverb modifies a verb and may tell how, when, or where an action took place. An adverb may come before or after the verb that it modifies. Ask your student to identify the words that are modified by the circled words. Then have him or her list other adjectives and adverbs that could be used. Discuss the different meanings that different words have.

3 **IDENTIFY** Now play a game with your student to help him or her distinguish adjectives from adverbs. Write 10 adjectives and 10 adverbs on note cards and place them in a box. Invite your student to select a card. After reading the word, ask him or her to identify whether it is an adjective or an adverb. Then invite him or her to think of a word that it could modify and use both words correctly in a sentence. Continue until your student has selected all the cards.

4 **PRACTICE** Distribute Student Learning Page 5.A. Read the instructions with your student and allow time for him or her to cut out the pieces of construction paper and work with the sentences for awhile. Invite your student to read any sentences that he or she finds particularly interesting. Encourage your student to be creative and even silly with the sentences.

5 **REINFORCE** To reinforce your student's usage of adjectives and adverbs, have him or her write in a journal. Encourage your student to use adjectives and adverbs to describe his or her feelings and thoughts. If your student writes in a journal regularly, suggest that he or she choose one day's writing and write a story.

Branching Out

TEACHING TIP

To further practice using adjectives, play a quick game of *I Spy* with your student. Choose an object in the room and give your student three adjectives that describe it. He or she can then ask if other adjectives also describe the object. Continue until your student guesses the object. Then reverse roles and invite your student to spy an object in the room.

CHECKING IN

To assess your student's understanding of adjectives and adverbs, invite your student to select a piece of his or her writing. Ask your student to read the selection to tell how it could be improved by enhancing the sentences with adjectives and adverbs.

Build Your Own Sentences

To build your own sentences, follow the instructions.

❏ Cut out small rectangles from red construction paper. Then write each of the words in the six sentences on its own piece of red paper.

❏ Next, cut out small rectangles from blue construction paper. Write each of the adjectives on its own piece of blue paper.

❏ Finally, cut out small rectangles from yellow construction paper. Write each of the adverbs on its own piece of yellow paper.

❏ Now put all your pieces of paper to use! Lay out the sentences using the red pieces of paper. Then insert blue adjectives and yellow adverbs to make the sentences more interesting. See how many sentences you can come up with. Have fun!

Sentences

The boy went into the house.
The ball bounced over the fence.
The car turned into the parking lot.
The woman looked at the picture.
The horse ran into the woods.
The alien landed on the planet.

Adjectives	Adverbs
shiny	angrily
new	frantically
boring	bumpily
tall	sadly
creepy	noiselessly
crowded	quickly
little	carefully
amazing	nervously
brown	loudly

What's Next? You Decide!

Now it's your turn to choose what to do next in the lesson.
Read the activities and decide which one you want to do—
you may want to try them both!

Use the Power of Adjectives

STEPS

Adjectives can be used to describe both positive and negative qualities of a person, place, or thing. There are many adjectives that we would like to hear someone use to describe us, such as smart, funny, and interesting. There are also adjectives that we wouldn't like someone to use about us, such as smelly or mean. This activity will help you learn about the power of these words.

❑ Think of a person, place, or thing you really like a lot. It may be a favorite pet, sports team, food, or book.

❑ Write one or two paragraphs describing what you like so much. Use at least 10 positive adjectives in your essay.

❑ Now copy the essay but use negative adjectives that mean the opposite of the positive ones you first used (use a dictionary or thesaurus for help if you need to).

❑ Now read each of the two essays aloud. How do the adjectives affect the tone of the essay?

Make an Adjective Collage

MATERIALS

❑ 1 posterboard

❑ old magazines

❑ 1 pair scissors

❑ glue

❑ markers or colored pencils

STEPS

❑ Choose an adjective that could describe many of the objects you can find pictured in a magazine. Some examples are shiny, expensive, or tasty. Be creative!

❑ Write your adjective in large letters in the middle of your posterboard.

❑ Look through old magazines for pictures of objects that fit the adjective you chose. Cut out these pictures and glue them to the posterboard.

❑ Display your adjective collage for others to enjoy.

❑ If you want to, make another collage of objects that could be described by the opposite of your adjective. For example, if you made a collage of large things, you might make another collage of small things.

Discovering Biographies

*We can often learn about the wonders of our world
through the story of a unique and interesting life.*

OBJECTIVE	BACKGROUND	MATERIALS
To help your student understand the features of a biography and to have him or her read an excerpt from one	Many events in a person's life happen during important periods in history. Reading biographies can help us create images of real events from the past. In this lesson, your student will read a biographical excerpt set during a time in early American history. He or she will also learn about the genre of biographical writing.	■ Student Learning Pages 6.A–6.C ■ 1 copy Web, page 356

VOCABULARY
BIOGRAPHY a true story of a person's life as told by another person

Let's Begin

1 **INTRODUCE** Explain to your student that he or she will explore a genre of literature called **biography.** Point out the following features of a biography:

- A biography tells the true story of a person's life. It includes events that happened in real life.
- Most biographies describe events in chronological order.
- A biography usually includes the most important and interesting events in the life of the person.

    Invite your student to think of a person he or she feels would have an interesting biography. Discuss why he or she chose this person.

2 **BUILD BACKGROUND** Tell your student that the selection he or she is about to read is an excerpt from a biography about Thomas Jefferson. Distribute the KWL Chart on Student Learning Page 6.A. Invite your student to note any facts he or she knows about Jefferson in the first column of the chart.

3 **PREVIEW AND EXPAND** Invite your student to preview the selection title on Student Learning Page 6.B. Clarify any concepts he or she doesn't understand. Then ask your student to think of some questions he or she has about Jefferson's life. Invite your student to write the questions in the second column of the KWL Chart.

DID YOU KNOW?

Did you know that Thomas Jefferson was also an inventor? Among the things he invented were a type of plow, a lever used to open double doors, such as on a bus, and many other things.

ENRICH THE EXPERIENCE

You may want to help your student explore biographies in different forms of media, such as videocassettes.

ENRICH THE EXPERIENCE

As your student shows interest, have him or her continue reading the book *Thomas Jefferson and the American Ideal,* by Russell Shorto (Barron's Educational Series, Inc., 1987).

FOR FURTHER READING

Founding Fathers . . . and Mothers: A Field Trip to 18th Century America with Cassettes, by Stacey Marolf, Laurie Pessano, and Peter Evans, ill. (Good Company Players Educational Division, 1999).

Thomas Jefferson (Childhood of the Presidents), by Joseph Ferry (Mason Crest Publishers, 2003).

4 **READ AND MONITOR** Distribute Student Learning Page 6.B. Alternate between reading aloud to your student and having him or her read to you. Monitor your student's reading as needed. Reread and review any text he or she doesn't understand. Review multiple-meaning words in the selection to aid your student's vocabulary development. Some of these words are *state, crops, down, place, back, run, might, felt,* and *coach.*

5 **PREDICT AND DRAW CONCLUSIONS** Explain that your student can use his or her own knowledge and clues from the text to guess information. Invite your student to use this strategy to draw conclusions about Jefferson's traits. Then invite him or her to predict what might happen in the next chapter and why he or she thinks this. Then discuss paragraph development. Have him or her look at the first two paragraphs on Student Learning Page 6.B. Discuss how each starts and ends and the information in the middle.

6 **SUMMARIZE** Invite your student to review the information he or she had listed in the third column of the KWL Chart while reading the selection. Then ask your student to use this information to summarize the important ideas of the selection.

7 **CONNECT** Remind your student that James Madison kept an important secret from his good friend Thomas Jefferson. Invite your student to imagine how Jefferson may have felt when he found out that he was a presidential candidate! Discuss a time when your student was tricked by a friend. Suggest that your student write about this in his or her journal.

8 **PLAN AND WRITE** Invite your student to write a paragraph describing a person, place, event, or object. Distribute a copy of the Web found on page 356 to use for brainstorming ideas. Remind your student to use vivid adjectives and adverbs to help readers visualize his or her writing. (See Lesson 1.5 for a review.) Have him or her think about the development of the paragraphs from Step 5.

9 **REVIEW** Ask your student to proofread his or her paragraph for correct punctuation, spelling, and sentence structure.

Branching Out

TEACHING TIP

Point out resources that your student can use in writing his or her paragraph. For example, you may want to guide your student through a thesaurus to help him or her choose vivid words.

CHECKING IN

Assess your student's understanding by having him or her discuss the importance of biographies with you.

Chart Your Knowledge

Complete the KWL Chart as you read the selection.

K List what you **k**now about the topic in the first column.

W List what you **w**ant to know about the topic in the second column.

L List what you **l**earned about the topic in the third column.

A Portrait of Thomas Jefferson

K What I Know	W What I Want to Know	L What I Learned

Read a Biography

Thomas Jefferson and the American Ideal
by Russell Shorto

At the end of that year, 1793, Thomas gave up his position as secretary of state and returned to Monticello. It was a pleasure for him to spend time with his daughters again. By now Patsy was married. She and her husband and their two children all lived at Monticello and the house was alive with the cries and laughter of children.

It was a long time since Thomas had lived at Monticello. Plenty of work needed doing. The crops had not been rotated properly and the fields were scarred by erosion. While the house had been completed, Thomas was eager to tear part of it down and rebuild. His mind was still full of images of the magnificent houses of Europe. He had seen so many artful and impressive buildings that at one point he had wanted to leave Europe immediately just to get home to Monticello and begin building all over again. In France, he had taken careful notes of all the designs he liked. He now had a whole new plan for Monticello outlined.

With boyish eagerness, Thomas set about rebuilding. Soon the place was alive with the clanging of hammers and the shouts of builders. Thomas had a brick factory built which was shortly producing bricks by the ton. "We are now living in a brick kiln," Thomas wrote to a friend. He also set up a nail factory which turned out ten thousand nails a day.

Meanwhile, back in Philadelphia, James Madison was a very busy man. He knew that Washington was not going to run for a third term. He had also learned that John Adams was determined to become the second president.

Adams, Hamilton, and others who believed in a strong federal government had been given a name. They were called the Federalists, and their party was called the Federalist party.

(CONTINUED) ➤

Jefferson, Madison, and those who believed that citizens and their local governments should have the power—and that a strong Federal government was dangerous—were called Anti-Federalists, or Republicans.

The two parties opposed each other even more than Democrats and Republicans do today. The system of government was still very young and, as with a baby, it needed time to grow

Thomas Jefferson was born on April 13, 1743, and became the third president of the United States.

(CONTINUED)

and become strong. Each party feared the policies of the other might kill the country. Men and women felt that the next election was critical to the direction of American democracy.

Thus, James Madison had a big question on his mind: If Adams was going to be the Federalist candidate for president, who would be the Republican candidate?

As far as Madison was concerned, there was only one man in America who was popular enough to win: Thomas Jefferson. But Jefferson would not run. Madison did a great deal of thinking. Finally, he came up with a plan. He would campaign for Jefferson for president without Jefferson knowing about it!

Thomas Jefferson was probably the only presidential candidate in our history who spent his entire campaign building a house. By the time he found out what was going on, the election was so close that he couldn't stop the campaign. He was in the running.

At that time the law said that whoever got the most votes would be president, and the second-place man would be vice president. Thomas remembered all too clearly how he had not been strong enough as governor of Virginia. He was worried now. He secretly hoped he would come in second.

He did. It was a close election, with 71 electoral votes for Adams and 68 for Jefferson. Thomas got what he wanted—the vice presidency—but now he was in a tough position. He and Adams were no longer very friendly to one another—in fact, they almost never spoke. They represented opposing political points of view. Now they had to run the government together!

On inauguration day, Thomas decided it would be best to arrive in Philadelphia quietly, by public coach, so Adams, the new president, would get all the attention. Besides, he thought, nobody would be too interested in the vice president.

He did not realize that there were many people in the country who still believed in the principles of the revolution. These men and women agreed with Jefferson that the best government was one that would not interfere in the lives of citizens. Jefferson had always put his faith in the decency of

(CONTINUED)

ordinary people, not in institutions. Many people understood this. Thomas Jefferson, author of the Declaration of Independence, was their hero. He was the one man who truly understood the rights they had fought for. They were determined to show how they felt about him.

Just outside Philadelphia the coach had to stop. The road was completely jammed with people. There was so much noise that Jefferson and the other passengers got out to see what the commotion was.

People clogged the road, and a company of soldiers stood at attention. Across the street was a banner saying "JEFFERSON, THE FRIEND OF THE PEOPLE." The soldiers saluted him. The cannons fired sixteen rounds. Everyone cheered.

What's Next? You Decide!

Now it's your turn to choose what to do next in the lesson. Read the activities and decide which one you want to do—you may want to try them both!

Make a Multimedia Time Line

MATERIALS

- ❏ construction paper
- ❏ 2–3 sheets posterboard
- ❏ markers
- ❏ photographs of your life
- ❏ 1 audiocassette and/or videocassette player
- ❏ glue

STEPS

Make a time line of your life that people can see, hear, and touch!

- ❏ Choose four to six important events in your life. Describe each event on a separate sheet of construction paper. Add the date on which the event happened.
- ❏ Glue two or three of the descriptions onto separate sheets of posterboard. Put them in chronological order.
- ❏ Decorate the posters. Draw pictures or add photos of each event. Add stickers, ribbons, poems, sayings, or whatever you can think of. Be creative!
- ❏ Ask someone to help you find an audio and/or video recording that expresses something about your life. This can be favorite music or a home video.
- ❏ Put the posters by the audiocassette and/or videocassette player in

correct time order. If you like, you can spread them out across a room. You also can put objects related to the events near the posters, such as a special trophy.

- ❏ Invite your friends and family to take a multimedia tour of your life!

Create a Biographical Storybook

MATERIALS

- ❏ construction paper
- ❏ colored pencils or markers
- ❏ glue or stapler

STEPS

The story of a person's life can be described with pictures as well as words.

- ❏ Make storyboards about an interesting time in someone's life.
- ❏ Draw a picture using colored pencils or markers for each important event on construction paper. Write about each event.
- ❏ Put the storyboards in chronological order. Place a blank sheet of construction paper at the front and back of your storyboards.
- ❏ Glue or staple the sheets of paper together to make a storybook.
- ❏ Design a creative cover for your book. Don't forget to give your book a title.

Exploring Drama

Drama brings stories to life before a reader's eyes.

OBJECTIVE	BACKGROUND	MATERIALS
To help your student read drama and understand the nature of dramatic literature	Drama is a genre of literature that can be enjoyed by all ages. When a student reads a play, he or she can visualize the action taking place. In this lesson, your student will read an excerpt from a play and learn more about the genre.	■ Student Learning Pages 7.A–7.C ■ 14 note cards

Let's Begin

1 **INTRODUCE** Begin by explaining to your student that he or she will be learning about a genre of literature called drama. Ask your student to think of his or her favorite television show or movie. Have a discussion with your student about how the actors in a movie or television show know how to act and what to say. Explain that actors read a script, which includes the words they are to say and the actions they are to perform. Explain that some stories are written as plays so that they can be acted out onstage.

2 **EXPLAIN** Tell your student that plays generally have the following elements:

■ Characters, or the people in the play. A list of characters usually appears at the beginning of a script.

■ A setting or settings, or where and when the story takes place.

■ Dialogue, or the words the characters say. A character's name appears before the lines that he or she is to speak.

■ Stage directions, which tell the actors what to do, where to move, and how to speak their lines. These may be shown in italics or parentheses.

■ Scenes, which are smaller divisions of a play that generally take place at one setting.

3 **READ** Explain to your student that there are four characters in the excerpt he or she will be reading on Student Learning Page 7.A. Explain that three of these characters are narrators, who are not actually in the story but explain what is happening. The narrator is important because he or she tells things that the reader can't know just from the dialogue. Ask your student which parts he or she would like to read. Then read the excerpt with him or her.

ENRICH THE EXPERIENCE

The study of drama can be enhanced by an outing to see a play onstage. Find a suitable play that is being performed locally and take your student to see it.

A BRIGHT IDEA

As your student shows interest, have him or her join a theater or drama group to learn firsthand how to put on a play.

PROMOTING LITERACY

LESSON 1.7

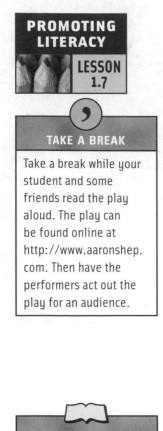

TAKE A BREAK

Take a break while your student and some friends read the play aloud. The play can be found online at http://www.aaronshep.com. Then have the performers act out the play for an audience.

FOR FURTHER READING

Cool Characters for Kids: 71 One-Minute Monologues, by Janet B. Milstein (Smith and Kraus, 2002).

Don Quixote in America: Plays in English and Spanish, Grades 1–6, by Resurreccion Espinosa; Charles Frink and Dorothy Louise Hall, eds. (Greenwood Publishing Group, Inc., 2002).

One Fine Day: A Radio Play, by Elizabeth Van Steenwyk and Bill Farnsworth, ill. (William B. Eerdmans Publishing Company, 2003).

Shakespeare for Kids: His Life and Times: 21 Activities, by Colleen Aagesen (Chicago Review Press, 1999).

4 **DISCUSS** Remind your student of the story elements discussed in Step 2. Ask him or her to identify the characters [Ray Sunshine and the narrators] and setting [a cold day on a street by a billboard] in the excerpt. Explain that the plot of a story is made up of the events that take place and usually includes a problem and a solution. Ask your student to determine what problem is presented in the excerpt.

5 **CONCLUDE AND PREDICT** Have your student reread the last line of dialogue in the excerpt. Ask him or her to conclude if Slappy's sign-painting days are really done. Point out that Narrator 1's saying it looked "as if" they were done suggests otherwise. Ask your student to predict what might happen in the rest of the story.

6 **COMPARE AND CONTRAST** Remind your student that comparing things means telling how they are the same, while contrasting things means telling how they are different. Invite your student to contrast Ray Sunshine's reaction to the billboard when it is new with his feelings about it a couple of days later. If your student keeps a writing journal, have him or her write a few paragraphs comparing and contrasting two things. You can offer an idea related to the play, such as which does he or she feel would make a better billboard for the travel agency, a cold, snowy scene or a hot, sunny scene like the one Slappy painted.

7 **EXAMINE CAUSE AND EFFECT** Remind your student that a cause is the reason an event takes place. The resulting event is the effect. In this excerpt, most of the effects are caused by Slappy's paintings. Give your student the following example:

Cause: Slappy painted a man and a woman on the beach under a hot sun.

Effect: People came to the street by the billboard to sunbathe.

Invite your student to tell the effects of these causes in the story: Slappy painting the sun on the billboard hotter and Slappy painting a storm cloud on the billboard. Now have your student complete Student Learning Page 7.B.

Branching Out

TEACHING TIP

When reading the story with your student, help him or her decode unfamiliar words and meanings using phonics and context clues.

CHECKING IN

Invite your student to write a short, one-scene play that includes all of the elements discussed in Step 2.

Discover Drama

The Legend of Slappy Hooper
An American Tall Tale
by Aaron Shepard

NARRATOR 1: Folks were getting scared to hire Slappy. But at last he got a job from the Sunshine Travel Agency.

NARRATOR 2: The billboard was to show a man and woman on a beach, toasting under a hot sun. Slappy painted it the day after a big snowstorm.

RAY SUNSHINE: Wonderful!

NARRATOR 3: . . . said Mr. Ray Sunshine.

RAY SUNSHINE: Why, that sun makes me feel hot! And look! The snow on the sidewalk is melting!

NARRATOR 3: But a couple of days later, Slappy got a call.

RAY SUNSHINE: Slappy, your sign is *too good.* Get down here right away!

NARRATOR 1: When Slappy arrived, he saw that the sidewalk and street in front of the billboard were covered with beach chairs. People sat around in swimsuits and sunglasses, sipping lemonade and splashing suntan lotion.

RAY SUNSHINE: They're blocking traffic, and the mayor blames me! Besides, they won't need my travel agency if they take their vacations here! You've got to *do* something, Slappy.

NARRATOR 2: So Slappy set up his gear and got to work. He painted the sun on the billboard much hotter. Before long, the crowd was sweating buckets and complaining of sunburn. Then everyone packed up and left.

RAY SUNSHINE: Good work, Slappy! *(gasps and points)* Look at that!

(CONTINUED)

NARRATOR 2: The man and woman on the *billboard* were walking off, too!

NARRATOR 3: Just then, a lick of flame shot up the wall of the building across the street. Slappy's sign had set it on fire! In a few minutes, fire trucks clanged up and firefighters turned hoses on the flames.

RAY SUNSHINE: Slappy! Try something else!

NARRATOR 1: Slappy got back to work. He painted a storm cloud across that sun. But he had to jump clear when the cloud shot bolts of lightning!

NARRATOR 2: Then the storm broke.

NARRATOR 3: Slappy's cloud rained so hard, the billboard overflowed and flooded all of Main Street!

RAY SUNSHINE: *Never again,* Slappy Hooper!

NARRATOR 1: After that, no one *on earth* would hire Slappy. It looked as if his sign-painting days were done.

Play the Game Because

Copy each of the 14 effects onto a note card. Place them in a box.
Select one at random. Think of something that may have happened to
cause the effect you chose. Then put the card back and choose another
card. (If you choose the same card again, just think of another cause.)
Be creative. There are no wrong answers in this game!

There is spaghetti on the baby's head because . . .

Frances can't go rollerblading today because . . .

My mother has a headache because . . .

The apartment is very dark because . . .

The only thing in the refrigerator is pickles because . . .

There is an elephant walking down my street because . . .

The children are very quiet because . . .

The man did not go to work today because . . .

There are footprints on the ceiling because . . .

Eddie is giggling because . . .

Selena covered her eyes because . . .

The window is open because . . .

The clown is crying because . . .

Kaelyn is holding a snake because . . .

**When you have thought of causes for these effects, make up some
effects of your own and give them causes!**

What's Next? You Decide!

Now it's your turn to choose what to do next in the lesson.
Read the activities and decide which one you want to do—
you may want to try them both!

Create a Come-to-Life Billboard

MATERIALS

❑ 1 posterboard
❑ markers, crayons, or paint

STEPS

In the story, the billboard that Slappy Hooper painted became real, and it had surprising effects! Suppose that you have Slappy's ability to paint things that come to life.

❑ Think of something that you would like to paint on a billboard.
❑ Sketch out your drawing in your notebook first.
❑ Then draw or paint your idea on the posterboard.
❑ Now write a paragraph or two telling what would happen when this billboard comes to life!
❑ Or, if you prefer, act out what would happen if your billboard came to life.
❑ You can write a script for your billboard and include many characters.
❑ Invite friends or family to read the script with you.
❑ Don't forget to include props and costumes.
❑ Perform your story of the billboard coming to life for an audience.

Analyze Advertisements

MATERIALS

❑ magazines with advertisements
❑ 1 sheet unlined paper
❑ markers or colored pencils

STEPS

In the excerpt you just read, Slappy was hired by the Sunshine Travel Agency to paint a billboard that would make people want to go on vacation. Think about why Slappy painted two people on a beach in the hot sun. Since it was cold and snowy, the billboard made people want to go somewhere warm. Companies create advertisements to make people want their products.

❑ Look through magazines and find advertisements for eight products.
❑ With a friend or family member, answer the following questions for each ad:
  ▪ What product is being advertised?
  ▪ How will the advertisement make people want the product?
  ▪ Do you think this advertisement will work? Why or why not?
  ▪ Now select one of the products advertised.
  ▪ Think about how you could create a different advertisement for the same product.
  ▪ Draw the different advertisement on the unlined paper.

Reading Poetry

Through its smells, tastes, and textures, the world around us calls us to express our thoughts and feelings through the unique genre of poetry.

OBJECTIVE	BACKGROUND	MATERIALS
To help your student identify and understand the various elements of poetry	Poetry is a unique genre in which various elements are used to express a feeling, tell a story, or describe something. Poems have a rhythm and often use language that helps the reader create a picture of a poem's subject. In this lesson, your student will read a poem and learn about the genre.	■ Student Learning Pages 8.A–8.B ■ 1 favorite children's poem

VOCABULARY

RHYTHM a pattern of beats

RHYME when words have the same last sounds

SIMILE a comparison of two things using the words *like* or *as*

METAPHOR a comparison of two things without using the words *like* or *as*

ONOMATOPOEIA a word that sounds like the word it describes

ALLITERATION repeating the same sound or letter in a group of words

STANZAS lines of poetry grouped together

Let's Begin

1 **INTRODUCE** Begin this lesson by reading aloud a children's poem of your choice to your student. Choose a poem that your child can understand and appreciate. Ask your student to close his or her eyes as you read the poem several times. Invite your student to share his or her initial responses to the poem.

2 **REVEAL** Share with your student that he or she is going to explore the genre of poetry. Ask your student to make a KWL Chart. He or she should make a three-column chart in a notebook with "What I Know" as the heading of the first column, "What I Want to Know" as the heading of the second column, and "What I Have Learned" as the heading of the third column. Now have your student write what he or she already knows about poetry in the first column. Next have your student write what he or she wants to know about poetry in the second column.

3 **DISCUSS** Discuss with your student how poetry differs from fictional stories he or she has read. Share how poetry has **rhythm.** Clap your hands and stomp your feet to establish a rhythm. Invite your student to join in. Ask your student to make up his or her own rhythm and have him or her teach you it.

4 **DISCUSS** Tell your student that a poet uses many different elements in poetry. In addition to rhyme and rhythm, a poet might use figurative language elements such as a **simile** (she runs as fast as lightning) or a **metaphor** (my bedroom is a junkyard). A poet might also use **onomatopoeia** (buzz) or **alliteration** (Laura laid down lazily). Challenge your student to think of his or her own examples of each of these elements.

5 **READ** Tell your student that reading poetry takes practice. Oftentimes a poet divides a poem into **stanzas** to help create a particular form. Distribute Student Learning Page 8.A. Ask your student to count how many stanzas are in the poem "Owl." [five] Invite your student to read the poem two times out loud. Then have your student identify in "Owl" some of the elements of poetry he or she has learned about. Finally, have your student write in a journal about what he or she thinks the poem means. Encourage him or her to read other poems and write about how they make him or her feel in the journal.

6 **REVIEW AND PRACTICE** Invite your student to revisit his or her KWL Chart. What did your student already know about poetry? Was he or she right? What questions did your student have about poetry? Were your student's questions answered in the lesson? In the third column of the chart, ask your student to write down what he or she has learned about poetry. Distribute Student Learning Page 8.B and invite your student to continue exploring the genre of poetry.

Branching Out

TEACHING TIP

Creating a picture in one's head can be difficult for some people. If your student struggles to explain what he or she imagines while reading a poem, invite him or her to make a drawing of the picture before verbally explaining it.

CHECKING IN

To assess your student's understanding of the lesson, ask your student to identify the three most important things he or she learned. Challenge your student to share why he or she chose those three things.

Rejoice in Poetry

Owl
by Eve Merriam

Who
who
who did it
who?

Who spilled the beans
who broke the news
who stepped into
somebody's shoes?

Who
who
who did it
who?

Who slipped the word
who hit a snag
who let the cat
out of the bag?

Who did the deed
who gets the blame
who is the culprit
What is your name?

What's Next? You Decide!

Now it's your turn to choose what to do next in the lesson. Read the activities and decide which one you want to do— you may want to try them both!

Host a Poetry Reading

MATERIALS

❑ construction paper

❑ markers and colored pencils

STEPS

Invite your family and friends to share their favorite poems!

❑ Set up a date and time for everyone to get together.

❑ Ask each person to choose a poem to read at the party. You'll want to make invitations for the big event! Use construction paper, markers, and colored pencils to make your invitations.

❑ Before others begin reading the poems they brought, share with them what you have learned about poetry.

Magazine Mania

MATERIALS

❑ old magazines or newspapers

❑ 1 pair scissors

❑ glue

❑ construction paper

STEPS

Many poems are very colorful and make it easy for the reader to create a picture in his or her mind. Make a collage based on a poem.

❑ Read a poem of your choice three or four times.

❑ Each time you read the poem, try to imagine a picture in your head that matches the words.

❑ Next use the scissors to cut out pictures and words you find in the magazines and newspapers that you feel show the picture you saw in your head.

❑ Glue the pictures to the construction paper to create a collage that shows what you think the poem means.

❑ Hang your collage where others can see it.

PROMOTING LITERACY

LESSON 1.9

Identifying Subjects and Predicates

Subjects and predicates are the building blocks of a complete sentence.

OBJECTIVE	BACKGROUND	MATERIALS
To have your student identify and write sentences with subjects and predicates	Every complete sentence has a subject and a predicate. A subject tells who or what a sentence is about. A predicate tells what the subject of a sentence is or does. Sentences with similar subjects can be joined, as can sentences with similar predicates. In this lesson, your student will identify and write sentences with simple and complete subjects and predicates.	■ Student Learning Pages 9.A–9.B ■ index cards

VOCABULARY

COMPLETE SUBJECT all the words that tell who or what a sentence is about

SIMPLE SUBJECT the main words in a complete subject

COMPLETE PREDICATE all the words that tell what the subject is or does

SIMPLE PREDICATE the main words in a complete predicate

Let's Begin

1 **INTRODUCE** Begin this lesson by explaining to your student that a sentence has two parts. Explain the meanings of the vocabulary words **complete subject** and **simple subject.** Show your student the following sentence. Tell him or her that the complete subject is underlined. The simple subject is double underlined.

The horses from the ranch gracefully ran down the open field.

Now ask your student to point out the simple subject [tourists] and the complete subject [the curious tourists] of the following sentence:

The curious tourists carefully looked at the famous painting.

2 **EXPLAIN** Share the meanings of the vocabulary words **complete predicate** and **simple predicate.** Show your student the

A BRIGHT IDEA

For fun grammar practice and quizzes, have your student visit http://www.eduplace. com/kids/hme. Click on Grades K–5 and then Grammar Blast to find activities for fourth-grade grammar students.

following sentence. Tell him or her that the complete predicate is underlined. The simple predicate is double underlined.

The children on the slide waited their turn to go down.

Now ask your student to point out the simple predicate [wilted] and the complete predicate [slowly wilted in the summer sun] of the following sentence:

The dry, browning plant slowly wilted in the summer sun.

3 **DISCUSS** Tell your student that sentences with similar subjects can be combined. Add that sentences with similar predicates can also be combined. Tell your student that the conjunction *and* is used to join subjects and predicates. Show him or her the following examples:

Cats are nice. + Cats are furry. ➔ Cats are nice and furry.

I collect rocks. + I collect stamps. ➔ I collect rocks and stamps.

The boy laughs. + The girl laughs. ➔ The boy and girl laugh.

Bats can fly. + Birds can fly. ➔ Bats and birds can fly.

Tell your student to write three sentences that have a joined subject and three sentences that have a joined predicate.

4 **DISTRIBUTE** Direct your student to Student Learning Page 9.A. Invite your student to read the directions aloud. Ask your student if he or she has any questions about the activity. Have your student complete the first exercise with you.

5 **REVIEW** After he or she has completed Student Learning Page 9.A, go over it with your student. Ask him or her to write new sentences using some of the subjects and predicates given on the page.

Branching Out

TEACHING TIP

If your student is having trouble identifying the simple and complete predicate of a sentence, review verbs with him or her. Remind your student that a predicate always includes a verb that shows action or state of being.

CHECKING IN

To assess your student's understanding of the lesson, have him or her write three complete sentences and identify the subject and predicate in each one. Then have your student choose a favorite book. Ask him or her to find two examples of simple and complete subjects and simple and complete predicates.

Become a Subject and Predicate Detective

Someone has hidden the complete subjects and predicates in the sentences. Find the complete subject and predicate in each sentence. Circle the complete subject and underline each complete predicate.

1. Families and friends gather during the festivities.

2. Everyone eats pizza and popcorn to celebrate.

3. Friends play games and music to have fun.

4. The food and drink is all eaten.

5. A large kite sailed across the sky.

Here's another mystery for you to solve. Someone has borrowed the complete subjects and predicates from these sentences. Fix each sentence using the clues in the word box. Be sure to capitalize the beginning of each sentence.

| play basketball all day | the two stray cats | changed into a butterfly |
| the brave pilot | the determined hiker | has a flat tire |

6. The girls on the playground _____.

7. _____ jump down from the tree.

8. _____ flew the small plane.

9. My bike _____.

10. _____ climbed Mt. Everest.

11. The caterpillar _____.

All whales, dolphins, and porpoises are known as cetaceans. This is a group of mammals that live in the sea. They give birth to live young, which they feed with their own milk. They also breathe air at the water's surface through lungs.

Cetaceans are warm-blooded, which means that their body temperature remains relatively constant. Some animals, such as fish and lizards, are cold-blooded; their temperature changes according to the temperature of their environment.

Dolphins are toothed whales but different enough to form their own group. Species with a body length of more than nine feet are usually called whales, and species smaller than this are known as dolphins. Of course, there are a number of exceptions; the smallest whale, the dwarf sperm whale, is smaller than the largest dolphin, the bottlenose. Despite its much greater length of some thirty feet, the killer whale is also considered a dolphin.

All cetaceans have the same basic body shape. Like all toothed whales, dolphins have a blowhole in the top of their heads; rubbery, hairless skin; and a powerful fluke or tail that drives the animal through the water. Dolphins are excellent swimmers, and their streamlined shape and smooth skin reduce friction with the water.

Bottlenose Dolphins

The name "bottlenose" comes from the animal's large, rounded beak, which is like the shape of an old-fashioned bottle. The color pattern varies on bottlenose dolphins, but they are typically brownish gray with a back darker than their underside. They vary in length from six to thirteen feet. Although mostly a coastal species, bottlenose dolphins are often seen in open waters riding the bow waves of ships. They are powerful swimmers and can reach speeds of fifteen miles an hour. The species is common in all seas from cold to tropical waters. They eat a wide variety of fish, squid, and octopuses, preferring shallow-water and bottom-dwelling species.

Bottlenose dolphins have a lifespan of over thirty years. Not surprisingly, they have a long adolescence and don't reach maturity until ten to twelve years old. A female may have up to eight calves in her lifetime.

(CONTINUED)

Bottlenoses are natural acrobats, which makes them the most popular performers in sea aquariums. They have adapted well to life in captivity, and they are the best studied species of dolphin. They are also the most well known—Flipper, star of the popular television series, was a bottlenose dolphin! Whenever anyone was in trouble, Flipper would come to the rescue.

Other Species

Most dolphins can be recognized by distinctive patterns on their bodies, particularly on the underside. In fact, of the remaining species of dolphin, a number of them are named after their appearance, such as the spotted and striped dolphins.

(CONTINUED) ▶

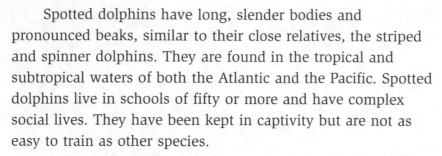

Spotted dolphins have long, slender bodies and pronounced beaks, similar to their close relatives, the striped and spinner dolphins. They are found in the tropical and subtropical waters of both the Atlantic and the Pacific. Spotted dolphins live in schools of fifty or more and have complex social lives. They have been kept in captivity but are not as easy to train as other species.

Occasionally bonds form between spinners and spotted dolphins, with each group taking turns to keep a lookout for sharks. Spinners hunt at night while spotted dolphins rest before taking over the "day shift."

The spinner dolphin is named after its habit of leaping out of the water and performing double twists and flips in the air. Spinners live in similar places to spotted dolphins and they are both very fast swimmers. Unlike spotted dolphins, spinners feed on fish and squid found in deep water.

Most of the day is spent resting close to shore, but spinner dolphins come alive in the late afternoon, leaping and splashing about. This is a sign for the rest of the animals to start moving. There is more activity as a hunting group is organized until, finally, the whole school heads out to sea.

Write an Informational Paragraph

An informational paragraph is often divided into three parts. Read the
list and then follow the directions.

1. A topic sentence begins the paragraph. The sentence states the main idea
of the paragraph.

2. The body of the paragraph presents facts that support the main idea.

3. The concluding sentence restates the main idea.

**Plan a paragraph about an animal you're interested in. Include interesting facts
about the animal and why you chose it.**

Topic sentence: _____

_____

_____

Supporting Fact 1	**Supporting Fact 2**	**Supporting Fact 3**
_____	_____	_____
_____	_____	_____
_____	_____	_____
_____	_____	_____
_____	_____	_____

Concluding sentence (restate main idea): _____

_____

**Now use the information to write an organized paragraph on a separate sheet of
paper. Remember to check your spelling and punctuation.**

What's Next? You Decide!

Now it's your turn to choose what to do next in the lesson. Read the activities and decide which one you want to do— you may want to try them both!

Research, Learn, and Write

MATERIALS

❑ 10–15 index cards

STEPS

Learn more about a topic that really interests you.

❑ Think about topics that interest you.

❑ Make a list of these topics.

❑ Then decide which one you would like to learn more about.

❑ Visit a library, read reference books, or interview an expert over the phone.

❑ You can also use the Internet to learn more about your topic.

❑ As you collect information, take notes using the notetaking skills presented in this lesson.

❑ Share what you have learned by writing an informational paragraph.

Make a Dolphin Mobile

MATERIALS

❑ 3–4 pictures of dolphins from old magazines

❑ reference books

❑ construction paper

❑ glue

❑ string

❑ 1 hole punch

❑ 1 hanger

STEPS

Make a dolphin mobile!

❑ Cut out the pictures of dolphins. If the pictures are thin, glue them on construction paper to make them stronger.

❑ Use reference books to determine what type of dolphin is pictured.

❑ Label each picture with the dolphin's name, such as "Bottlenose."

❑ Punch a hole in each picture.

❑ Then tie one end of a string to it.

❑ Tie the other end of each string to the hanger.

❑ Tie them so that the pictures hang at different lengths.

❑ Hang your mobile where others can enjoy it.

Reading and Writing a News Article

News articles help us connect to what's happening in the world around us.

OBJECTIVE	BACKGROUND	MATERIALS
To have your student read and write a news article	How do you find out the latest news? While television offers a convenient way to learn about the news, newspapers and magazines remain popular media for communicating current events. In this lesson, your student will learn the features of a good news article. Your student will also practice writing news articles.	■ Student Learning Pages 11.A–11.B ■ 1–2 newspaper or magazine articles from current publications ■ 1 sheet construction paper (optional) ■ markers (optional)

Let's Begin

1 **INTRODUCE** Select one or two recent news articles to share with your student. Be sure the articles are age appropriate and focus on engaging topics. Some popular children's magazines are *American Girl, Boy's Life, Cricket, Muse, National Geographic World, Sports Illustrated for Kids,* and *Ranger Rick.* You can also go to http://www.nationalgeographic.com/kids and *Time* magazine at http://www.timeforkids.com. Ask your student to talk about why newspapers and magazines are important.

2 **READ** Invite your student to read along as you slowly read the articles aloud. Read each headline first. Then ask your student if the headline grabbed his or her attention. Invite your student to explain his or her answer. Then point out that headlines often contain clues that help readers predict what a news article is about. Invite your student to predict the important ideas of the articles.

3 **EXPLAIN** Point out that many news articles begin with attention-grabbing sentences. Look again at the articles as you read them with your student. Read the first sentences. Ask your student if they grabbed his or her attention. Invite your student to explain his or her answer.

ENRICH THE EXPERIENCE

Help your student identify the Ws that aren't obvious in the article. For example, the article doesn't mention a specific time or setting. However, the words *recently* and *now* help the reader guess a general time frame for the article. Also, specific names aren't mentioned in the article, but the words *scientists*, *researchers*, and even *horses* can indicate who the article is about.

FOR FURTHER READING

Craft Lessons: Teaching Writing K–8, by Ralph Fletcher and JoAnn Portalupi (Stenhouse Publishers, 1998).

Expository Writing, Grades 4–8, by Tara McCarthy (Scholastic Trade, 1999).

The Young Journalist's Book: How to Write and Produce Your Own Newspaper, by Nancy Bentley, Donna Guthrie, and Katy Keck Arnsteen, ill. (Millbrook Press Trade, 2000).

4   **EXTEND**   Explain to your student that he or she should look for the five Ws when reading a news article. Tell your student that the five Ws often appear early in the article. The five Ws of an article answer the following questions:

- **Who**—Who is the article about? Who is mentioned in the article?
- **What**—What is the article about? What important events happened?
- **Where**—Where did the events take place?
- **When**—When did the events take place?
- **Why**—Why did the events happen? Why did the author write the article?

Explain that news writers answer the five Ws of an article in a way that is clear, concise, and to the point. Challenge your student to review the articles you read and identify the details that answer the five Ws.

5   **PRACTICE**   Invite your student to read the news article "Keeping a Cool Head" on Student Learning Page 11.A. Ask him or her to point out the features discussed in Steps 2–4. Ask your student to tell how this article compares to the previous articles he or she read.

6   **SUMMARIZE AND DRAW CONCLUSIONS**   Invite your student to summarize the article. Remind him or her that summaries include the most important ideas of a text. Readers sometimes draw conclusions as they summarize text. An example is "Horses have special ways of keeping cool." Invite your student to draw a conclusion as he or she summarizes the article in two or three sentences.

7   **USE QUOTATIONS**   Explain to your student that news articles often include direct quotations, which are the exact words a person said. Then distribute Student Learning Page 11.B.

Branching Out

TEACHING TIPS

Although this lesson may only take one to two hours to complete, be sure to give your student enough time to read the article and write his or her own article.

CHECKING IN

To assess your student's understanding of news articles, ask questions about the five Ws after he or she has finished reading an article.

Read a News Article

Keeping a Cool Head

Horses can't horse around when it comes to the heat they generate galloping at full speed. Becoming overheated could cause them to suffer brain damage.

Until recently, scientists were baffled as to how horses keep a cool head, because they don't have the same mechanism for cooling exercise-heated blood that other fast-moving animals have.

Now researchers at Canada's University of Saskatchewan in Saskatoon have discovered horses' secret: "air bags"! The artery that carries most of the blood to a horse's brain passes over two air-filled pouches at the base of a horse's skull. The air in the pouches cools the "hot blood"—like a built-in air-conditioning system.

Write Your Own News Article

Write a news article about something that's happened to you this past week, or about some other event. Complete the chart to brainstorm ideas. Then write your article on a separate sheet of paper.

My News Article

Features	My Ideas
Attention-grabbing headline	
Attention-grabbing opening sentence	
Facts that answer the five-W *Who?*	
Facts that answer the five-W *What?*	
Facts that answer the five-W *Where?*	
Facts that answer the five-W *When?*	
Facts that answer the five-W *Why?*	
Direct quotations (exact words said)	

More Fun Ideas

❏ A lot of news articles have pictures with captions. Use markers to draw your own picture to go with your news article. Write a caption that explains the picture.

❏ If you'd like, type your news article on a computer. Ask someone to help you choose a font that looks like a font used in newspapers or magazines.

❏ Design your own newspaper page. Put the parts of your article together on a sheet of construction paper. Use bigger letters for your headline.

❏ Think of a name for a newspaper that might publish your article. An example is *The Student's Daily News.*

Understanding Prepositions and Conjunctions

Conjunctions and prepositions are the little words that make sentences clearer and more interesting.

OBJECTIVE	BACKGROUND	MATERIALS
To help your student understand the use and functions of prepositions and conjunctions	Although prepositions and conjunctions often are short words, they are an important part of language. Students are often confused by these words because they are abstract and can be used in many ways. In this lesson, your student will learn about conjunctions and prepositions and their functions in language.	■ Student Learning Pages 12.A–12.B ■ tape ■ 36 index cards

VOCABULARY

PREPOSITIONS words that relate a noun or pronoun to another word in a sentence
CONJUNCTIONS words that join other words together in a sentence

Let's Begin

1 **REVIEW** Invite your student to think about the different types of words he or she has learned about. Help him or her recall what nouns, pronouns, verbs, adjectives, and adverbs are. (Review Lessons 1.3, 1.4, and 1.5, if necessary.) Explain that all of these are parts of speech. Tell your student that this lesson is about two more parts of speech, **prepositions** and **conjunctions.** Invite your student to copy this sentence into a notebook:

Two fast squirrels ran across the street and climbed up a tree.

Have your student identify the part of speech of each word in the sentence, circling those words he or she doesn't know.

2 **EXPLAIN** Point out to your student that many of the words in the sentence he or she circled are prepositions or conjunctions. Reveal that the words *across* and *up* are prepositions, which usually indicate a relationship of time or place. For example, the phrases *across the street* and *up a tree* both tell where the squirrels went. Other prepositions, such as *after* and *until,* might tell when something happened. Read the following prepositions

ENRICH THE EXPERIENCE

Have your student work with the Grammar Gorilla at http://www.funbrain.com/grammar for fun quizzes and practice with prepositions, conjunctions, and other parts of speech. Click on *advanced.*

PROMOTING LITERACY

LESSON 1.12

A BRIGHT IDEA

To demonstrate that prepositions are abstract, select a few words from Student Learning Page 12.A and ask your student to define them. He or she will find it difficult!

FOR FURTHER READING

Grammar Puzzles and Games Kids Can't Resist (Grades 3–6), by Karen Kellaher (Scholastic Prof Book Div, 2000).

Prepositions and Conjunctions, by Beth Bridgman, ed. (EDCP, 1998).

Under, over, by the Clover: What Is a Preposition?, by Brian P. Cleary and Brian Gable, ill. (Lerner Publishing Group, 2002).

out loud and ask your student to tell whether each indicates time or place:

above [place]	across [place]	before [time or place]
until [time]	during [time]	between [time or place]

3 **ELABORATE** Ask your student to again look at the sentence from Step 1. Point out that each of the prepositions is related to a noun. These nouns are called the object of the preposition. Objects of prepositions can also be pronouns. The preposition, the noun or pronoun, and all the words in between make up a prepositional phrase. Give the following examples of prepositional phrases:

above the fireplace	between the tall buildings
during morning recess	behind me

Invite your student to find the noun or pronoun in each of these phrases that serves as the object of the preposition.

4 **DISTRIBUTE** Distribute Student Learning Page 12.A. Help your student read and follow the directions to complete the exercise.

5 **EXTEND** Tear a sheet of paper in half and ask your student what he or she would do if the paper were important. Invite your student to repair your torn sheet of paper with tape. Explain that just as tape can join things together, there are some words that can join other words and whole sentences together. Ask your student to refer once again to the sentence from Step 1. Invite him or her to look at the word *and*. Explain that this word is a conjunction.

6 **PRACTICE** Tell your student that the most common conjunctions are *and, or,* and *but*. Other conjunctions include *because, since, if,* and *unless*. Read the following sets of sentences aloud to your student. Invite him or her to create one sentence using a conjunction to connect or combine the two sentences.

Roy went to the store. Sal went to the store.
[Roy and Sal went to the store.]

I like candy. Candy gives me a headache.
[I like candy, but it gives me a headache.]

Branching Out

TEACHING TIP

For more practice with prepositions, write each preposition on Student Learning Page 12.A on an index card. Place them in a box, ask your student to select one, and have him or her think of a sentence using that word.

CHECKING IN

To assess your student's understanding of conjunctions, ask your student to write six sentences that employ a conjunction. Then have your student explain how the conjunction functions in each sentence.

Use Prepositions

Why is the cat **on** my head?

Why is this girl **under** me?

Read the list of prepositions.

about	between	inside	over
above	beyond	into	since
across	by	like	through
after	down	near	to
around	during	of	under
at	except	off	until
before	for	on	up
below	from	out	with
beside	in	outside	without

Now select five prepositions. Use each one in a sentence. Write the sentences on the lines. Circle the preposition and underline the object of the preposition.

1. _____

_____

2. _____

_____

3. _____

_____

4. _____

_____

5. _____

What's Next? You Decide!

Now it's your turn to choose what to do next in the lesson.
Read the activities and decide which one you want to do—
you may want to try them both!

Make a Preposition Treasure Hunt

MATERIALS

❑ several small slips of paper

❑ 1 piece "treasure"

STEPS

Use the prepositions you have learned to create a treasure hunt for a friend or family member.

❑ Choose a small object to serve as treasure. Hide the treasure somewhere in the room.

❑ Write a clue using a preposition that tells the hunter where the treasure is. Label this No. 1.

❑ Hide clue No. 1 in a different place than the treasure.

❑ Write a new clue telling the person where the hidden clue is. Label this No. 2. Hide clue No. 2 in a different place.

❑ Continue writing, numbering, and hiding clues until you think there are enough clues. You should have at least five clues.

❑ Don't hide the last clue you write. Give this to the person who will be hunting for the treasure.

❑ Explain to him or her that the number on this paper is the number of clues that need to be found to find the treasure.

❑ Sit back and watch your hunter find the treasure!

Try to Live Without Conjunctions

STEPS

Conjunctions are little words that get a lot of use!

❑ Remember, the most common conjunctions are *and, or,* and *but*.

❑ Test yourself to see if you could live without these three conjunctions.

❑ While you're talking today, try not to use any of these words.

❑ You may be surprised—it's harder than it sounds!

❑ Keep track of how many times you actually say them. How many times?

❑ Then test yourself the next day.

❑ Again, keep track of how many times you say them.

❑ On which day did you say those words the most?

Using Interjections

Need to get someone's attention? Then use an interjection!

OBJECTIVE	BACKGROUND	MATERIALS
To have your student understand how to identify and use interjections	An interjection is a word or phrase that is used in a sentence to show strong feeling or to emphasize a point. Most interjections are placed at the beginning of sentences. They are usually followed by a comma or an exclamation point. In this lesson, your student will study how to identify, punctuate, and use interjections.	■ Student Learning Pages 13.A–13.B ■ markers or colored pencils

VOCABULARY

INTERJECTIONS words used to express strong feelings
INTONATION the rise and fall of a person's voice

Let's Begin

 INTRODUCE Begin the lesson by reading the following sentences to your student:

Wow, I really like your shirt.
Oh! I just broke my favorite mug!

Invite your student to share his or her ideas about how the sentences are similar.

2 **INSTRUCT** Tell your student that he or she will learn how to use **interjections.** Show your student the example sentences above. Explain that the underlined words are interjections. Tell your student that interjections are used to express strong feelings. They may also be used when someone wants to express something forcefully. Ask your student to read the sentences aloud. Encourage him or her to read the interjections with feeling and emphasis.

ENRICH THE EXPERIENCE

Have your student check out the Grammar Gorillas at the Web site http://www.funbrain.com/grammar.

3 **EXPLAIN** Tell your student that interjections are generally used at the beginning of sentences. They can be punctuated with commas or exclamation points. Exclamation points are used to indicate greater emotion or force in a statement. Commas are used to express a statement with less emotion or force. Ask your student to write two sentences with interjections, one with a comma and one with an exclamation point. Tell him or her to use *wow* and *oh*.

PROMOTING LITERACY

LESSON 1.13

TAKE A BREAK

Give your student a break by letting him or her choose a book to read silently. Call the silent reading time something fun or inspiring, such as REAL (Reading Enlightens All Learners). Encourage your student to apply the lesson by encouraging him or her to look for interjections in the text.

FOR FURTHER READING

A Child's Garden of Grammar, by Tom M. Disch and Dave Morice, ill. (University of Michigan Press, 2002).

Fantastic! Wow! And Unreal!: A Book About Interjections and Conjunctions, by Joy Peskin (Puffin Books, 2000).

---

4   **ELABORATE** Tell your student that the **intonation** of a person's voice changes when an interjection is spoken. Explain that intonation refers to the rise and fall of a person's voice. Read the following sentences, which contain the same words. Point out how the intonation of your voice changes for the interjection with the exclamation point and the interjection with the comma.

> No, I don't want to do that.
> No! I don't want to do that!

Invite your student to read the sentences he or she wrote in Step 3 out loud. Encourage him or her to use correct intonation.

5   **PRACTICE** Read the following sentences aloud one at a time. After reading each one, invite your student to say the interjection in the sentence.

> Oh, I didn't know that.
> Yum! This apple tastes great!
> Ugh! This meal is awful.
> Wow, that movie was long.
> Cool! How did you do that?
> Hah! I don't believe it.
> Well, I'm not sure.
> Yeah! My team won!

6   **REINFORCE** Read the sentences above aloud again. Have your student write each one in a notebook after you read it. Be sure he or she uses the correct punctuation depending on your intonation. Don't let your student peek at the page!

7   **DISTRIBUTE** Direct your student to Student Learning Page 13.A. Read the directions together. Encourage your student to use markers or colored pencils to draw colorful pictures for his or her comic strip.

Branching Out

TEACHING TIP

Be sure your student doesn't confuse interjections with one-word commands, such as *Wait!* or *Listen!* Point out that these commands consist of imperative verbs. However, interjections don't call for carrying out an action. If you'd like to brush up on your grammar, go to http://www.grammarlady.com.

CHECKING IN

To assess your student's understanding of the lesson, ask him or her to write down three important things he or she learned. Challenge your student to share why he or she chose those things.

Create a Comic Strip

Make a funny and interesting comic strip! Draw a picture in each box to show part of an event. Write what the characters say in speech bubbles. Use at least four interjections to show your characters' feelings.

What's Next? You Decide!

Now it's your turn to choose what to do next in the lesson.
Read the activities and decide which one you want to do—
you may want to try them both!

Play a Game with Interjections

MATERIALS

❏ 10–12 index cards

❏ 1 stopwatch

STEPS

Invite your family and friends to play a game using interjections.

❏ Write down 10 to 12 exciting events on index cards. Use one index card for each event.

❏ Display one index card. Have players write down sentences with interjections about the event.

❏ Players have only one minute to write their sentences for the event. Use a stopwatch to keep track of time.

❏ Give a point to the player who wrote the most sentences for the event. Keep track of the points on a sheet of paper.

❏ Repeat until all the index cards have been displayed.

❏ Count each player's points at the end of the game and declare a winner!

Write and Perform a Play

MATERIALS

❏ props

❏ costumes

❏ 1 audiocassette tape (optional)

❏ 1 audiocassette recorder (optional)

STEPS

Write a short play that is one to three minutes long. Write your play about something exciting, such as an adventure.

❏ Write down the words that each character will say. If you are not sure how to arrange your sentences, ask someone to show you an example of a play.

❏ Use as many interjections as you can to show the characters' feelings.

❏ When you are done writing, ask someone to help you make copies of your play for all the characters.

❏ Perform your play for friends and neighbors. Use creative props and costumes if you can. You might even want to record interesting sounds on an audiocassette and use them as sound effects!

Investigating Irregular Verbs

Any irregular verb will tell you—some rules are meant to be broken.

OBJECTIVE	BACKGROUND	MATERIALS
To help your student understand and use irregular verbs	Learning grammar rules helps us understand how to spell and pronounce words. However, there are exceptions to rules that must be memorized. Your student learned that he or she can form the past tense of many verbs by adding –*ed* to them. In this lesson, your student will learn about different types of verbs that don't follow this rule— irregular verbs.	■ Student Learning Pages 14.A–14.B ■ 1 copy Web, page 356 ■ 1 dictionary ■ 2–3 copied pages from a favorite book ■ 1 highlighter

Let's Begin

1 **REVIEW** Remind your student that a verb is a word that shows the action of a sentence. Invite him or her to brainstorm some verbs using a copy of the Web found on page 356. Then invite him or her to insert each verb into the following sentences. Have your student say the completed sentences out loud.

> I _____ each day.
> Yesterday, I _____.

2 **DISCUSS** Ask your student to explain how he or she changed the verbs to the past tense. Help him or her see that in many cases a verb can be changed to the past tense by simply adding –*ed* to it. Challenge him or her to find a verb from the Web or think of a verb for which this rule isn't true.

3 **EXPLAIN** Tell your student that there are verbs that form the past tense in different ways. These verbs are called irregular verbs. It's necessary to memorize the spelling of past tense irregular verbs. Point out some examples of irregular verbs, such as *run, win,* and *swim.* Ask your student to think about how he or she would change these verbs to complete the sentence "Yesterday, I _____." [Yesterday, I ran. Yesterday, I won. Yesterday, I swam.]

4 **PRACTICE** Invite your student to make a chart in his or her notebook. Have him or her label the first column "Present

A BRIGHT IDEA

To encourage your student to write and practice using the past tense, suggest that he or she keep a journal. Allow time for your student to write freely about events that happened each day. Encourage your student to look back at past journal entries to see how events in his or her life have changed.

FOR FURTHER READING

Fun with Grammar: 75 Quick Activities and Games That Help Kids Learn About Nouns, Verbs, Adjectives, Adverbs, and More: Grades 4–8, by Laura Sunley (Scholastic Professional Books, 2002).

Hot Fudge Monday: Tasty Ways to Teach Parts of Speech to Students Who Have a Hard Time Swallowing Anything to Do with Grammar, by Randy Larson (Cottonwood Press, 1998).

Tense," the second column "Past Tense," and the third column "Dictionary Check." Under the first column, have your student write this list of words: do, bring, catch, see, leave, know.

5   **COMPLETE**   Ask him or her to complete the second column with the past tenses of these verbs. Then have your student use a dictionary to check the answers. (Tell your student that he or she can find the past tense forms of irregular verbs by looking up the base verb in the dictionary.) If the answer is correct, ask your student to place a check mark in the third column. If it's incorrect, have him or her write the correct past tense form in the column.

6   **DISTRIBUTE**   Distribute Student Learning Page 14.A. Read the directions with your student. Then invite him or her to circle the incorrect verbs and write the correct spellings on the lines at the bottom of the page.

7   **CONTINUE**   For more practice with irregular verbs, together with your student go to http://english-zone.com and click on Irregular Verbs.

Branching Out

TEACHING TIP

Your student may feel overwhelmed by the thought of having to memorize irregular verbs. Remind him or her that people use these verbs in speech every day without even realizing it. When writing irregular verbs, encourage him or her to read what has been written aloud to see if it sounds right.

CHECKING IN

To assess your student's understanding of irregular verbs, have him or her read a few pages from a favorite book. Copy two or three pages that have irregular verbs. Invite him or her to circle all the verbs and highlight those that are irregular. Help your student with any difficulties that arise.

Proofread a Paragraph

Read the paragraph. There are nine verbs that are in incorrect form. Circle the incorrect verbs. Then write them correctly on the lines at the bottom of the page.

Carl waked up and looked out the window. It had snowed a lot last night, and everything was covered in white. Carl jumped out of bed, got dressed, and goed downstairs. He quickly eated some cereal and brushed his teeth. Then he went outside. The snow feeled crunchy under his feet. He jumped into the snow and maked a snow angel. Then he went to his friend Alex's house to play. Together, the two boys builded a big snowman. Then Alex haved a great idea. "I'll ask my mom to take us sledding!" said Alex. The two boys runned to Alex's house. A few minutes later, Alex's mom drived them to the big hill.

1. _____

2. _____

3. _____

4. _____

5. _____

6. _____

7. _____

8. _____

9. _____

What's Next? You Decide!

Now it's your turn to choose what to do next in the lesson.
Read the activities and decide which one you want to do—
you may want to try them both!

Write a Letter

MATERIALS

❏ 1–2 sheets stationery

❏ 1 letter-sized envelope

❏ 1 U.S. postage stamp or
1 airmail stamp

❏ 1 pair scissors

STEPS

❏ Write a letter to a friend or relative to practice using past tense verbs. Use your favorite stationery.

❏ In your letter, tell what you have been doing in the past week, month, or year.

❏ Read your letter when you have finished writing.

❏ Note all of the past tense verbs you used. You may be surprised at how much you use irregular verbs!

❏ If you'd like, mail your letter.

❏ Ask someone to help you prepare an envelope and use the correct postage stamp to mail the letter.

❏ Drop your letter in a nearby mailbox or take it to a post office.

❏ After some time has passed, you may get a response!

Play a Memory Game

MATERIALS

❏ 15 index cards

❏ markers or colored pencils

❏ 1 pair scissors

STEPS

Make a memory game to play with friends. This game will help you remember how to spell irregular verbs.

❏ Cut each index card in half to make 30 cards of the same size.

❏ Write the present tense of one irregular verb on 15 of the cards.

❏ On the other 15 cards, write the past tense of each of these verbs.

❏ Spread the cards out on a table and turn them facedown.

❏ Each player should take turns turning over two cards. If the cards show two forms of the same verb, the player should take them. The player should then take another turn.

❏ If the cards show different verbs, put them back on the table. It's the next player's turn.

❏ Keep playing until all the cards have been collected. The person with the most cards wins!

Comparing and Contrasting

Ever wonder if two similar things are created equal?
In this lesson, your student will learn to be the judge.

OBJECTIVE	BACKGROUND	MATERIALS
To teach your student how to write a compare/contrast paper	On many occasions you've probably considered how two things are similar and different. If you had put your thoughts on paper, how would you have presented your ideas? When you compare and contrast two things, it helps to organize ideas clearly and logically. In this lesson, your student will learn how to write a compare/contrast paper.	■ Student Learning Pages 15.A–15.B ■ 1 copy Venn Diagram, page 355 ■ 1 soccer ball ■ 1 basketball

VOCABULARY
COMPARE to find how things are alike **CONTRAST** to find how things are different

Let's Begin

1 **INTRODUCE** To prepare your student for the lesson, review the meanings of the words **compare** and **contrast.** Then invite your student to name two things that are alike and two things that are different.

2 **BEGIN** Tell your student that some things have qualities that are both alike and different. Provide an example by showing two related objects, such as a basketball and a soccer ball. Ask, *How are these two things alike?* [They are both balls. They are both round. They both can bounce. You can play games with both of them.] Then ask, *How are these two things different?* [They are different sizes. They are different colors. They are used in different sports. You use a basketball with your hands; you use a soccer ball with your feet.]

3 **ELABORATE** Examine two things that have some qualities in common. You might compare and contrast a dog and a cat, snow skiing and water skiing, or any pair you can think of. Distribute a copy of the Venn Diagram found on page 355. Ask your student to complete the Venn Diagram by writing similarities in the overlapping part of the two circles and differences in the parts of the circles that don't overlap. Have your student note at least two examples in each part of the diagram.

ENRICH THE EXPERIENCE

With your student, head to the Young Writers' Clubhouse at http://www.realkids. com/club.shtml. If you'd like, you can help your student publish his or her paper online at http://www.kidsnews. com.

4 **EXPAND** To provide an interesting analysis of how two things can be very alike and yet very different, compare and contrast twin siblings. Discuss any twins that your student knows from real life, books, articles, or movies. Point out how even identical twins can have very different talents, likes, dislikes, and personality traits!

5 **ORGANIZE** Tell your student that he or she can use a Venn Diagram to plan a compare/contrast paper. Ask your student to select two or three similarities and two or three differences.

6 **DRAFT** Help your student begin drafting his or her compare/ contrast paper. Tell him or her that the paper will have two paragraphs. The first paragraph will explain how the two things are alike. The second paragraph will explain how the two things are different. Explain that each paragraph should begin with a topic sentence, which tells what the paragraph is about. The topic sentence usually gives the main idea of a paragraph. For a compare/contrast paper, a topic sentence might be something like "Soccer balls and basketballs are similar in many ways." Ask your student to write a topic sentence for the first paragraph of the paper.

7 **SUPPORT** Explain that each main idea in a paragraph must be supported by details that show how the main idea is true. An example of a supporting detail for the topic sentence in Step 6 might be "First, both types of balls are round." Point out the transition word *first.* Explain that your student can use transition words to help ideas flow smoothly. Other transition words are *second, third, next,* and *finally.* Ask your student to write supporting details for the first paragraph. Then have your student complete his or her paper. Review it and then distribute Student Learning Page 15.A.

FOR FURTHER READING

Craft Lessons: Teaching Writing K–8, by Ralph Fletcher and JoAnn Portalupi (Stenhouse Publishers, 1998).

Paragraph Writing Made Easy, by Rosemary Shiras and Susan Cary Smith (Scholastic Professional Books, 2001).

The Writer's Express: Grades 4–5, by Rebekah Woodie (Instructional Fair, 1999).

Branching Out

TEACHING TIP

To help your student become more comfortable with comparing and contrasting, organize information in different ways. For example, list the qualities of each of two things in a two-column chart. Then have your student match the similarities. Explain that the qualities that don't match are differences.

CHECKING IN

To assess your student's understanding of the lesson, have him or her orally compare and contrast two things.

Write a Compare/ Contrast Paper

Read the list of ideas. Then choose two things from one of the ideas (or two things you know about). Write a compare/contrast paper on a separate sheet of paper. Use the model to help you. The introduction and conclusion are optional.

List of Ideas

❏ **Entertainment:** Compare and contrast two movies or television shows. Or compare and contrast the movie version of a story with the book version.

❏ **Literature:** Compare and contrast two different stories or books.

❏ **Characters:** Compare and contrast two characters from a story. You may also compare and contrast two real people from history, or even two people whom you know personally.

❏ **Places:** Compare and contrast two different cities or towns, two different houses or apartments, or two different vacation spots. You can also compare and contrast two different places where you play, or two rooms in your house.

❏ **Food:** Compare and contrast two different foods or dishes. You may compare and contrast two different types of food, or two different restaurants.

Model

First Paragraph (Introduction): Tell what the entire paper is about. Begin with an attention-grabbing sentence, joke, question, or something unexpected.

Second Paragraph (Body): _____ and _____ are similar in many ways. First, _____. Second, _____. Finally, _____.

Third Paragraph (Body): _____ and _____ are different in many ways. First, _____. Second, _____. Finally, _____.

Fourth Paragraph (Conclusion): Summarize the main ideas using different words. Tell how comparing and contrasting the two things is helpful.

What's Next? You Decide!

Now it's your turn to choose what to do next in the lesson. Read the activities and decide which one you want to do—you may want to try them both!

Play a Com/Con Game

STEPS

Here's a compare/contrast game that you can play anytime and anywhere.

- ❑ Think of two objects.

- ❑ Choose some ways that the two objects are similar.

- ❑ Choose some ways that the two objects are different.

- ❑ In the Com game, tell the other players, "I am thinking of two objects. They are alike because _____." See if the other people can think of the two objects.

- ❑ In the Con game, tell the other players, "I am thinking of two objects. They are different because _____."

- ❑ See if the other people can think of the two objects.

- ❑ In the Com/Con game, tell the other players, "I am thinking of two objects. They are alike because _____, and they are different because _____."

- ❑ See if the other people can think of the two objects.

Become a Compare/Contrast Detective

MATERIALS

- ❑ 8 sheets construction paper
- ❑ markers or colored pencils

STEPS

You might enjoy sneaking around your house or neighborhood to discover comparisons and contrasts.

- ❑ Look around your home, yard, or neighborhood. Observe some things around you.

- ❑ Draw a thing you observed on a sheet of construction paper. Then label it.

- ❑ List the thing's qualities next to the picture. For example, you might list for a dog "animal, brown, short hair, playful, likes people and other animals."

- ❑ Repeat this process for seven more things. When you're finished, place the eight sheets of construction paper side by side.

- ❑ Choose any two sheets. Look at the two different pictures and lists. See if you can find ways that the two things are alike and different.

- ❑ You can shuffle the sheets and try again.

Writing a Problem/ Solution Paragraph

Solutions are best discovered by examining all sides of an issue.

OBJECTIVE	BACKGROUND	MATERIALS
To have your student understand and compose a problem/solution paragraph	A problem/solution paragraph states a problem and then examines possible solutions for solving it. The writer states the pros and cons for each solution considered. Like other paragraphs, a problem/solution paragraph has a topic sentence, supporting details, and a concluding sentence. In this lesson, your student will study and write a problem/solution paragraph.	■ Student Learning Pages 16.A–16.B

VOCABULARY

PROBLEM   an issue or question that needs to be answered
SOLUTION   an answer to a problem
PROS   the reasons for choosing a solution
CONS   the reasons against choosing a solution

Let's Begin

1   **INTRODUCE** Begin the lesson by reading aloud the following paragraph:

Should I stay out late or should I try to get home on time? Staying at my friend's house is one solution because I want to keep playing this video game. My friend's mom said it was okay to stay. The downside is that my parents may ground me for staying out late. Also, it's scary and dangerous to bike home in the dark. The other solution is to leave now and get home at the time my parents asked me to. If I'm home on time, my parents will be proud of me and trust me. It's safer to bike at this time of day. The downside is that I have to quit the video game just as I'm getting good at it. I think the best solution is to leave now so I get home on time. That way my parents won't worry about me.

   Ask your student what decision he or she would make and to explain why.

DID YOU KNOW?

Did you know that studying problem/solution paragraphs can prepare your student for writing persuasive essays? After your student masters writing problem/solution paragraphs, he or she will feel more comfortable writing paragraphs that present arguments for and against a certain opinion.

FOR FURTHER READING

A Child's Calendar, by John Updike (Holiday House, Inc., 1999).

Craft Lessons: Teaching Writing K–8, by Ralph Fletcher and JoAnn Portalupi (Stenhouse Publishers, 1998).

Paragraph Writing Made Easy, by Rosemary Shiras and Susan Smith (Scholastic Professional Books, 2001).

2 **REVEAL** Share with your student that he or she is going to explore how to write a problem/solution paragraph. Ask your student what a **problem** is. Then ask your student what a **solution** is. Invite him or her to give an example that shows the meaning of each vocabulary word.

3 **QUESTION** Reread the paragraph on the previous page. Ask, *What problem is stated in the paragraph?* [the writer doesn't know whether he or she should go home or stay at his or her friend's house] Point out that the first line of the paragraph is the topic sentence. It states the problem. Tell your student that the writer of a problem/solution paragraph explains possible solutions to the problem. Invite your student to identify the two solutions in the paragraph above. [stay at his or her friend's house or go home on time]

4 **SHARE** Tell your student that after stating each solution, the writer explains the **pros** (reasons for choosing a solution) and **cons** (reasons against choosing a solution). Challenge your student to identify the pros and cons of the first solution. [pros: writer can keep playing video game, friend's mom said it was okay to stay; cons: parents may ground writer for being late, it's scary and dangerous to ride bike in the dark] Then have your student identify the pros and cons of the second solution. [pros: parents will trust and be proud of writer, it's safer to bike; cons: writer has to quit the video game] Finally, ask your student which solution the writer chose. [to go home]

5 **DISTRIBUTE** Direct your student to Student Learning Page 16.A. Tell your student that he or she will now have the opportunity to write his or her own problem/solution paragraph. Have your student read the directions out loud. Answer any questions your student has about the activity. When your student has finished writing the paragraph, check it for correct spelling, punctuation, and sentence structure. Help your student make any corrections as needed.

Branching Out

TEACHING TIP

Use an analogy to help your student understand the parts of a paragraph. Compare a peanut butter sandwich to a paragraph. The top piece of bread is the topic sentence, the peanut butter in the middle is the details, and the bottom piece of bread is the concluding sentence.

CHECKING IN

To assess your student's understanding of the lesson, invite him or her to take on the role of teacher. Invite him or her to suppose that you are the student. Then challenge him or her to teach you how to write a problem/solution paragraph.

Make a Choice

Suppose it's your birthday. Your family asks you to choose the type of party you want. You can have a small party where you eat lunch at a restaurant and then go out to a movie. Or you can have a big party at home where you eat lunch and play your favorite games. Take notes about the pros and cons of each choice. Then write a problem/solution paragraph on a separate sheet of paper.

PROS

1. Small party:

_____

_____

_____

_____

_____

2. Big party:

_____

_____

_____

_____

CONS

1. Small party:

_____

_____

_____

_____

_____

2. Big party:

_____

_____

_____

_____

What's Next? You Decide!

Now it's your turn to choose what to do next in the lesson. Read the activities and decide which one you want to do—you may want to try them both!

Give a Speech

 MATERIALS

❑ 1 audiocassette tape

❑ 1 audiocassette recorder

STEPS

Should children have to do chores at home? Write a problem/solution speech to answer this question.

❑ Fold a sheet of paper in half.

❑ On one side of the paper write the answer "Children should not have to do chores at home." On the other side of the paper write the answer "Children should have to do chores at home."

❑ Write the pros and cons of each answer in the correct column.

❑ Choose the answer that you agree with.

❑ Then prepare a speech where you give the reasons that support your opinion. Use your notes on the pros and cons.

❑ Prepare your speech. Then record it on an audio player.

❑ Play your speech for family and friends. Ask them if they agree with the solution you chose.

❑ Invite them to share their reasons for their answer.

Make a Persuasive Advertisement

 MATERIALS

❑ 1 posterboard

❑ markers

STEPS

The mayor of your town wants to build a shopping mall where there is a large park. Some people agree with her plan. Some people don't. What do you think?

❑ Decide if you want the mayor to build the shopping mall or keep the park. Then make a poster on posterboard advertising your opinion.

❑ Write a headline in big letters that tells what you'd like the mayor to do. Examples are "Save the Park!" or "Don't Stall. Build the Mall!"

❑ Draw a picture and write a list of reasons on your advertisement to support your opinion.

❑ If you want to keep the park, write the pros for keeping it and the cons for replacing it with the mall.

❑ If you want the mall built, write the pros for building it and the cons for not building it.

❑ Present your advertisement to friends and family. Ask them to share if your advertisement led them to agree with your opinion.

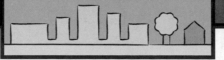

In Your Community

To reinforce the skills and concepts taught in this section,
try one or more of these activities!

Attend a Town Meeting

Together with your student attend a town meeting or debate where local issues and possible solutions will be discussed. If possible, educate your student about the issues that will be discussed so he or she will have a better understanding of the issues to be debated. During the meeting, help your student take notes. Together, write the issues discussed and list the pros and cons of each solution. Encourage your student to write other possible solutions that weren't discussed. After the meeting or debate, see if your student can meet some of the people involved in the discussion to find out why they supported the solutions they did.

Visit a Newspaper or Magazine Office

Show your student the steps between writing and publishing by visiting a local newspaper or magazine office. Contact a local office to arrange a tour of the facilities. See if your student can spend time with a writer, an editor, a printer, or a circulation representative. Have that person explain to your student his or her role and responsibilities in newspaper or magazine production. Take the news article that your student wrote in Lesson 1.11 and ask the newspaper or magazine professional what section of the newspaper or magazine it would fit into.

To Be or Not to Be: That Is the Question

Attend a play at your local high school or playhouse. If possible contact the director of the play or visit your library to obtain the script of the play. Use the script to show your student how the play is transferred from the printed page to the stage. For example, show your student how stage directions in the script are reflected in the acting. Make sure your student is able to identify drama characteristics, such as acts, scenes, and settings. If your student conveys an interest in the stage, see how he or she could get involved in drama in your community. Aside from acting, there are many behind-the-scenes jobs that your student can be involved in to gain memorable and invaluable stage experience.

Explore the World of Biography

Have your student research and write a short biography of a famous or important person from your town. Your student should make a list of important events, places, and objects discovered during his or her research. Then take your student on a field trip. For example, see if you can take your student to the chosen person's childhood home, a place where a historical event happened, or a museum that contains items of historical importance to your town. If possible take pictures at every stop. Discuss with your student the importance of what you are viewing at each location. Then have your student write a biography using the research information and the places and things viewed. Add the pictures to illustrate the final draft.

Host a Poetry Reading

Together with your student select a day in the near future on which he or she can gather together friends and family to host a poetry reading. The reading could take place at your home, a community center, or the library. (Be sure to ask the community center or library in advance of selecting the day.) Put together a list of guests to invite. If you'd like, have your student make his or her own invitations to send. Encourage the guests to bring one or two poems to read in front of the other guests. Poems can be of their own creation or just a few favorites. Don't forget to provide enough seating. You may want to supply refreshments.

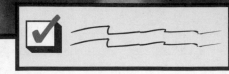

We Have Learned

❏ **Fiction**
❏ reading and analyzing fiction
❏ characteristics of fiction

❏ **Writing an Essay**
❏ using details to support and explain
❏ understanding introduction, body, conclusion

❏ **Tale**
❏ reading and analyzing a tale
❏ characteristics of tales
❏ orally retelling a story

❏ **Biography**
❏ reading and analyzing a biography
❏ characteristics of a biography

❏ **Drama**
❏ reading and analyzing drama
❏ characteristics of drama

❏ **Poetry**
❏ reading and analyzing poetry
❏ characteristics of poetry

❏ **General Nonfiction**
❏ reading and analyzing nonfiction
❏ characteristics of nonfiction

❏ **Taking Notes**
❏ identifying main-idea clues: heads, subheads, boldfaced text
❏ recognizing and organizing important information

❏ **Writing an Informational Paragraph**
❏ using topic sentence that states main idea
❏ organizing facts and details
❏ using facts and details to support main idea

❏ **News Article**
❏ reading and analyzing a news article
❏ characteristics of a news article
❏ writing a news article

❏ **Writing a Compare/Contrast Paper**
❏ comparing and contrasting two or more things
❏ using a clear topic sentence and details to support idea

❏ **Grammar**
❏ subjects, predicates
❏ adjectives, adverbs
❏ nouns, pronouns
❏ prepositions, conjunctions, interjections

❏ **Writing a Problem/Solution Paragraph**
❏ understanding pros and cons
❏ choosing the best solution

We have also learned:

_____

_____

Math

Math

Key Topics

Understanding Place Value

MATH
LESSON
2.1

It's time to put numbers in their place!

OBJECTIVE	BACKGROUND	MATERIALS
To help your student understand place value, ordering, number patterns, and rounding	Developing number sense builds a strong foundation for performing operations with numbers. In this lesson your student will study place value and learn to compare and order numbers, find number patterns, and round numbers.	■ Student Learning Pages 1.A–1.B ■ 1 posterboard ■ markers or colored pencils ■ 1 small dry-erase board (optional)

VOCABULARY

PLACE-VALUE CHART a chart that identifies the place values of the digits in a number

Let's Begin

PLACE VALUE THROUGH HUNDREDS

1 **MODEL** Use place-value blocks to help your student understand place value. Look at the place-value model together.

2 **DISCUSS** Show your student the blocks above. Have your student decide how many hundreds, tens, and ones are shown. [2 hundreds, 3 tens, and 6 ones] Ask, *What number is shown?* [236]

PLACE VALUE THROUGH MILLIONS

1 **EXPLORE** Explain that a **place-value chart** can help you read and write numbers. Look at the place-value chart together. If your student has a dry-erase board, you may wish to have him or her copy the chart onto the board.

A BRIGHT IDEA

You may wish to purchase a small dry-erase board for your student to use throughout this lesson and other math lessons.

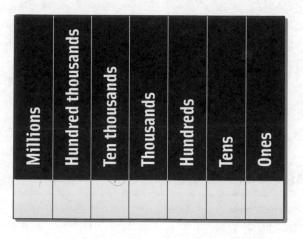

Millions	Hundred thousands	Ten thousands	Thousands	Hundreds	Tens	Ones

2 **EXPLAIN** While you're looking at the place-value chart, explain that the ones place is on the far right side. The place value increases from right to left. Write the number 2,369. Ask, *What digit is in the ones place?* [9] *What digit is in the tens place?* [6] *What digit is in the hundreds place?* [3] *What digit is in the thousands place?* [2]

3 **WRITE** Have your student make a copy of the place-value chart in his or her notebook and write each number below in the chart.

459   2,381   14,650   46,718   309,721   4,326,507

4 **EXPAND** Look at the number 2,381 together. Explain that knowing the place value of a digit tells you the value of the digit. Say, *The 1 is in the ones place, so its value is 1. The 8 is in the tens place, so its value is 80.* Ask, *What is the value of the 3?* [300] *What is the value of the 2?* [2,000]

COMPARE AND ORDER NUMBERS

1 **EXPAND** Explain that you can use what you know about place value to compare and order numbers. Ask, *Which is greater, 2,439 or 2,394? Use a place-value chart to help find the answer.* [2,439]

2 **DISCUSS** Explain that you can use symbols to show that one number is greater than or less than another. Tell your student about the greater-than symbol (>) and the less-than symbol (<). Write 2,439 > 2,394 and 2,394 < 2,439. Have your student copy these number pairs into a notebook and write > or < for each.

813   831 [<]   1,425   1,245 [>]
26,819   28,619 [<]   309,112   309,121 [<]

3 **PRACTICE** Have your student put the following numbers in order from least to greatest. Encourage your student to use a place-value chart if he or she needs to.

46,723   64,327   46,237   64,732

EXACT NUMBERS OR ESTIMATES

1   **EXPLAIN** Explain that when you are solving a word problem, you usually need an exact answer. However, sometimes you only need an estimate. Describe this situation to your student: *The Ruiz family traveled 832 miles on their summer vacation. The Dalt family traveled 697 miles. About how many more miles did the Ruiz family travel than the Dalt family?*

2   **DISCUSS** Ask, *Do you think this problem needs an exact answer or an estimate?* [estimate] If your student answers *estimate,* ask, *How do you know?* [the problem asks about how many miles] If your student answers *exact,* ask, *Why do you think you need an exact answer?* Point out that the problem asks *about* how many miles. Explain that words such as *about* and *approximately* indicate that only an estimate is needed.

3   **ASK** Ask your student to decide whether an exact answer or an estimate is needed for each situation below.

    There are 293 players in the city softball league. There are 218 players in the city soccer league. How many more players are in the city softball league than in the city soccer league? [exact]

    Last year, 26,453 people visited the zoo and 22,893 people visited the amusement park. About how many more people visited the zoo than the amusement park last year? [estimate]

NUMBER PATTERNS

1   **EXPAND** Explain that understanding place value can also help you identify patterns in numbers. Have your student look at the number pattern below.

$$536, 546, \underline{\hspace{1.5cm}}, 566$$

2   **DISCUSS** Discuss the pattern with your student. Ask, *The digits in which place values are staying the same?* [hundreds and ones] *The digits in which place value are changing?* [tens]

3   **EXPLORE** Ask, *By how much are the tens changing each time?* [they are increasing by 1 ten] *What is the pattern?* [the pattern is increasing by 10 each time] *What is the missing number?* [556]

4   **REVIEW** If your student names the missing number incorrectly, review the material on place value. Write the numbers in a place-value chart to help your student see that the pattern is increasing by 10.

5   **EXPAND** Give your student another number pattern. Discuss which digits stay the same and which digits change. Ask what the pattern is and what the missing number is.

ROUND NUMBERS

1 **EXPLORE** Explain that you can use a number line to round numbers. Look at the number line with your student.

1,228

1,200   1,225   1,250   1,275   1,300

2 **EXPLAIN** Explain that when you want to round a number, you should look at the distances between numbers on either side of the number line. This helps you decide whether to round up or down. Have your student use the number line to round 1,228 to the nearest hundred.

3 **DISCUSS** Look at the number line with your student. Ask, *What two numbers is 1,228 between?* [1,200 and 1,300] Ask, *Is 1,228 closer to 1,200 or to 1,300?* [1,200] Explain that because 1,228 is closer to 1,200, you will round down to the nearest hundred. Ask, *What is 1,228 rounded to the nearest hundred?* [1,200]

4 **ASK** Have your student practice rounding by rounding each number below to the nearest ten.

718 [720]   **954** [950]   **2,382** [2,380]

Have your student round each number below to the nearest hundred.

608 [600]   **3,466** [3,500]   **28,729** [28,700]

Have your student round each number below to the nearest thousand.

987 [1,000]   **5,623** [6,000]   **17,395** [17,000]

A BRIGHT IDEA

If your student is having difficulty rounding, have him or her draw a number line and then cut it out. Explain that he or she can fold the number line in half to find the halfway point. If the number falls to the left of the halfway point, round down. If the number falls to the right of the halfway point, round up.

FOR FURTHER READING

Math Bridge: 4th Grade, by Tracy Dankberg, Jennifer Moore, and James Michael Orr (Rainbow Publishers, 1999).

Ready to Use Math Proficiency Lessons and Activities, 4th Grade, by Frances McBroom Thompson (John Wiley and Sons, 2003).

Branching Out

TEACHING TIP

If your student is not sure which digit to look at when deciding how to round, have him or her circle the digit in the value place he or she is rounding to. Then have him or her underline the digit to the *right* of the circled place. The underlined digit is the deciding digit.

CHECKING IN

Ask your student to write down any four-digit number. Then have him or her round to the nearest ten, hundred, and thousand.

Practice Finding Place Value

MATH

1.A

Write the value of the underlined digit.

1. 4,387 _____

2. 3,095 _____

3. 36,807 _____

Write > or < on the line.

4. 43,891 _____ 34,891

5. 87,459 _____ 87,594

Order the numbers from least to greatest.

6. 78,877   87,778   78,787   87,877   _____

7. Three friends played a computer game. Anna scored 72,456.
Javier scored 73,002. Hannah scored 72,588.

Who had the highest score? _____

Who had the lowest score? _____

Write the missing numbers. Use place-value patterns to help.

8. 41,398; 42,389; 43,189; _____; _____

Round each to the nearest hundred.

9. 3,459 _____

10. 25,438 _____

Round each to the nearest thousand.

11. 18,013 _____

12. 487,687 _____

What's Next? You Decide!

Now it's your turn to choose what to do next in the lesson.
Read the activities and decide which one you want to do—
you may want to try them both!

Make the Big Bucks

MATERIALS

- ❑ 20 $100 play-money bills
- ❑ 20 $1,000 play-money bills
- ❑ 1 $10,000 play-money bill
- ❑ 1 die

STEPS

Play this game with a friend or family member. Use play money from a board game or make your own with paper, scissors, and markers.

- ❑ Each player rolls the die and takes the number of $100 bills rolled. If you roll a five, take five $100 bills.

- ❑ Each time a player has 10 or more of one type of bill, he or she MUST trade it in for the next higher bill. If the player passes the turn to the next player without trading the money in, he or she must skip the next turn.

- ❑ Take turns until one player can trade for the $10,000 bill. The first player to "make the big bucks" wins.

Make the Wild Estimate

STEPS

- ❑ Think of five estimates to answer the following questions:

  - How tall is the tallest person in the world?

  - What is the driving distance in miles from New York City (east coast) to Los Angeles (west coast)?

  - How many doorways are in your house?

- ❑ Write the estimates in a notebook. These are tough questions, so don't worry if you have to make a wild estimate.

- ❑ Look up the answers in the back of the book.

- ❑ Compare the real answers to your estimates. Were you close? Are you surprised by the real answer?

- ❑ Think up five more wild questions you can make wild estimates for and try those.

- ❑ Share what you learned with a friend.

Adding Whole Numbers and Money

It all adds up!

OBJECTIVE	BACKGROUND	MATERIALS
To teach your student to use a variety of strategies to add whole numbers and money	Understanding how to add greater whole numbers and money is a fundamental skill in mathematics and is applicable to everyday life. In this lesson, your student will learn how to add two- and three-digit numbers, greater numbers, and money.	<ul><li>Student Learning Pages 2.A–2.B</li><li>10 buttons or counters</li><li>1–2 copies Grid, page 357</li></ul>

VOCABULARY
REGROUPING exchanging amounts of the same value to rename a number

Let's Begin

ADDITION FACTS

1 **EXPLORE** Tell your student that using addition facts he or she already knows is one way to solve an addition problem. Give your student 10 buttons or counters. Then have him or her make a group of 2 counters and a group of 6 counters. Say, *Use your counters to solve 2 + 6.* [8]

2 **EXPAND** Then say, *You know that 2 + 6 = 8. How can you use this addition fact to solve 4 + 6?* [add 2 more counters to the group of 2 to get 10 total; think of the problem as 2 + 6 + 2 to get 10]

ADDITION OF TWO- AND THREE-DIGIT NUMBERS

1 **EXPLAIN** Explain that when adding two- and three-digit numbers, your student must line up the ones, tens, and hundreds place-value columns. Then, starting with the ones column, he or she can add each place-value column as a separate addition fact. Give your student these addition problems:

$$\begin{array}{r} 15 \\ + 34 \\ \hline \end{array} \qquad \begin{array}{r} 132 \\ + 347 \\ \hline \end{array}$$

2 **PRACTICE** Have your student use a copy of the Grid found on page 357 to line up the problems correctly. Then have your student add the numbers in the ones column, the tens column, and the hundreds column. Ask, *What are the answers to the problems?* [49; 479]

3 **RELATE** Explain that your student can estimate sums to judge whether an answer is reasonable. For two-digit addition problems, round both numbers to the nearest ten. For three-digit problems, round both numbers to the nearest hundred. Then add the rounded numbers. Give your student the problems below. Have him or her estimate the sums.

36 + 42 [40 + 40 = 80]

589 + 202 [600 + 200 = 800]

71 + 694 [70 + 700 = 770]

312 + 99 [300 + 100 = 400]

4 **ASK** Have your student give the exact answers for the problems above. Then ask him or her to compare the estimated sums with the exact answers. Ask, *Based on your estimated sums, are your exact answers reasonable? Why?*

5 **MODEL** If your student needs help estimating sums, review how to round numbers. Refer to the numbers below. Tell your student to look at the number to the right of the place value that he or she is rounding to. If the number is equal to or greater than 5, round up. If it is less than 5, round down. Ask, *Which number would you look at to round 46 to the nearest ten?* [6] *139 to the nearest hundred?* [3] *To what numbers would you round 46 and 139?* [50 and 100]

Hundreds	Tens	Ones
0	4	6
1	3	9

6 **EXPLAIN** Tell your student that some addition problems require **regrouping.** Give your student this problem: *Alexana has $186. Bryce has $107. How much money do Alexana and Bryce have in all?*

7 **ASK** Have your student set up the problem correctly on a copy of the Grid found on page 357. Ask, *Does the problem require regrouping?* [yes] *How do you know?* [because the 6 and 7 in the ones column add up to 13, which is more than 9] Watch as your student solves the problem. [$293]

A BRIGHT IDEA

If your student needs more help with regrouping, use everyday objects to clarify the concept. Pens may stand for tens and buttons for ones.

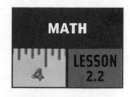

8 **MODEL** If your student **didn't solve the problem** correctly, demonstrate how to regroup. Show him or her how to group the numbers for addition as shown below. Ask, *In which place do the numbers add up to more than 9?* [the ones place] *What do they add up to?* [13] *What does the 1 represent?* [tens] *Where do you carry the 1?* [above the 8 in the tens column] Have your student add the tens and the hundreds. [293]

	1	
Hundreds	**Tens**	**Ones**
1	8	6
+ 1	0	7
		3

ADDITION OF GREATER NUMBERS

1 **EXPAND** Explain that adding greater numbers is similar to adding two- and three-digit numbers. Point out that there are more place values to pay attention to, so it's important to line up the columns correctly. Tell your student that five-digit numbers have thousands and ten-thousands places. A comma always follows the thousands place. Ask, *How can you use the commas to set up the problem 19,885 + 30,121?* [the commas show the thousands place; use them to align the place values]

2 **MODEL** Have your student find the answer to the problem in Step 1. [50,006] Observe his or her regrouping technique. Then have your student practice by completing these problems:

$$
\begin{array}{r} 12{,}689 \\ + \ 67{,}421 \\ \hline [80{,}110] \end{array}
\qquad
\begin{array}{r} 45{,}076 \\ + \ 86{,}632 \\ \hline [131{,}708] \end{array}
$$

ADDITION OF DOLLARS AND CENTS

1 **RELATE** Explain that when adding money it's also important to line up the decimals. Give your student the list of prices below. Ask him or her to write the problems in a notebook and align the decimals. Suggest that he or she draw a line between the numerals in each column.

$20.00
$9.53
$67.12
$.75
$165.09
$2.26
$400.80
$.04
$595.76
$1.00

GET ORGANIZED

Have your student add zeros to those prices that do not have a ones or tens place value, e.g., $00.75. This will help him or her stay organized when adding each column.

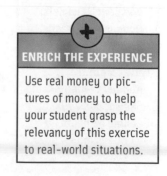
ENRICH THE EXPERIENCE

Use real money or pictures of money to help your student grasp the relevancy of this exercise to real-world situations.

MATH

LESSON
2.2
4

2 **EXPLORE** Explain that adding money requires regrouping cents into dollars. Point out that one dollar ($1.00) is made up of 100 cents. Explain that when adding 50 cents and 75 cents, the sum is more than 100 cents and so is written or spoken as a combination of dollars and cents. In other words, 50 cents plus 75 cents is one dollar and 25 cents. Ask, *Suppose you have six quarters. How many cents do you have?* [150 cents] *How would you say that in dollars and cents?* [one dollar and 50 cents] Work with your student to show that six quarters equals $1.50.

3 **ASK** Ask your student to solve this problem: *You have $9.00. A movie ticket costs $4.75. A medium popcorn costs $3.50. Do you have enough money for both?* [yes]

4 **PRACTICE** Distribute Student Learning Page 2.A for additional practice.

Branching Out

TEACHING TIP

Encourage your student to estimate the sum of addition problems before he or she gives the exact answer. This will help your student decide whether his or her exact answer is reasonable.

CHECKING IN

Give your student this problem:

$$\$1.35 + \$.45 = \text{_____}$$

Ask your student to explain in words the steps he or she would take to solve the problem.

FOR FURTHER READING

Coin County: A Bank in a Book, by Jim Talbot (Innovative Kids, 1999).

Let's Add Bills (Dollars and Cents), by Kelly Doudna (Sandcastle, 2002).

Power Math Whole Numbers: Addition and Subtraction 1995, by Connie Eichhorn (Globe Fearon, 2002).

Practice Addition

Form numbers using all of the numbers in the parentheses.
What is the largest number you can form by adding both lines?

1. _____ (3, 8, 4)   2. _____ (2, 9, 7, 1)

   + _____ (1, 1, 2)   + _____ (5, 6, 3, 2)

   _____   _____

Add.

3.   325   4.   1,155
    + 498   + 402

5.   578   6.   99
    + 313   + 87

7. Which sum is closest to 900? _____

Read the word problems. Then solve.

8. Corrine has 12 dimes and 38 pennies. Michelle has $1.05. Who has more money?

   _____

9. Keith wants to buy a new bicycle and helmet. The bicycle costs $127.99. The helmet costs $26.75. Estimate how much money Keith will need for both items.

   _____

10. Last year, a total of 25,006 people attended a football game in the town of Sportsdale. The year before that, 28,765 people attended a football game in Sportsdale. How many people attended football games during both years?

    _____

What's Next? You Decide!

Now it's your turn to choose what to do next in the lesson. Read the activities and decide which one you want to do— you may want to try them both!

Plan a Party!

MATERIALS

❑ 3 slips paper reading $20, $35, $100

❑ 1 paper or plastic bag

STEPS

❑ Place the slips of paper in a bag and shake it.

❑ Choose one slip of paper. This is how much money you may spend on party supplies.

❑ Think of five items you probably have enough money to buy for the party.

❑ Estimate the price of each item and add them together. Do you have enough money to buy all the items?

❑ Research the prices of these items. Use the Internet, the newspaper, or go to the store. Write down the prices.

❑ Check your answer by adding the actual price of each item.

Decode the Secret Message

STEPS

❑ Solve each addition problem.

❑ Write the letter that matches each answer to learn the secret message.

3,405 +5,124	201 +669	27 +71
_____	_____	_____
333 +498	1,479 +3,652	13 +47
_____	_____	_____

831 = W	60 = N
5,131 = I	870 = O
98 = U	8,529 = Y

❑ What was the secret message?

❑ See if you can come up with your own secret code.

Subtracting Whole Numbers and Money

What you take away matters!

OBJECTIVE	BACKGROUND	MATERIALS
To teach your student subtraction with whole numbers and money	Mastering basic subtraction facts builds a strong foundation for subtraction with two- and three-digit numbers, greater numbers, and money. In this lesson, your student will practice basic subtraction facts and apply subtraction strategies to greater numbers and money.	■ Student Learning Pages 3.A–3.B ■ 1 copy Grid, page 357

Let's Begin

SUBTRACTION WITH TWO- AND THREE-DIGIT NUMBERS

1 **REVIEW** Have your student practice basic subtraction facts. Ask your student to write and solve the following subtraction problems in a notebook:

$9 - 4 = $ ____	$12 - 6 = $ ____	$11 - 5 = $ ____
$8 - 3 = $ ____	$7 - 5 = $ ____	$10 - 6 = $ ____
$13 - 8 = $ ____	$12 - 7 = $ ____	$15 - 8 = $ ____
$14 - 6 = $ ____	$17 - 9 = $ ____	$16 - 7 = $ ____

2 **EXPAND** Explain that knowing basic subtraction facts is important for learning subtraction with two- and three-digit numbers. Check your student's answers to the problems above. Have him or her correct any errors before moving to subtraction with two- and three-digit numbers.

3 **EXPLAIN** Explain that when subtracting two- and three-digit numbers, it's important to set up the problem correctly. Tell your student, *It's important to line up numbers according to their place value. Ones should be lined up with other ones. Tens should be lined up with other tens. Hundreds should be lined up with other hundreds.* Describe this situation to your student: *The theater had 483 tickets available for the eight o' clock performance. It sold 374 tickets. How many tickets were left?*

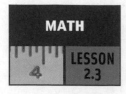

MATH

LESSON
4   2.3

A BRIGHT IDEA

If your student is having trouble with regrouping, have him or her make place-value blocks to use when regrouping. Use large squares of paper for the hundreds blocks, thin strips of paper for the tens blocks, and small squares of paper for the ones blocks.

---

4 **ASK** Have your student write out the problem. Ask, *Will this problem require regrouping?* [yes] Have your student subtract the two numbers. Observe his or her regrouping methods. Check the final answer. [109] If your student **solved the problem** correctly, have him or her complete problems 1–4 on Student Learning Page 3.A for more practice.

5 **MODEL** If your student **didn't solve the problem** correctly, have him or her look at the numbers below to help with regrouping. Write the number 483 in the chart and model for your student the steps to follow for borrowing. Ask, *After you regroup, what new numbers do you have in the place-value chart?* [4 hundreds, 7 tens, 13 ones] *Now what is your answer when you subtract?* [109] If your student still has an incorrect answer, check his or her subtraction.

Hundreds	Tens	Ones
	7	13
4	8̸	3̸

SUBTRACTION WITH GREATER NUMBERS

1 **EXPLAIN** Explain that the strategies your student used to subtract two- and three-digit numbers can be used to subtract numbers with more than three digits. Describe this situation to your student: *The population in Gina's town was 29,936 last year. This year the population is 28,014. How many more people lived in Gina's town last year?* Explain that estimation is helpful when subtracting greater numbers. Ask, *What numbers do you get if you round each number in the problem to the nearest thousand?* [30,000 and 28,000]

2 **ESTIMATE** Ask your student to estimate the answer to the problem. [about 2,000] Explain to your student that this estimation can be used to check his or her answer to the problem. Have your student write out the problem.

3 **SOLVE** Ask, *Will this problem require regrouping?* [no] Have your student subtract the two numbers to solve the problem. [1,922]

4 **CHECK** Have your student check his or her answer using the estimate from above. If your student **solved the problem** correctly, have him or her complete problems 5–7 on Student Learning Page 3.A for more practice.

5 **MODEL** If your student **didn't solve the problem** correctly, have him or her use a place-value chart to ensure the numbers are lined up correctly. Write the number 29,936 in the place-value chart. Then write the number 28,014 below it in the place-value chart. Ask, *Now what is your answer when you subtract?* [1,922] If your student still has an incorrect answer, check his or her subtraction.

SUBTRACTION ACROSS ZEROS

1 **EXPLAIN** Explain that when the larger (or top) number in a subtraction problem has zeros in it, the problem will require regrouping. Describe this situation to your student: *There are 800 seats in the auditorium. There are people sitting in 678 seats. How many seats are empty?*

2 **ASK** Have your student write out the problem. Ask, *What should you do when you are subtracting from a number with a zero in the ones place?* [regroup by taking 1 ten and making it 10 ones] Then ask, *What should you do when there is also a zero in the tens place?* [move to greater place values until you find a nonzero number, then regroup] Have your student subtract the two numbers. Observe his or her regrouping methods. Point out that he or she will need to regroup hundreds to tens and then regroup tens to ones before subtracting the ones column. Check the final answer. [122]

3 **MODEL** If your student **didn't solve the problem** correctly, have him or her use a place-value chart to help with regrouping. Write the number 800 in the chart and model for your student the steps to follow for borrowing. Ask, *After you regroup, what new numbers do you have in the place-value chart?* [7 hundreds, 9 tens, 10 ones] *Now what is your answer when you subtract?* [122] If your student still has an incorrect answer, check his or her subtraction.

SUBTRACTION WITH MONEY

1 **EXPAND** Explain that you can subtract money using the same strategies your student used for subtracting two- and three-digit numbers and greater numbers. Ask, *How is subtracting $2.34 from $4.56 like subtracting three-digit numbers?* [these are three-digit numbers with a decimal and a dollar sign]

2 **EXPLAIN** Explain that when subtracting money, it's important to set up the problem correctly. This includes lining up the decimal points. Tell your student, *Always line up money amounts according to dollars and cents. Dollars are on the left side of the decimal point and cents are on the right side of the decimal point. Always line up the decimal points.* Describe this situation to your student: *Alex had $5.63. He spent $3.54. How much money did he have left?*

3 **ASK** Have your student write out the problem. Remind him or her to line up the decimal points. Having your student use a copy of the Grid found on page 357 might help him or her set up the problem correctly. Ask, *Will this problem require regrouping?* [yes] Have your student subtract the two numbers. Observe his or her regrouping methods. Check the final answer. [$2.09] Make sure the decimal point is in the correct place and that the answer includes a dollar sign. If your student **solved**

MATH

LESSON 2.3

A BRIGHT IDEA

To reinforce subtracting with money, try using real coins. Have your student pretend to be a store cashier. You can pretend to buy something and have your student count back the change to you. Then have your student solve the same problem with pencil and paper.

FOR FURTHER READING

Nimble with Numbers, by Leigh Childs and Laura Choate (Dale Seymore Publications, 1998).

Ready to Use Math Proficiency Lessons and Activities, 4th Grade, by Frances McBroom Thompson (John Wiley and Sons, 2003).

the problem correctly, have him or her complete problems 8–12 on Student Learning Page 3.A for more practice.

4 **MODEL** If your student **didn't solve the problem** correctly, help him or her with regrouping. Write the problem and demonstrate how to regroup $5.63. Cross out the 3 and write 13 above it. Cross out the 6 and write 5 above it. Ask, *Now what is your answer when you subtract?* [$2.09] If your student still has an incorrect answer, check his or her subtraction.

$$\begin{array}{r} {\scriptstyle 5\ 13} \\ \$5.63 \\ -\ 3.54 \\ \hline \end{array}$$

Branching Out

TEACHING TIP

If your student is making subtraction errors, review basic subtraction facts. Give your student a number, such as 12, and have him or her write 5 different subtraction sentences that involve subtracting another number from 12. Repeat this exercise with any subtraction facts with which your student is having difficulty.

CHECKING IN

Have your student write his or her own problem using the number sentence 1,438 − 1,247. Observe as your student uses regrouping to solve the problem.

Subtract Whole Numbers and Money

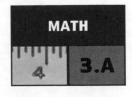

MATH

3.A

Subtract.

1.   75
      − 28

2.   83
      − 66

3.   98
      − 17

4.   254
     − 167

5.   832
     − 478

6.   555
     − 281

Estimate first. Then subtract.

7.   3,419
    − 1,289

8.   42,302
    − 36,814

9.   74,391
    − 55,218

Subtract.

10. $0.76
     − $0.34

11. $2.56
     − $1.43

12. $8.07
     − $4.39

13. The city improvement group plans to plant 3,525 new trees
    around the city. So far, it has planted 1,498 trees. How many
    more trees does it need to plant?

    _____

14. Monique had $6.54. She spent $3.95 on lunch. How much money
    does she have left?

    _____

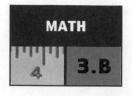

What's Next? You Decide!

Now it's your turn to choose what to do next in the lesson.
Read the activities and decide which one you want to do—
you may want to try them both!

Make Change

MATERIALS

❏ several coins and bills

❏ 1 posterboard

❏ crayons or markers

STEPS

Ask a friend or family member to help
you with this activity.

❏ Suppose you are the cashier at a
school supply store. Make a price
chart on the posterboard that shows
all the items you sell and their costs.

❏ Make a bank for yourself and give
some bills and coins to your friend
to use in the activity.

❏ Have your friend be a customer who
comes in to buy an item. He or she
should hand you more money than
the item costs.

❏ Decide how much change the person
should receive and make the correct
change.

❏ If you have difficulty making
change, write the subtraction
problem on paper and solve.

Watch the Weather

MATERIALS

❏ 1 Fahrenheit thermometer

STEPS

❏ Place a thermometer outside. The
thermometer should show the
temperature in degrees Fahrenheit.

❏ Create a five-day chart in your
notebook.

❏ Check the temperature at 9:00 A.M.
and 3:00 P.M. each day for five days
in a row.

❏ Record the temperatures for each
day in the chart.

❏ Find the difference in temperature
between 9:00 A.M. and 3:00 P.M. for
each day.

❏ On which day was the difference
in temperature the greatest?

❏ On which day was the difference
in temperature the least?

❏ Based on what you observed over
the last five days, do you think the
temperature differences tomorrow
will be larger, smaller, or about the
same?

❏ Share your observations with an
adult.

Multiplying Whole Numbers

Want more? Multiply!

OBJECTIVE	BACKGROUND	MATERIALS
To help your student understand multiplication concepts and master multiplication facts	Understanding the concepts behind multiplication will help your student master multiplication facts, which will build a strong foundation for multiplying and dividing greater numbers. In this lesson, your student will learn how multiplication can be used to add like groups and how multiplication facts relate to each other.	■ Student Learning Pages 4.A–4.B ■ 1 copy Grid, page 357

VOCABULARY

ARRAYS arrangements of rows with the same number of items in each row; an egg carton is an array of two rows of six

FACTORS the numbers that are being multiplied; in $2 \times 7 = 14$, 2 and 7 are factors

PRODUCT the answer to a multiplication problem; in $2 \times 7 = 14$, 14 is the product

Let's Begin

MULTIPLICATION WITH 2 AND 4

1 **EXPLORE** Explain that multiplication is used to add like groups. Ask your student how many apples he or she would need if you both wanted two apples. Have your student explain how he or she arrived at the answer. Then ask how many apples you would need if each of you wanted four apples. Ask your student to explain how he or she figured out the problem.

2 **EXPLAIN** Have your student draw the following **arrays** in his or her notebook:

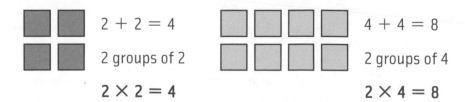

$2 + 2 = 4$	$4 + 4 = 8$
2 groups of 2	2 groups of 4
$2 \times 2 = 4$	$2 \times 4 = 8$

Explain how the first array shows two groups of two. Mention that he or she can add to find the total items ($2 + 2 = 4$) or he or she can use the multiplication fact $2 \times 2 = 4$. The second

array shows two groups of four. Show that the total number of items can be found by adding (4 + 4 = 8) or by using the multiplication fact 2 × 4 = 8. Ask, *How is multiplication like addition?* [multiplication is a way to add groups that have the same number of items]

3 DRAW Tell your student to draw an array for 4 × 3 in his or her notebook. [four rows of three] Then ask your student to write a multiplication sentence for the array. Show him or her how to write a multiplication sentence by multiplying the total number of groups by the number of objects in each group. The array has four groups of three: 4 × 3 = 12.

4 PRACTICE Have your student draw another illustration for 4 × 3, such as four groups of three stars. Again, help your student write a multiplication sentence for what he or she sees. Point out that in 4 × 3 = 12 the numbers 4 and 3 are **factors.** Twelve is the answer, or **product.** Draw arrays or other illustrations for multiplication facts using 4 as a factor (4 × 9, 4 × 6, etc.) and have your student write multiplication sentences for each.

5 COMPARE Encourage your student to write the following problems in his or her notebook:

2 × 3 = 6	2 × 5 = 10	2 × 7 = 14
4 × 3 = 12	4 × 5 = 20	4 × 7 = 28

Then ask your student, *If you have two groups of three, how many items do you have?* [6] *If you have four groups of three, how many items do you have?* [12] *When you went from two groups to four groups, how did the number of groups change?* [the number of groups doubled] *After the number of groups in the problem was doubled, what happened to the product?* [it doubled] Ask your student what patterns he or she sees in the problems and discuss. [when you double one of the factors, the product doubles]

MULTIPLICATION WITH 3 AND 6

1 ASK Explain that multiplication can be used to add any number of like groups. Have your student solve the following problem:

Henry has 3 dogs. It costs $3 to have the pet groomer cut a dog's hair. Henry is taking all 3 dogs for a haircut. How much money will he spend?

Ask your student to explain how he or she solved the problem.

2 REINFORCE Reinforce multiplication concepts by having your student draw an array and tell you the number sentences for the problem. [three rows or groups of three; 3 + 3 + 3 = 9; 3 × 3 = 9] Ask your student to make up a new story problem for the multiplication fact 3 × 3 = 9.

DID YOU KNOW?

Explain to your student that the word *of* usually indicates multiplication. That is, the phrase "two groups *of* four" means 2 × 4.

3 **REVIEW** Have your student write the following problems in his or her notebook:

$3 \times 2 = 6$	$3 \times 4 = 12$	$3 \times 8 = 24$
$6 \times 2 = 12$	$6 \times 4 = 24$	$6 \times 8 = 48$

Ask your student what patterns he or she sees in the problems and discuss. [when you double one of the factors, the product doubles]

4 **PRACTICE** Create story problems for your student to solve using multiplication sentences with factors of 3 and 6. Encourage your student to explain the strategy he or she used to solve each problem. Then have your student create story problems of his or her own.

MULTIPLICATION WITH 5 AND 10

1 **MODEL** Reveal that groups of five or ten can be added together by multiplying. Explain that counting by fives and tens will help your student multiply by those numbers. Have your student trace around his or her two hands and label each finger from 1 to 10.

Point to each finger as your student counts by fives. Discuss how multiplying by five is like adding groups of five or counting by fives.

Model how to use the drawing to solve 7×5. Say, *7×5 is seven groups of five, so I can count by fives seven times.* Point to each finger as you and your student count: 5, 10, 15, 20, 25, 30, 35. Repeat the activity, but count by tens and solve 4×10.

2 **PRACTICE** Give your student other multiplication problems with factors of 5 and 10 to solve. Have him or her point to each finger as he or she counts.

MULTIPLICATION WITH 7, 8, AND 9

1 **OBSERVE** Explain to your student that he or she can use any of the strategies he or she feels comfortable with to solve multiplication problems. Remind your student that he or she can add, draw arrays, or draw other pictures to help him or her solve multiplication problems. Give your student the following multiplication problems to solve: 3×9, 7×8, and 5×7. Ask your student to explain his or her strategy. If your student **solved the problems** correctly, proceed to the next section, Relations Between Multiplication Facts.

2 **RETEACH** If your student **didn't solve the problems** correctly, help him or her solve the problems by drawing arrays or other pictures. Have your student say aloud, "3×9 is three groups of nine, 7×8 is seven groups of eight," and so on. You may wish to distribute a copy of the Grid found on page 357 to make it easy to show arrays. Continue working with various multiplication facts until your student is comfortable solving multiplication problems.

GET ORGANIZED

Graph paper is an easy and efficient way for students to show arrays. By coloring a box for each object, he or she can keep the rows and columns straight.

RELATIONS BETWEEN MULTIPLICATION FACTS

1 **EXPLORE** Explain that each multiplication fact has a corresponding fact made by reversing the factors being multiplied. For example, $9 \times 5 = 45$ and $5 \times 9 = 45$ are corresponding facts. Have your student draw the following arrays: two rows of seven and seven rows of two. Then have your student write a multiplication fact for each array. [$2 \times 7 = 14$, $7 \times 2 = 14$] Ask, *How are the arrays and multiplication facts similar?* [each array contains the same number of objects arranged differently; each multiplication fact has the same factors written in reverse order]

2 **RELATE** Give your student various multiplication problems to solve. Ask him or her to write and solve the multiplication problem and then reverse the factors to find the multiplication fact that corresponds to the problem he or she solved.

3 **DISTRIBUTE** Have your student complete Student Learning Page 4.A for more practice.

Branching Out

TEACHING TIP

Encourage your student to memorize all of the basic multiplication facts (multiplying with factors from 1 to 10). This will greatly enhance his or her success with division and with multiplying greater numbers. You may wish to set up a reward system to motivate your student to commit the facts to memory.

CHECKING IN

You can assess your student's understanding of multiplying whole numbers by having your student write a story problem for 9×7. Then have him or her solve the problem and explain how he or she arrived at the product.

FOR FURTHER READING

The Best of Times: Math Strategies That Multiply, by Greg Tang and Harry Briggs, ill. (Scholastic Trade, 2002).

The Grapes of Math, by Greg Tang (Scholastic Trade, 2001).

Making Multiplication Easy, by Meish Goldish (Scholastic Trade, 1999).

Practice Multiplication

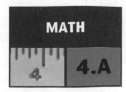

Write a multiplication sentence for each.

1. Three rows of six _____

2. Seven rows of four _____

3. Draw an array for 8 × 5.

Multiply.

4.   7
     × 6

5.   2
     × 9

6.   8
     × 4

7.   3
     × 4

8.   8
     × 8

9.   5
     × 10

Solve.

10. Maria has 7 cats. Maria's grandmother knitted kitten mittens for each of the cats' paws. How many mittens did Maria's grandmother knit?

_____

What's Next? You Decide!

Now it's your turn to choose what to do next in the lesson. Read the activities and decide which one you want to do— you may want to try them both!

Roll the Dice

MATERIALS

❏ 2 dice

❏ at least 36 counters (buttons, soda tabs, toothpicks, and so on)

STEPS

Ask an adult to help you do this activity and check your work.

❏ Find at least 36 counters. You can use buttons, soda tabs, toothpicks, and so on. Be sure to check with an adult first before using.

❏ Roll each die.

❏ Look at the numbers that came up on each die.

❏ Write a multiplication sentence using the two numbers rolled as factors. For example, if you rolled a 6 and a 5, the multiplication sentence would be 6 × 5.

❏ Use the counters to lay out an array that matches your multiplication sentence.

❏ Reverse the factors and write another multiplication sentence.

❏ Build another array that matches your new sentence.

❏ If you'd like, play with another person. One of you can roll the dice and create multiplication sentences while one of you makes arrays.

Make a Multiplication Chart

MATERIALS

❏ 1–2 copies Grid, page 357

STEPS

❏ Write a multiplication sign in the top left-hand square of the Grid. Then write the numbers 1 to 10 across the top and 1 to 10 down the left side.

❏ Find the number 1 on the left side. Count across by ones, recording one number in each square.

❏ Now find the number 2 on the left side. Count across by twos, recording one number in each square.

❏ Complete each row by skip counting beginning with the first number in the row.

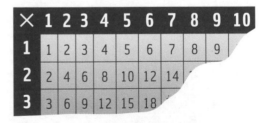

❏ Now use your chart to find the product of 3 × 7. Place one finger on row 3 and one on column 7.

❏ Follow the row and column with your fingers until they intersect. The intersection of row 3 and column 7 is the product of 3 × 7.

Multiplying Greater Numbers

Give a child the proper tools and he or she will do great things.

OBJECTIVE	BACKGROUND	MATERIALS
To teach your student to multiply two-, three-, and four-digit numbers	You need 212 napkins for the banquet. Will 16 packages of 18 be enough? Multiplying is a skill that we use every day. We often need to multiply numbers greater than the basic facts. In this lesson, your student will use his or her knowledge of the basic multiplication facts to multiply greater numbers.	■ Student Learning Pages 5.A–5.B

Let's Begin

MULTIPLICATION WITH MULTIPLES OF 10, 100, AND 1,000

1 **MODEL** Show your student how to count by tens to find the multiples of 10: 10, 20, 30, 40, and so on. Multiplying by multiples of 10 is simpler if you break the multiple into groups of ten. Model how to solve this problem:

$$6 \times 20 \qquad 20 = 2 \text{ tens}$$
$$6 \times 2 \text{ tens} = 12 \text{ tens} \qquad 12 \text{ tens} = 120$$

2 **EXPAND** Mention that to find the multiples of 100, count by hundreds. Model how to solve 9×300 using the methods in Step 1. Then give your student a few problems to solve using those methods.

3 **BUILD** Ask your student, *If you can count by tens to find multiples of 10, and you can count by hundreds to find multiples of 100, how can we find multiples of 1,000?* [count by thousands] Model how to solve $10 \times 5,000$ using the same methods. Ask your student to think of a multiplication sentence that uses a multiple of 1,000 as a factor. Ask him or her to explain how to solve the problem.

4 **PRACTICE** Ask your student to figure the following: 300 times his or her age; 6,000 times the number of people in your family; and 90 times the number of bedrooms in your home.

A BRIGHT IDEA

If your student needs help visualizing tens, hundreds, or thousands, you can make place-value blocks by cutting graph paper into strips and squares.

MATH

LESSON 2.5

MULTIPLICATION WITH GREATER NUMBERS

1 **ESTIMATE** Ask your student to estimate the answer to the following problem:

Ben is planting 12 rows of squash plants in his garden. He will plant 8 squash plants in each row. About how many squash plants will he need? [8 is almost 10; 12 is close to 10; 10 × 10 = 100; Ben will need about 100 squash plants]

2 **MODEL** Explain that it's easier to multiply greater numbers vertically. Model how to arrange the numbers vertically.

12 × 8	12 = 1 ten and 2 ones 8 = 8 ones	The ones must be in the same column.
1 12 × 8 ___ 6	Multiply by the ones. 2 × 8 = 16 16 is 1 ten and 6 ones	The 6 ones are recorded in the ones column. The 1 ten is placed, or carried, to the top of the tens column.
1 12 × 8 ___ 96	Multiply by the tens. 8 × 1 = 8 8 tens + 1 ten = 9 tens	

3 **OBSERVE** Ask your student to multiply greater numbers, such as 216 × 4. Observe as he or she solves each problem.

MULTIPLICATION WITH TWO-DIGIT NUMBERS

1 **DISCUSS** Mention that multiplying by two-digit numbers requires more steps than multiplying by one-digit numbers. Ask your student, *How do you think multiplying 13 × 12 would be different than multiplying 13 × 2?*

2 **TEACH** Ask your student to estimate the answer to 13 × 24. [13 is close to 10; 10 × 24 = 240] Explain that 13 × 24 is 4 groups of 13 and 20 groups of 13. Guide your student through the steps of multiplication he or she learned above: multiply by the ones, multiply by the tens, and add the products. Show your student how 13 × 24 = 312.

Branching Out

TEACHING TIP

Use graph paper or a copy of the Grid found on page 357 to align vertical multiplication problems. One digit in each box will keep the columns aligned.

CHECKING IN

Have your student walk you through a two-digit multiplication problem. Ask him or her to explain the steps.

GET ORGANIZED

Have your student go to the Web site http://www.multiplication.com for games and activities on multiplication and times tables. While he or she is online, you can get organized for the next day's math instruction.

FOR FURTHER READING

Marvelous Multiplication: Games and Activities That Make Math Easy and Fun, by Lynette Long (John Wiley, 2000).

Mighty-Fun Multiplication Practice Puzzles, by Bob Hugel (Scholastic, Inc., 2001).

Multiplication and Division, by Lucille Caron and Philip M. St. Jacques (Enslow Publishers, Inc., 2001).

Multiply Greater Numbers

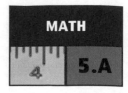

Fill in the flow chart to solve the problem 36 × 24.

1. **Step 1: Multiply by the ones.**

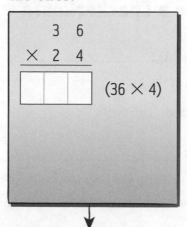

```
    3  6
  × 2  4
  ┌──┬──┬──┐
  │  │  │  │   (36 × 4)
  └──┴──┴──┘
```

Step 2: Place a zero in the ones column.

```
    3  6
  × 2  4
  ┌──┬──┬──┐
  │  │  │  │   (36 × 4)
  └──┴──┴──┘
          0
```

Step 3: Multiply by the hundreds.

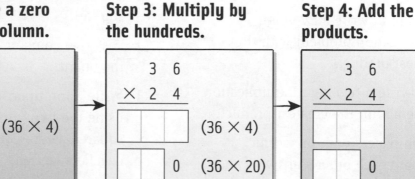

```
    3  6
  × 2  4
  ┌──┬──┬──┐
  │  │  │  │   (36 × 4)
  └──┴──┴──┘
  ┌──┬──┐
  │  │  │  0   (36 × 20)
  └──┴──┘
```

Step 4: Add the products.

```
    3  6
  × 2  4
  ┌──┬──┬──┐
  │  │  │  │
  └──┴──┴──┘
  ┌──┬──┐
  │  │  │  0
  └──┴──┘
  ┌──┬──┬──┐
  │  │  │  │
  └──┴──┴──┘
```

Multiply.

2. 316
   × 2

3.   72
   × 9

4.   16
   × 11

5.   32
   × 44

Solve.

6. There are 23 rows of chairs set up for the town meeting. Each row has 18 chairs. How many chairs have been set up?

_____

Student Learning Page 5.A: Multiply Greater Numbers **113**

What's Next? You Decide!

Now it's your turn to choose what to do next in the lesson. Read the activities and decide which one you want to do— you may want to try them both!

Use Your Phone Number

STEPS

❏ Write your phone number in your notebook.

❏ Use the digits in your phone number to write multiplication problems.

❏ Ask an adult to write multiplication problems, too. See who can write the most problems.

❏ Estimate to write a two-digit multiplication problem with the smallest product.

❏ Now write a two-digit multiplication problem with the greatest product.

❏ Switch papers with the adult. Estimate each other's answers and then solve the problems.

555−1234

1,234
× 5
‾‾‾‾‾

12 × 34 = _____

43
× 5
‾‾‾‾

Use a Checkerboard

MATERIALS

❏ 1 checkerboard

❏ 2 coins or checkers

STEPS

❏ Write or tape two-digit numbers on each square of your checkerboard.

❏ Use a different number for each square.

❏ Toss two coins or checkers onto the board.

❏ Write a multiplication sentence using the two numbers on the squares where your coins or checkers landed.

❏ Toss the coins or checkers again.

❏ Write a new multiplication problem.

❏ Which problem will have a larger product? Estimate to decide.

❏ Find out if your guess is correct by solving the problems.

MATH

LESSON 2.6

Dividing Whole Numbers

Division will be a breeze for the student who has mastered the multiplication table.

OBJECTIVE	BACKGROUND	MATERIALS
To introduce your student to the basic idea of division and the patterns of division facts	Division facts and multiplication facts are fact families. As in multiplication, there are useful patterns between division facts. In this lesson, your student will learn to recognize the patterns between various division facts and become more familiar with remainders.	■ Student Learning Pages 6.A–6.B ■ 40 counters (or similar objects, such as pennies)

VOCABULARY
QUOTIENT the answer in a division problem; in $14 \div 6 = 2$ R2, 2 R2 is the quotient
DIVIDEND the number in a division problem that is divided; in $14 \div 6 = 2$ R2, 14 is the dividend
DIVISORS the number in a division problem that you divide by; in $14 \div 6 = 2$ R2, 6 is the divisor
REMAINDER   the part of the dividend that's left over if your quotient is not a whole number; in $14 \div 6 = 2$ R2, R2 is the remainder

Let's Begin

INTRODUCTION TO DIVISION

1 **DISCUSS** Start by having your student arrange 24 counters in an array of 6 rows and 4 columns. Have him or her write the equation $24 \div 4 = 6$ in his or her notebook. Model the equation by emphasizing the phrase "four groups of six." Next, have your student write $24 \div 8$ and ask him or her to find the relationship between $24 \div 4 = 6$ and $24 \div 8$. Look for your student to note that the 8 means there will be *twice* as many groups as in the first equation. This means that each group will have *half* as many counters, so $24 \div 8 = 3$. Tell your student to try to show this with the counters. If necessary, guide him or her to divide the 4 groups of 6 counters into 8 groups of 3 counters.

2 **EXPAND** Repeat the method in Step 1 using these sets of equations:

$$40 \div 5 = 8 \qquad 16 \div 8 = 2 \qquad 20 \div 5 = 4$$
$$40 \div 10 = \underline{\qquad} \qquad 16 \div 4 = \underline{\qquad} \qquad 20 \div 10 = \underline{\qquad}$$

Begin by having your student arrange an appropriate array for the first equation in each group. Then ask him or her to write the first equation in his or her notebook. Model how to change the array to the second equation. Ask, *What do you notice about the total number of counters?* [the total is the same for each equation] If your student needs help, explain using phrases such as "twice as many groups with half as many counters" or "five groups of four is the same as ten groups of two." Have your student visually model your explanation by physically moving the counters. After your student understands this idea, have him or her create his or her own example of these patterns with 12 counters. [12 ÷ 3 = 4 and 12 ÷ 6 = 2 or 12 ÷ 2 = 6 and 12 ÷ 4 = 3]

DIVISION STRATEGIES

1 **EXPLAIN** Tell your student that there are several ways to solve basic division problems. Explain that the most important way is to know the basic fact families that relate multiplication and division. Throughout this lesson, if your student is having difficulty with any basic facts, take the time to review a multiplication table or a particularly troublesome fact (such as 56 ÷ 8 = 7, 56 ÷ 7 = 8, 7 × 8 = 56, 8 × 7 = 56). Have your student write and say a fact family to help him or her memorize the facts. Remind your student, *If you know one fact, you know the other three facts.* Ask your student which fact family he or she needs the most practice with.

2 **REVIEW** Explain that recognizing patterns between different division facts, as your student did earlier with counters, can also help solve division problems. Have your student write 28 ÷ 4 = 7 in his or her notebook. Ask, *How can you use the relationship between 4 and 2 to solve 28 ÷ 2?* [because 2 is half of 4, the answer to 28 ÷ 2 will be twice as much as 7] Explain that the answer to a division problem is called the **quotient.** If your student has trouble understanding this idea, guide him or her through simple examples and use counters. Next, have your student write the equations 36 ÷ 4 = 9 and 36 ÷ 2 = _____ in his or her notebook. Have him or her find the quotient of 36 ÷ 2 and explain which multiplication fact he or she used. [36 ÷ 2 = 18, 2 × 9 = 18]

3 **OBSERVE** Confirm that your student understands how the relationship between 2 and 4 helps predict the quotient when the **dividend** is the same. Similar relationships are true when you divide by 3 and 6, or when you divide by 5 and 10. Instruct your student to write the following sets of equations:

6 ÷ 3 = 2	30 ÷ 10 = 3
6 ÷ 6 = _____	30 ÷ 5 = _____
60 ÷ 6 = 10	100 ÷ 10 = 10
60 ÷ 3 = _____	100 ÷ 5 = _____

Ask your student to explain each equation and discuss the relationship of each set of **divisors.** Have your student explain how you can use the relationship between each set of equations to predict the quotient. [1, 20, 6, 20]

4   **EXPAND** Start by having your student arrange 6 counters in 1 group. Ask him or her to write the equation 6 ÷ 3 = 2 in his or her notebook. Model the equation with counters while saying aloud to your student, *6 divided into 3 groups of 2.* Then have your student gather the counters into 1 group. Add 6 more counters while saying, *Now we double the amount of counters and divide by 3.* Have your student write the equation 12 ÷ 3 = _____. Show your student how to compare the equations and observe that, when you double the dividend, you can predict that the quotient will double. Have your student show this by dividing the counters into 3 groups of 4. Ask, *Can you predict what the quotient is by comparing the dividends?*

$$12 ÷ 3 = 4 \qquad 10 ÷ 5 = 2 \qquad 24 ÷ 3 = 8$$
$$24 ÷ 3 = \underline{\hphantom{00}} \qquad 20 ÷ 5 = \underline{\hphantom{00}} \qquad 48 ÷ 3 = \underline{\hphantom{00}}$$

Have your student discuss with you the relationship of the dividends of each set of equations. Ask him or her to explain how he or she can use the relationship between each set of equations to predict the quotient. [8, 4, 16]

RULES OF DIVISION

1   **PRESENT** Start by telling your student to arrange 9 counters to show the equation 9 ÷ 3 = 3. Your student should divide the counters into 3 groups of 3. Next, have your student gather the counters into 1 group and ask him or her to show the equation 9 ÷ 9 = 1. Your student should divide the counters into 9 groups of 1. Finally, have your student gather the counters into 1 group and ask him or her to show the equation 9 ÷ 1 = 9. Help your student realize that the counters are already in 1 group of 9. Ask, *Which rules of division did you just show?* [any number divided by itself equals 1; any number divided by 1 equals itself]

2   **DISCUSS** Gather the counters into 1 group and ask your student to show 9 ÷ 0. Explain to your student that something can't be divided into zero groups. Ask, *Which rule of division did you just show?* [a number can't be divided by zero] Finally, discuss with your student how you could show the rule "zero divided by any number equals zero" with counters. The best solution would be to have your student clear all the counters away and observe that zero counters can only be divided into zero groups. Ask your student to retell the rules of division, and discuss the ideas.

REMAINDERS

1 **PRESENT** Ask your student to write the following word problem in his or her notebook: *A baker sells her rolls in boxes. Each box holds 6 rolls. A customer buys 38 rolls. How many boxes does the baker need?* [7 boxes] *If the baker always fills up each box before packing the next box, how many rolls will be in the last box?* [2 rolls] Ask, *What division problem do you need to solve to find the answers to each question?* [38 ÷ 6 = _____]

2 **EXPAND** Have your student explain why he or she used 38 ÷ 6 = _____ as the equation to solve. If your student didn't come up with the correct equation, use 38 counters and show how the groups of 6 represent the divisor in the equation. Have your student solve the equation and say which multiplication fact he or she used to help find the **remainder.** [6 × 6 = 36 or 6 × 7 = 42]

3 **EXPLAIN** Ask, *Did you need to know the remainder of 38 ÷ 6 to answer both questions?* [no, only for the second question] Have your student explain why knowing the remainder is only important for solving the second question.

4 **DISTRIBUTE** Have your student complete Student Learning Page 6.A for more practice.

Branching Out

TEACHING TIP

Prepare your student for future lessons by introducing him or her to fractions. Show some simple examples, such as $\frac{12}{3} = 4$. Explain that your student can think of the fraction as being equivalent to the equation 12 ÷ 3 = 4 and that the line in the fraction can be thought of as a division sign.

CHECKING IN

To assess your student's understanding of this lesson, pose the following types of questions to your student: *The quotient of 24 ÷ 7 has a remainder of 3. What is the remainder if the dividend is 25?* [4] *What is the remainder if the dividend is 27?* [6] *What is the remainder if the dividend is 28?* [no remainder, because 28 is evenly divided by 7; 28 ÷ 7 = 4]

ENRICH THE EXPERIENCE

Point out to your student that not every number divided by itself is 1. Zero cannot be divided by itself because the rules of division say that you cannot divide by zero.

FOR FURTHER READING

Dazzling Division: Games and Activities That Make Math Easy and Fun, by Lynette Long (John Wiley, 2000).

Hot Math Topics: Multiplication and Division, by Carole Greenes, Rika Spungin, and Linda Schulman (Dacey Dale Seymour Publications, 1999).

Multiplication and Division (Math Success), by Lucille Caron and Philip M. St. Jacques (Enslow Publishers, Inc., 2001).

Practice Division

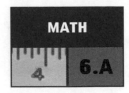

Divide.

1. $54 \div 9 =$ ___ 6

2. $48 \div 8 =$ ___ 6

3. $64 \div 8 =$ ___ 8

4. $63 \div 7 =$ ___ 9

5. $26 \div 4 =$ ___ 6 R2

6. $19 \div 2 =$ ___ 9 R1

Solve by comparing the equations.

7. $60 \div 10 = 6$

$60 \div 5 =$ ___

8. $42 \div 6 = 7$

$42 \div 3 =$ ___

9. $90 \div 9 = 10$

$90 \div 3 =$ ___

Complete.

10. Find the missing quotients in each table. (Remember: dividend ÷ divisor = quotient.)
Write your answers on a separate sheet of paper.

Divisor: 6

Dividend	Quotient
43	7 R1
54	a
32	b
14	2 R2
28	c

Divisor: 7

Dividend	Quotient
61	8 R5
43	d
15	2 R1
38	e
24	f

Divisor: 9

Dividend	Quotient
79	8 R7
23	g
48	h
78	j
70	7 R7

Challenge yourself. Use reasoning to answer.

11. If you know that $a \div b = 3$, can you predict what $2a \div 2b$ equals? Explain why
you think so and give an example.

___

___

What's Next? You Decide!

Now it's your turn to choose what to do next in the lesson. Read the activities and decide which one you want to do— you may want to try them both!

Play the Small Remainder Game

MATERIALS

❑ 2 small objects (such as pennies or beans) to toss

❑ the table below

6	7	8	0	3
5	2	1	TOSS AGAIN	1
9	4	6	8	5
9	TOSS AGAIN	3	5	7

STEPS

❑ Find a dividend by tossing two pennies on the table. If the first penny lands on a 4 and the second penny lands on a 5, the dividend is 45. If the first penny you toss is a zero, then your number will be a one-digit number.

❑ Now divide your number by any one-digit number you want. Make sure that the quotient is less than 10 and has as small a remainder as possible.

❑ For example, if you toss a 73, then write $73 \div 9 = 8$ R1 or $73 \div 8 = 9$ R1. If you toss a 12, there are lots of good answers that don't have any remainder, like $12 \div 4 = 3$ or $12 \div 6 = 2$.

❑ Write at least 10 equations. Then have an adult check your work.

Create Story Problems

MATERIALS

❑ colored pencils

STEPS

❑ Write your own division story problems.

❑ If you need ideas, talk to an adult about times when he or she uses division during a normal day.

❑ You can also use the words in the groups below to help you.

eggs	cakes	cups	flour
players	cards	game	deal
hours	bike	miles	ride

❑ Use colored pencils and paper to draw a picture of your story problems.

❑ Have someone else solve your story problems.

Dividing Greater Numbers

It's easy to divide greater numbers when you know the basic facts of division.

OBJECTIVE	BACKGROUND	MATERIALS
To review for your student the basics of division and introduce dividing greater numbers	Dividing greater numbers is built upon basic division facts. More concentration and organization are often needed to find the quotient. In this lesson, your student will practice estimates and dividing by multiples of 10 and will learn to use those skills to find quotients with confidence.	■ Student Learning Pages 7.A–7.B

Let's Begin

ESTIMATES AND MULTIPLES OF 10

1 **INTRODUCE** Tell your student that dividing with greater numbers is simple when working with multiples of 10. Have him or her write the equation $798 \div 19 =$ _____ in his or her notebook. Help your student review how to round the numbers to multiples of 10. Then have him or her rewrite the equation as $800 \div 20 =$ _____ and solve it to produce an estimate. [40]

2 **LEARN** Direct your student to write the following equations in his or her notebook:

$3 \times 4 = 12$ $12 \div 3 =$ _____
$4 \times 30 = 120$ $120 \div 40 =$ _____
$3 \times 40 = 120$ $120 \div 3 =$ _____
$30 \times 40 = 1,200$ $1,200 \div 30 =$ _____

Have your student find the quotients using the multiplication facts given. Ask your student, *What rule can you make for dividing with multiples of 10?* [the number of zeros in the quotient equals the number of zeros in the dividend minus the number of zeros in the divisor]

3 **DISCUSS** Have your student prove that the rule for dividing with multiples of 10 is true. Instruct him or her to write down similar patterns to the one above (such as $18 \div 6$, $180 \div 6$, and $180 \div 60$). Check that your student can predict the correct quotient. Talk with your student about why the rule makes sense.

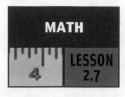

4 **EXTEND** Reintroduce the original problem to your student: 798 ÷ 19 = _____. Ask him or her if the estimate of the quotient [800 ÷ 20 = 40] is higher or lower than the actual quotient [42]. Have your student think about what happens if the dividend is less and the divisor is more. Model to your student that rounding the dividend up and rounding the divisor down will result in an estimate that is greater than the actual quotient.

5 **PRACTICE** Have your student write these in his or her notebook and find estimates for each. [6, 12, 10, 3]

$$23\overline{)184} \qquad 19\overline{)239} \qquad 28\overline{)311} \qquad 62\overline{)178}$$

DIVISION BY HAND

1 **MODEL** Tell your student that finding exact quotients for division problems can be done by hand. Walk your student through this example, asking him or her to estimate the quotient. [812 ÷ 18 ≅ 40]

$$
18\overline{)812}^{\,?} \qquad
\begin{array}{r} 4 \\ 18\overline{)812} \\ -72 \\ \hline 9 \end{array}
\;\leftarrow 4 \times 18
\qquad
\begin{array}{r} 45R2 \\ 18\overline{)812} \\ -72\downarrow \\ \hline 92 \\ -90 \\ \hline 2 \end{array}
\;\leftarrow 5 \times 18
$$

Have him or her estimate how many times 18 goes into 81. [4] Then have your student multiply 18 × 4. [72] Put the 4 in the appropriate place and show how to subtract and bring down the 2. Have your student estimate how many times 18 goes into 92. Have him or her multiply 18 × 5. [90] Explain to your student that the leftover 2 is a remainder. Instruct him or her to compare the exact quotient to the estimate.

2 **CHECK** Show your student how to check the answer. Have him or her multiply 45 × 18. [810] Ask your student, *Do you think the quotient is correct?* [yes, because 810 + 2 = 812] Give your student division problems to complete in his or her notebook.

3 **DISTRIBUTE** Have your student complete Student Learning Page 7.A for more practice.

Branching Out

TEACHING TIP

After your student solves a division problem such as 808 ÷ 8 = 101, have him or her solve the problem 808 ÷ 4 = 202. Then ask your student if he or she sees a pattern.

CHECKING IN

Have your student solve a simple problem such as 540 ÷ 5 by hand. [108] Make sure that he or she can correctly place the zero in the quotient.

Practice Division

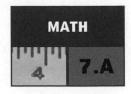
Divide.

1. 300 ÷ 6 = _____

2. 300 ÷ 50 = _____

3. 3,000 ÷ 5 = _____

4. 3)54

5. 22)92

6. 25)632

7. 32)910

Solve.

8.

÷		=
162	60	4 R5
306	30	6 R6
153	40	4 R43
125	50	7 R13
283	20	4 R2
÷		=

❏ The path shown is 125 ÷ 30 = 4 R5.

❏ Make a path by connecting the dividends and divisors to their correct quotients.

❏ Each number can only be used in one path.

9. A roller coaster carries 48 people each time it runs. If 1,536 people rode the roller coaster during the day, how many times did the ride run?

_____

What's Next? You Decide!

Now it's your turn to choose what to do next in the lesson. Read the activities and decide which one you want to do— you may want to try them both!

Divide at the Supermarket

MATERIALS

❑ 1 receipt from a recent shopping trip to the grocery store

STEPS

❑ Choose any item from the receipt.

❑ Find out the amount of money it cost.

❑ Write the price in pennies. For example, if the item cost $5.43, write down the price as 543 pennies.

❑ Find the item in your house, and find out how many ounces it weighs.

❑ Ask an adult to round the weight to the nearest ounce or to show you how to read the weight on the box. (One pound is equal to 16 ounces.)

❑ Divide the number of pennies by the number of ounces. This tells you how many pennies the item cost for each ounce.

❑ Do this for other items on the receipt. Are you surprised at how much they cost?

Find an Average Using Division

MATERIALS

❑ 1 ruler

STEPS

❑ Find four or five items in your house to measure.

❑ Use a ruler to find the length of each item rounded to the nearest inch.

❑ Record the length of each item in your notebook.

❑ Find the total number of inches by adding the lengths.

❑ Divide the total length by the number of items you measured.

❑ The quotient of this equation is the average length (in inches) of the items you measured.

❑ Find three more items.

❑ Measure each one to the nearest inch and add those lengths to your total. Now find the average length of all of your items.

❑ Is the average less than or greater than the first average?

Comprehending Fractions

Mastering fractions takes only a fraction of your time!

OBJECTIVE	BACKGROUND	MATERIALS

To help your student understand fractions and how to add and subtract them	Fractions give your student the chance to consider parts that make up a whole. Mastering fractions will also prepare your student to work with decimals. In this lesson, your student will learn what fractions represent and how to add and subtract these values.	■ Student Learning Pages 8.A–8.B
		■ 6 strips cardboard, each the same size, divided and labeled as follows:
		  ❑ no divisions, labeled 1
		  ❑ divided into two equal parts, each part labeled $\frac{1}{2}$
		  ❑ divided into three equal parts, each part labeled $\frac{1}{3}$
		  ❑ divided into four equal parts, each part labeled $\frac{1}{4}$
		  ❑ divided into six equal parts, each part labeled $\frac{1}{6}$
		  ❑ divided into eight equal parts, each part labeled $\frac{1}{8}$

VOCABULARY

REGION a whole, continuous object

SET a whole made up of separate equal parts

NUMERATOR the top number in a fraction

DENOMINATOR the bottom number in a fraction

EQUIVALENT FRACTIONS two fractions with equal values

MIXED NUMBER a number consisting of a whole number and a fraction

Let's Begin

INTRODUCTION TO FRACTIONS

1 **ILLUSTRATE** Explain to your student that fractions show the equal parts of a **region** or a **set.** Have your student draw a circle in his or her notebook. Say to him or her, *Four people want to decorate this cake. How can they divide it so that each of them can decorate the same amount of the cake?* [the cake can be divided into four equal parts] Have your student draw lines dividing the circle into four parts. Then have him or her shade one part of the circle.

2 **EXPLAIN** Tell your student that the fraction $\frac{1}{4}$ represents the shaded part because there is one part shaded out of the four total parts of the circle. Explain to him or her that the **numerator** of the

fraction describes the number of parts each person may decorate. Ask, *What is the numerator of $\frac{1}{4}$?* [1] Then explain that the **denominator** of the fraction describes the total number of equal parts in the cake. Ask, *What is the denominator of $\frac{1}{4}$?* [4] Have your student tell you in words what part of the cake each person will decorate. [each person will decorate one part out of four]

3 **DESCRIBE** Have your student copy the following picture in his or her notebook:

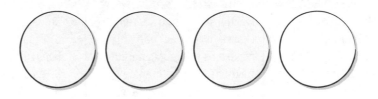

Then describe to your student that a fraction can also be part of a set. Have him or her tell you the number of shaded circles [3] and the number of total circles [4]. Then ask, *What fraction represents the shaded part of this set?* [$\frac{3}{4}$]

EQUIVALENT FRACTIONS AND COMPARISONS

1 **PREVIEW** Instruct your student to draw two equal-sized squares in his or her notebook. Have him or her divide one of the squares into two equal rectangles and the other into four equal squares. Direct your student to shade half of each square. Explain that these fractions are called **equivalent fractions** because the same part of each square is shaded. Ask, *What fraction represents each shaded area?* [$\frac{1}{2}$, $\frac{2}{4}$] Then have your student explain how each shaded region can represent the same amount of space. [both squares have half shaded]

2 **DISCUSS** Model for your student how to use the cardboard fraction strips to determine if two fractions are equivalent. Explain that he or she can also tell which of two fractions is greater using the fraction strips. Take a $\frac{1}{3}$ strip and show your student how to compare it to the $\frac{1}{6}$ strip. Discuss with your student how he or she can tell that $\frac{1}{3}$ and $\frac{2}{6}$ are equivalent fractions.

3 **PRACTICE** Give your student the cardboard fraction strips. Have him or her use the strips to answer the following questions: *Are $\frac{1}{2}$ and $\frac{4}{8}$ equivalent fractions?* [yes] *Which fraction is greater, $\frac{3}{8}$ or $\frac{1}{4}$?* [$\frac{3}{8}$]

MIXED NUMBERS

1   **EXPLAIN**   Explain to your student that a **mixed number** is made up of both a whole number and a fraction. Model a mixed number to him or her by showing $1\frac{1}{2}$ glasses of water. Tell your student that drawing a picture can help solve problems with mixed numbers. Describe the following situation: *A family orders 2 pizzas. Each pizza has 8 equal slices. The family eats 13 slices of pizza. What mixed number represents how many of the pizzas the family ate?*

2   **ASK**   Have your student draw a picture of the 2 pizzas in his or her notebook. Then direct him or her to shade in the number of slices that the family ate. Ask, *What is the fraction for one slice of pizza?* $[\frac{1}{8}]$ *How many total slices are in both pizzas?* [16] *How many slices did the family eat?* [13] *What fraction represents the total number of slices the family ate?* $[\frac{13}{16}]$

3   **RELATE**   Show your student that because 8 slices is 1 full pizza, $\frac{8}{8}$ is equal to 1. The other 5 slices are a part of the 8 total slices of the other full pizza, or $\frac{5}{8}$. Ask, *What mixed number shows the number of pizzas the family ate?* $[1\frac{5}{8}]$

ADDITION AND SUBTRACTION OF FRACTIONS AND MIXED NUMBERS

1   **PREVIEW**   Tell your student that before fractions can be added or subtracted, they must have like denominators. Ask, *Which pairs of these fractions have like denominators:* $\frac{2}{3}$, $\frac{4}{9}$, $\frac{1}{9}$, $\frac{6}{7}$, $\frac{3}{3}$, *and* $\frac{1}{6}$? $[\frac{2}{3}$ *and* $\frac{3}{3}$; $\frac{4}{9}$ *and* $\frac{1}{9}]$

2   **EXPLAIN**   Explain to your student that when fractions have like denominators, the numerators are added and the denominator stays the same. Help him or her understand that the sum or difference of the numerators is written above the like denominator. Ask, *What is* $\frac{3}{4} - \frac{2}{4}$? $[\frac{1}{4}]$ *How did you get the answer?* [I subtracted only the numerators and placed the difference over the like denominator of 4]

MATH

LESSON 2.8

A BRIGHT IDEA

Invite the visual learner to draw a rectangle for each fraction. The number of squares in the rectangle represents the denominator. The number of shaded squares represents the numerator. Your student can then add or subtract the shaded squares.

3 **MODEL** Tell your student that some problems have fractions with unlike denominators. Explain to him or her that before adding or subtracting these fractions, a like denominator must be found. Model using the cardboard fraction strips to find a like denominator for $\frac{1}{2} + \frac{1}{3}$. Have your student order the fraction strips from greatest to least. Show your student that whole sections of the $\frac{1}{6}$ fraction strip fit evenly beneath both the $\frac{1}{2}$ and $\frac{1}{3}$ strips.

4 **FOLLOW THROUGH** Follow through with the $\frac{1}{2}$ and $\frac{1}{3}$ fraction strips. Ask, *How many $\frac{1}{6}$ pieces fit exactly under $\frac{1}{3}$?* [2] *How many $\frac{1}{6}$ pieces fit exactly under $\frac{1}{2}$?* [3]

5 **ASK** Ask, *Using the fraction strips, what common denominator do $\frac{1}{2}$ and $\frac{1}{3}$ share?* [6] Then have your student solve $\frac{1}{2} + \frac{1}{3}$. $\left[\frac{5}{6}\right]$ Observe your student to ensure that he or she adds only the numerators and places the sum over the like denominator.

6 **DISTRIBUTE** Distribute Student Learning Page 8.A to your student for more practice with fractions.

Branching Out

TEACHING TIPS

❑ Encourage your student to draw pictures of fractions in addition or subtraction problems. This will help him or her visualize the values he or she is working with.

❑ Using fractions with food can sometimes make understanding the concepts of half, quarter, third, eighth, and so on easier to grasp. While making a meal you can ask your student questions such as what size of a portion a third of the food or a quarter of the food might be.

CHECKING IN

Give your student this problem: $\frac{3}{4} - \frac{1}{3}$. $\left[\frac{5}{12}\right]$ Quiz your student on the steps he or she would take to solve it.

FOR FURTHER READING

Fabulous Fractions: Games, Puzzles, and Activities That Make Math Easy and Fun, by Lynette Long (John Wiley, 2001).

Making Fractions (Math for Fun), by Andrew King (Copper Beach Books, 1998).

Work with Fractions

Match each picture with the correct fraction.

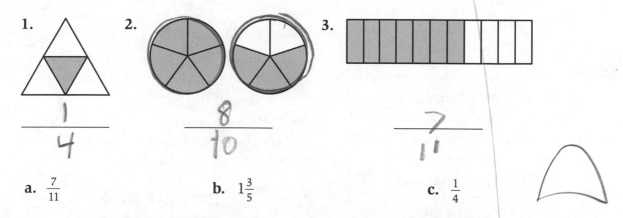

1. $\dfrac{1}{4}$

2. $\dfrac{8}{10}$

3. $\dfrac{7}{11}$

a. $\dfrac{7}{11}$

b. $1\dfrac{3}{5}$

c. $\dfrac{1}{4}$

Circle the greater fraction in the first pair. Write that fraction on the next line. Then circle the greater fraction in that pair. Write that fraction on the next line. Then circle the greater fraction in the last pair.

4. $\dfrac{1}{8}$ $\dfrac{1}{3}$

5. _____ $\dfrac{6}{9}$

6. _____ $\dfrac{2}{6}$

7. Which fraction in problems 4–6 is the greatest? Rewrite it in simplest form.

_____ 6 _____

8. List the fractions in problems 4–6 in order from least to greatest.

_____

Read the word problems. Use your fraction strips to help you solve them.

9. John and Daisy are reading the same book. John has read $\dfrac{2}{3}$ of the book, and Daisy has read $\dfrac{5}{6}$ of the book. Who has read more of the book?

_____ John _____

10. In Rosy's family, $\dfrac{3}{4}$ of the people have blue eyes. In Nina's family, $\dfrac{1}{6}$ of the people have blue eyes. Which family has the greater fraction of people with blue eyes? How much greater is the fraction?

_____

What's Next? You Decide!

Now it's your turn to choose what to do next in the lesson.
Read the activities and decide which one you want to do—
you may want to try them both!

Double a Recipe

MATERIALS

- ❏ ingredients shown below
- ❏ 1 oven
- ❏ 1 cookie sheet

Maple Walnut Cookies

_____ $\frac{1}{4}$ cup canola oil

_____ $\frac{2}{3}$ cup maple syrup

_____ $1\frac{1}{2}$ tsp. vanilla extract

_____ 2 cups flour

_____ $1\frac{1}{2}$ tsp. baking powder

_____ $\frac{1}{8}$ tsp. salt

_____ $\frac{1}{2}$ cup chopped walnuts

_____ oil spray

---

1. Preheat oven to 350°F.
2. Mix the oil, maple syrup, and vanilla extract in a mixing bowl and beat until creamy.
3. In another bowl, mix the flour, baking powder, and salt. Add to the maple syrup mixture. Mix well.
4. Stir in walnuts.
5. Oil the cookie sheet.
6. Drop heaping teaspoons of dough on cookie sheet. Leave enough room for cookies to spread.
7. Bake 12 minutes and then cool.

STEPS

- ❏ Double the amounts of ingredients in the recipe. Write them on the lines on the recipe card.
- ❏ Have an adult work with you to bake the cookies and enjoy!

Roll the Dice!

MATERIALS

- ❏ 1 pair dice
- ❏ colored pencils

STEPS

- ❏ Roll one die six times. List the numbers as numerators.
- ❏ Roll both dice six times. List the sum of the two numbers as denominators.
- ❏ Make six fractions out of the six pairs of numerators and denominators. Make sure the denominator is greater than the numerator in each fraction.
- ❏ Make three addition problems. Solve them.
- ❏ Make three subtraction problems. Solve them. (Always put the greater fraction first!)
- ❏ Use colored pencils to draw pictures representing each of your addition and subtraction problems.
- ❏ Roll the dice to find more numerators and denominators. Make fractions and add and subtract them. Have an adult check your work.

Understanding Decimals

Each of us is part of something bigger. Without our part the world would not be complete.

OBJECTIVE	BACKGROUND	MATERIALS
To give your student practice with place value and reading, adding, and subtracting decimals	Decimals are a part of everyday life. Our most common experience with decimals occurs when we work with money, but we also need to understand decimals in order to record temperatures, read stock market reports, and even find a station on the radio. In this lesson, your student will learn about place value, reading decimals, and relating fractions to decimals.	■ Student Learning Pages 9.A–9.B ■ 1 one-dollar bill ■ 10 dimes ■ 1 copy Grid, page 357 ■ 100 pennies

Let's Begin

FRACTIONS, MIXED NUMBERS, AND DECIMALS

1 **DISCUSS** Parts of a whole can be written as fractions. Fractions with a denominator (the bottom number of the fraction) of 10, 100, and 1,000 can be easily translated into decimals. Show your student a one-dollar bill. Ask, *How much is this?* [one dollar] *How many dimes are in one dollar?* [10] Have your student count out 10 dimes. Remove a dime and ask, *How many dimes did I take away?* [1] Ask your student to write a fraction that represents how many dimes you took away. [$\frac{1}{10}$] Ask your student, *How much is $\frac{1}{10}$ of a dollar?* [$0.10] Restate that fractions with a denominator of 10 can be easily written as decimals. Ask, *What does $0.10 mean?* [$\frac{1}{10}$ of a dollar]

2 **RELATE** On a copy of the Grid found on page 357, outline a 5-by-2-unit rectangle. Ask your student how many squares he or she sees in the rectangle. [10] Have your student color 3 of the squares. Ask, *What fraction of the rectangle did you color?* [$\frac{3}{10}$] Say, *Think about the dimes in our dollar. We wrote $\frac{1}{10}$ as $0.10. How could we write $\frac{3}{10}$ as a decimal?* [0.30 or 0.3] Explain that the zero on the right is only needed when working with money. Ask your student to write the decimal form of $\frac{5}{10}$. [0.5]

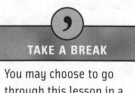

TAKE A BREAK

You may choose to go through this lesson in a few hours or take breaks throughout and spend a few days on it.

3 **EXPAND** Use the above steps to help your student understand writing decimals to the hundredths. Use 100 pennies and a 10-by-10-unit square on your Grid. Ask your student to write the decimal forms of $\frac{17}{100}$, $\frac{7}{100}$, and $\frac{70}{100}$. [0.17, 0.07, 0.70]

4 **MODEL** On the Grid outline 4 blocks of 10 squares each. Shade 3 of the blocks completely and 7 squares in the fourth block. Ask, *How many of the blocks are shaded?* [$3\frac{7}{10}$] Ask, *How do you think you could write $3\frac{7}{10}$ in decimal form?* [3.7] Give help and explain as needed. Then ask your student to write $5\frac{13}{100}$ in decimal form. [5.13]

PLACE VALUE

1 **DISCUSS** Understanding place value helps us determine how large a number is. We know that the value of numbers to the left of the decimal point gets larger as the numbers move away from the decimal point (ones, tens, hundreds, etc.). The value of the numbers to the right of the decimal point, however, gets smaller as the numbers move away from the decimal point: 0.001 is smaller than 0.01; 0.0001 is smaller than 0.001. Draw a place-value chart like the one below. Discuss the value of 1 in each place with your student. Have your student point to each place as he or she says *ones, tens, hundreds,* and so on.

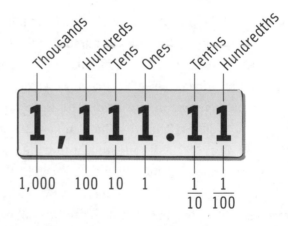

A BRIGHT IDEA

If your student has trouble determining whether tenths are bigger than hundredths, ask, *Would you rather have 0.1 of a day to play or 0.01 of a day to play?* [0.1 of a day, because it is a longer period of time than 0.01]

2 **READ NUMBERS** Read the number on the chart out loud for your student. Say, *one thousand, one hundred eleven, and eleven hundredths.* Point out that when reading a number the decimal point is read as "and." Write the following numbers on another sheet of paper and have your student read them out loud: 9,536.97; 500.1; 1,503.01; and 19.99.

3 **COMPARE** Ask your student, *Which is bigger, 0.01 or 0.001?* [0.01] Write 563.94 and 563.49. *If 0.01 is bigger than 0.001, which of these two numbers is bigger?* [563.94] Show your student how to line up the decimal points of the numbers he or she is comparing. Model how to compare digits beginning at the left. When the digits are the same, continue comparing to the right. At the point of two different digits, ask, *Which is bigger?*

> 563.9̲4   9 tenths is greater than 4 tenths, so 563.94 is
> 563.4̲9   greater than 563.49.

4   **PRACTICE**   Ask your student to choose the larger number in the following pairs of numbers. Have your student write each pair of numbers and insert the greater-than sign or less-than sign as appropriate. [47.12 < 48.12; 310.91 > 310.19; 1,560.87 > 1,500.87] Discuss how he or she arrived at the answer.

47.12   48.12

310.91   310.19

1,560.87   1,500.87

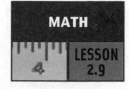

A BRIGHT IDEA

If your student has trouble distinguishing between the greater-than sign and the less-than sign, explain that the wide, or large, end always opens toward the larger number.

HOW TO ORDER NUMBERS

1   **DISCUSS**   Knowing how to compare decimals enables your student to order numbers from greatest to least and from least to greatest. Write the following numbers: 1.019; 1.202; and 1.013. Ask, *How will lining up the decimal points help us put these numbers in order?* [you can compare the digits in each place after you line up the decimal points]

2   **COMPARE**   Model how to put the numbers in order from greatest to least. Point out that, beginning at the left, all of the numbers in the ones column are the same. The greatest number in the tenths column is 2, so 1.202 is the largest number. The remaining numbers both have a 0 in the tenths column and a 1 in the hundredths column. In the thousandths place, 9 is larger than 3, so 1.019 is the second largest number. Write another series of numbers with decimals and have your student put the numbers in order from least to greatest.

1.2̲02

1.019̲

1.013̲

ESTIMATION AND ROUNDING

1   **INTRODUCE**   Explain that when adding or subtracting decimals, estimation can be used. Estimating helps you check if an answer is reasonable. Point out that estimation requires rounding. The rules for rounding decimals are the same as the rules for rounding whole numbers. Show your student how to round to the nearest whole number by looking at the tenths place. The number 74.9 rounds up to 75. Remind your student that the number 9 is rounded up. The number 62.4 rounds down to 62. Remind your student that 4 is rounded down. The number 6.5 rounds up to 7.0. Show your student that 5 gets rounded up. Ask your student, *Why do you look at the tenths place?* [when rounding to the nearest whole number, look at the number to the right of the ones place]

2 **PRACTICE** Read this problem to your student: *Mr. Markel filled his car with 9.72 gallons of gas. Round Mr. Markel's gas to the nearest gallon.* [10 gallons] Ask your student to explain how he or she rounded to the nearest whole number.

ADDITION AND SUBTRACTION WITH DECIMALS

1 **PREPARE** The procedure for adding and subtracting decimals follows the same rules as adding and subtracting whole numbers. Before you begin, all of the places must be aligned correctly. Lining up the decimal points will set up the problem correctly.

Have your student write out the problem 549.36 + 127.5 and align the decimals. Explain that a zero can be added as a placeholder in the hundreds column of 127.5. [127.50] Ask, *Why do you think it's okay to add a zero to this number?* [there are no hundredths, so we can write in a zero without changing the value; both numbers will have five digits and it will be easier to add]

2 **SOLVE** First have your student estimate the answer to the problem. Remind your student to round to the nearest whole number. [549 + 128 = 677] Then have your student solve 549.36 + 127.5. [676.86] Ask, *Is your answer reasonable?* [yes, the estimate was 677, which is close to 676.86]

3 **PRACTICE** Read this problem to your student: *Louis goes running every day. He keeps track of how far he runs each day and totals the miles at the end of the month. In September, Louis ran 47.9 miles. In October, he ran 51.3 miles. How many more miles did Louis run in October than in September?* [3.4 miles] Have your student estimate the answer first and then solve the problem. Then have your student complete Student Learning Page 9.A for more practice.

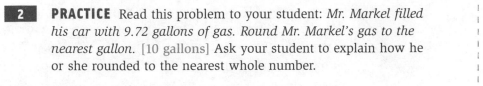

Branching Out

TEACHING TIPS

For more practice with adding and subtracting decimals, have your student add and subtract money problems. Provide play or real money for your student to use to check his or her work.

CHECKING IN

Give your student a list of four decimal numbers. Ask your student to put the numbers in order from greatest to least. Then have him or her find the difference between the largest and smallest number. Finally, have him or her add the two remaining numbers. Observe your student as he or she works, noting concepts that need review.

ENRICH THE EXPERIENCE

Have your student go through the house and look to see where decimals are used, for example, on food packages and with measurements.

FOR FURTHER READING

Math Phonics—Decimals: Quick Tips and Alternative Techniques for Math Mastery, by Marilyn B. Hein, Judy Mitchell, ed., and Ron Wheeler, ill. (Teaching and Learning Company, 1999).

Math Trek: Adventures in the Math Zone, by Ivars Peterson and Nancy Henderson (John Wiley, 1999).

Work with Decimals

Write each shaded area as a decimal.

1. _____ 2. _____

Write as decimals.

3. $36\frac{37}{100}$ _____ 4. four hundred twelve and five hundredths _____

Write the value of each underlined number.

5. 1,436.19 _____ 6. 4,000.01 _____ 7. 7,413.19 _____

Order the numbers from least to greatest.

8. 57.12   59.18   59.73   57.4

_____

Solve the problems.

9.   416.11
   + 98.39

10.   2,162.83
    − 594.93

11.   42.10
    − 16.07

12.   1,284.19
    + 2,307.73

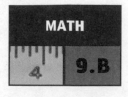

What's Next? You Decide!

Now it's your turn to choose what to do next in the lesson.
Read the activities and decide which one you want to do—
you may want to try them both!

Plan a Meal

MATERIALS

❑ 1 grocery store flyer or advertisement

STEPS

❑ Find a grocery store flyer from a newspaper.

❑ Choose two things that you like to eat from the flyer.

❑ Write the prices of the two items in your notebook and add them together. How much would you spend if you bought both items?

❑ Then choose five things from the flyer that you could use to make a meal for your family.

❑ Estimate to decide if you could buy the things for your meal with $20.00.

❑ Write the costs of the five items and add to find the exact total cost.

❑ Can you plan a meal for less than $10.00? Less than $5.00?

Build a Number

MATERIALS

❑ 3 dice

STEPS

❑ Roll three dice.

❑ Write down each of the numbers you see.

❑ Arrange the three numbers into ones, tenths, and hundredths to make the largest number possible. For example: 4.21.

❑ Write the numbers in your notebook.

❑ Roll until you have built five numbers.

❑ Order the numbers from greatest to least.

❑ Play the game again, but this time build the smallest numbers you can.

❑ Order the numbers from least to greatest.

❑ Challenge yourself and add the five numbers together.

❑ Check your answer with a calculator.

Investigating Measurement and Temperature

OBJECTIVE	BACKGROUND	MATERIALS
To teach your student about measuring length, weight, capacity, and temperature	Understanding measurement units helps students connect with real-world experiences. In this lesson, your student will apply customary and metric units of measurement to concrete examples and learn about measuring temperature in degrees Fahrenheit and Celsius.	■ Student Learning Pages 10.A–10.B ■ 1 inch ruler ■ 1 metric ruler ■ 1 scale ■ household objects to measure in inches, feet, yards, millimeters, and centimeters ■ household objects to measure in ounces, pounds, grams, and kilograms ■ household objects showing capacity, such as measuring cups and a gallon jug ■ 1 copy Venn Diagram, page 355

VOCABULARY
MASS the amount of matter an object has

Let's Begin

CUSTOMARY UNITS OF MEASUREMENT

1 **EXPLAIN** Explain to your student that length can be measured by customary units. Have your student copy the chart below in his or her notebook. Ask, *What does length measure?* [how long an object is]

Customary Units of Length	
inch (in.)	12 in. = 1 ft
foot (ft)	3 ft = 1 yd
yard (yd)	1,760 yd = 1 mi
mile (mi)	1 mi = 5,280 ft

2 **EXPLORE** Show your student objects that measure about 1 inch, 1 foot, and 1 yard, such as a postage stamp, a sheet of paper, and a baseball bat. Ask, *What other objects would you measure with each unit? What would you measure using miles?* [long distances]

3 **APPLY** Have your student estimate the lengths. Show him or her objects that can be measured with an inch ruler, such as a book. Then have your student use the ruler to measure the actual lengths of the objects. Invite your student to compare the estimated and actual measurements.

4 **RELATE** Tell your student that weight can be measured using the customary units of ounces (oz) and pounds (lb). Explain that 1 pound is equal to 16 ounces. Ask, *What does weight measure?* [how heavy an object is] *How do you know?* [I can use pounds to find my weight, and so on]

5 **DISPLAY** Explain to your student that a pencil weighs about 1 ounce and a can of beans weighs about 1 pound. Let your student hold these or similar objects. Have him or her make a list of objects that should be measured in ounces and another list of objects that should be measured in pounds.

6 **MODEL** Capacity can also be measured using customary units. Have your student copy the chart below into his or her notebook. Model for your student how to find measurements using such things as measuring spoons, cups, and a gallon jug. Ask, *Would you use gallons or tablespoons to measure water in a bathtub?* [gallons]

Customary Units of Capacity	
teaspoon (tsp)	3 tsp = 1 tbsp
tablespoon (tbsp)	16 tbsp = 1 c (dry)
fluid ounce (fl oz)	8 fl oz = 1 c (fluid)
cup (c)	2 c = 1 pt
pint (pt)	2 pt = 1 qt
quart (qt)	4 qt = 1 gal
gallon (gal)	1 gal = 8 pt

7 **PREVIEW** Have your student list the units in each category from least to greatest in his or her notebook. [length: inches, feet, yards, miles; weight: ounces, pounds; capacity: teaspoons, tablespoons, fluid ounces, cups, pints, quarts, gallons]

8 **EXPAND** Explain to your student that to change from larger to smaller units, the larger unit is multiplied. Tell him or her that to change from smaller to larger units, the smaller unit is divided. Use the capacity chart to show your student how to find the number of teaspoons in 2 tablespoons. [1 tbsp = 3 tsp; multiply both sides by 2 to find 6 teaspoons] Ask, *To change inches to feet, would you multiply or divide?* [divide]

9 **OBSERVE** Ask, *How many yards are in 6 feet?* [2 yards] *If you weigh 100 pounds 14 ounces, how many total ounces do you weigh?* [1,614 ounces] *How many pints are in 8 cups?* [4 pints]

METRIC UNITS OF MEASUREMENT

1 **RELATE** Explain to your student that length can also be measured by metric units. Have your student copy this chart into his or her notebook:

Metric Units of Length	
millimeter (mm)	100 mm = 1 cm
centimeter (cm)	100 cm = 1 m
meter (m)	1,000 m = 1 km
kilometer (km)	1km = 100,000 cm

2 **MODEL** Show your student some objects that measure about a millimeter, a centimeter, and a meter, such as a dime, a pen, and a door. Have your student use a metric ruler to measure the length of three objects in centimeters. Make sure the objects are of reasonable size. Ask, *Based on the chart, what would you measure with a kilometer?* [long distances]

3 **EXPLAIN** Explain to your student that **mass** means the amount of matter something has. Point out that metric units measure mass in grams (g) and kilograms (kg). Say, *1 kilogram is equal to 1,000 grams. A dime has a mass of about 1 gram. A hardcover book has a mass of about 1 kilogram.* Let your student hold these or similar objects. Then ask, *Would you use grams or kilograms to measure the mass of a car?* [kilograms]

4 **DESCRIBE** Tell your student that capacity can be measured in the metric units milliliters (mL) and liters (L). Say to him or her that 1 liter equals 1,000 milliliters. Display a teaspoon to your student and explain that it holds 3 milliliters. Then show him or her a two-liter bottle and explain its capacity. Ask, *Would you use liters or milliliters to measure the amount of water in a bottle cap?* [milliliters]

ENRICH THE EXPERIENCE

For a fun practice activity for measuring length in standard and metric units, go to http://www.funbrain. com/measure.

ENRICH THE EXPERIENCE

Metric units have prefixes that stand for multiples of 10. These prefixes can help your student recall the units' values. Have your student use a dictionary and read definitions of *milli-* (thousandth) and *centi-* (hundred or hundredth part). Then ask your student to use the length or mass chart to guess what *kilo-* means. [1,000]

5 **PREVIEW** Explain to your student that the metric system is based on tens. Then have your student list the metric units in each category from least to greatest in his or her notebook. [length: millimeters, centimeters, meters, kilometers; mass: grams, kilograms; capacity: milliliters, liters] Review with your student how to convert metric units of measurement. Ask, *Would we multiply or divide to change millimeters to centimeters?* [divide]

TEMPERATURE

1 **EXPLAIN** Tell your student that the customary system measures temperature in degrees Fahrenheit (°F). Explain to him or her that water freezes at 32°F and boils at 212°F. Then have your student estimate temperatures of hot, warm, and cold days. Have your student estimate the temperature on the coldest and hottest days where you live. Discuss the answers.

2 **EXTEND** Describe below-zero temperatures to your student. Explain to him or her that as it gets colder the numbers increase. Ask, *Which is warmer, –5°F or –25°F?* [–5°F] Model how to solve this problem: *How many degrees warmer is 10°F than –5°F?* [count up from –5°F to 0°F and then from 0°F to 10°F] Have your student solve the problem. [15°F]

3 **RELATE** Explain to your student that the metric system measures temperature in degrees Celsius (°C). Tell him or her that water freezes at 0°C and boils at 100°C. Have your student estimate temperatures of hot, warm, and cold days in degrees Celsius. Then have him or her use degrees Celsius to estimate the temperatures on the coldest and hottest days where you live. Then distribute Student Learning Page 10.A for more practice.

Branching Out

TEACHING TIP

Make a copy of the Venn Diagram found on page 355. Have your student compare degrees Celsius and degrees Fahrenheit. Your student may note that Celsius has lower numbers and is a metric unit and that Fahrenheit has greater numbers and is a customary unit. Both measure temperature, increase as it gets warmer, and decrease as it gets colder.

CHECKING IN

To assess your student's understanding of the lesson, have your student collect objects from around the house and measure them using different types of measurement. For example, he or she could measure a scarf's length in feet, inches, centimeters, and millimeters. Then have your student tell you which unit of measurement would be best suited for each object.

ENRICH THE EXPERIENCE

Your student can use the automatic metric converter at http://www.superkids.com/metric_converter.htm to quickly convert length, mass, and temperature measurements between standard and metric units.

A BRIGHT IDEA

For fun activities and experiments with temperature, try the book *Really Hot Science Projects with Temperature: How Hot Is It? How Cold Is It?* by Robert Gardner.

FOR FURTHER READING

Measurement Mania: Games and Activities That Make Math Easy and Fun, by Lynette Long (John Wiley, 2001).

Measuring Penny, by Loreen Leedy (Holt, Henry Books for Young Readers, 2000).

Temperature, by Alan Rodgers and Angella Streluk (Heinemann Library, 2002).

Practice Measurement

Complete the measurements in the squares. Then answer the question in the center diamond.

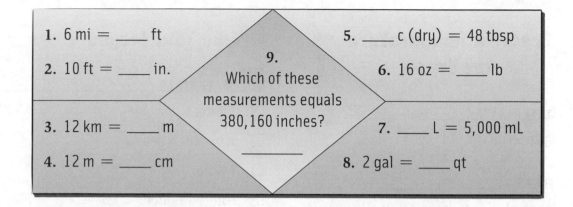

1. 6 mi = _____ ft

2. 10 ft = _____ in.

3. 12 km = _____ m

4. 12 m = _____ cm

9.
Which of these measurements equals 380,160 inches?

_____

5. _____ c (dry) = 48 tbsp

6. 16 oz = _____ lb

7. _____ L = 5,000 mL

8. 2 gal = _____ qt

Read the word problems. Then solve. Show your work.

10. Laurie wants to balance a scale. One side of the scale has a book that weighs 10 pounds 6 ounces. Which two items should Laurie put on the other side of the scale in order to balance it?

    a. A shoe that weighs 3 pounds 4 ounces

    b. A lamp that weighs 114 ounces

    c. A bowling ball that weighs 9 pounds 1 ounce

11. The coldest temperature ever recorded in Alaska was −80°F. The warmest temperature ever recorded in Alaska was 84°F. What is the difference between these two temperatures?

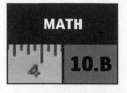

What's Next? You Decide!

Now it's your turn to choose what to do next in the lesson. Read the activities and decide which one you want to do— you may want to try them both!

Create a Temperature Bar Graph

MATERIALS

❑ 1 posterboard

STEPS

❑ Research the average temperatures in your city for each month of 2002. Use the Internet or the library. Find the temperatures in both degrees Fahrenheit and degrees Celsius.

❑ Create a temperature bar graph for the entire previous year. Show both degrees Fahrenheit and degrees Celsius. Ask an adult for help if you need to.

❑ Answer these questions:

1. Which month was the hottest?

2. Which month was the coldest?

3. Which two months had the closest temperatures? What was the difference in degrees Fahrenheit and in degrees Celsius?

4. Which two months had the greatest difference in temperature? What was the difference in degrees Fahrenheit and in degrees Celsius?

Take Your Measurements

MATERIALS

❑ 1 inch ruler

❑ 1 metric ruler

❑ 1 scale

❑ colored pencils

STEPS

❑ Use the inch and metric rulers to measure the following: how tall you are, how wide your hand is, how long your foot is, how long your arm is.

❑ Draw a picture of yourself using colored pencils. Write the measurements of your height, the width of your hand, and the lengths of your foot and arm on the picture.

❑ Use the scale to see how many pounds you weigh.

❑ Then figure out how many ounces you weigh.

❑ Estimate how many cups and milliliters of water you drink every day.

❑ Then estimate the number of pints and liters of water you drink every day.

Understanding Statistics and Probability

Organization is the key to success.

OBJECTIVE	BACKGROUND	MATERIALS
To teach your student different ways of organizing data and to predict probable outcomes	The world is full of information. We use this information, or data, in many ways. Learning how to organize and read data makes the information we collect more useful. In this lesson, your student will learn how to organize and interpret data. He or she will also learn a variety of uses for data, such as finding averages and probability.	■ Student Learning Pages 11.A–11.B ■ 9 counters, such as coins ■ 5 copies Grid, page 357 ■ 1 paper clip ■ 2 sheets construction paper ■ markers or colored pencils

VOCABULARY

RANGE   the difference between the least and greatest numbers in a data set

AVERAGE   the quotient of the total value of the numbers of a data set and the total number of numbers; the typical number of the data set

MODE   the number in a data set that occurs most often

Let's Begin

DATA DESCRIPTION

1   **INTRODUCE** Tell your student that once data is collected it can be used to make comparisons. Explain to him or her that the **range, average,** and **mode** are different ways of describing the data collected. Have your student use the following data for the exercises presented throughout the lesson.

Minutes Spent Practicing Math Facts

	Mon.	Tues.	Wed.	Thurs.	Fri.
Week 1	16	22	18	24	20
Week 2	16	18	18	18	20
Week 3	22	24	16	22	18
Week 4	17	23	20	18	14

2 **EXPLAIN** Have your student look at the data. Explain to him or her that one way to describe data is by finding the mode. Tell your student that the mode is the number that occurs most often. Ask, *How do you think we could organize this data so that we can find the mode?* [group the numbers together that are alike] Have your student experiment with various ways of doing this. Ask, *What is the mode of this data?* [18]

3 **TEACH** Ask, *What was the longest time the student spent practicing math facts?* [23 minutes] *What was the shortest amount of time?* [14 minutes] Tell your student that the difference between the greatest number and the least number is the range. Help him or her subtract to find the range. [9] Ask, *How can you use the range to describe the student's practice time?* [each day the student's practice time is always at most 9 minutes less or more than another day's practice time] Have your student find the range for each week's practice time. [Week 1: 8 minutes; Week 2: 4 minutes; Week 3: 8 minutes; Week 4: 9 minutes]

4 **DISCUSS** Ask your student, *What do you think the word* average *means?* Then read this problem to your student: *Alex received 3 birthday cards in the mail on Monday, 4 cards on Tuesday, and 2 cards on Wednesday. What is the average number of cards he received each day?* Have your student use 9 counters to represent the 9 cards. Model how to arrange the counters into 3 groups to find that the average is 3. Ask, *What are we doing when we find the average?* [changing unlike groups to even groups] Ask, *How do you think we could use division to find averages?* [add up all of the items and divide by the number of groups]

5 **MODEL** Show your student how to find the average practice time for Week 1: Add the practice times and divide by 5. [20 minutes] Have him or her find the average practice time for Week 2. [18 minutes]

6 **REVIEW** Give your student the following data group representing people's ages. Have him or her find the mode [9], range [7], and average [10].

12, 9, 10, 12, 9, 10, 13, 9, 6

INTRODUCTION TO GRAPHS

1 **EXPLAIN** Explain to your student that organizing data makes it easier to interpret. Explain that one way to organize data is by making a graph. There are many different kinds of graphs, such as bar graphs, line graphs, circle graphs, and pictographs. Use a copy of the Grid found on page 357 to show your student how to make a line graph using the sample data. Label the vertical axis with the number of minutes and the horizontal axis with the days of the week. Show your student how to plot the number of minutes practiced each day and how to draw lines to connect each point.

2 **ANALYZE** Ask, *How many days are shown on the line graph?* [5] *Which days did the student practice the same number of minutes?* [Tuesday, Wednesday, and Thursday] *How many more minutes did the student practice on Friday than on Monday?* [2 minutes]

3 **EXPAND** Model how to make a bar graph and pictograph using the practice time data. Have your student use copies of the Grid found on page 357 to make a bar graph. Each box can be worth 2 minutes or 5 minutes. Color enough boxes to equal each day's practice time. A simple picture, such as a star, can represent a certain number of minutes in a pictograph. Have your student draw the appropriate number of pictures to represent the practice time.

4 **CONTINUE** Now model circle graphs. Explain to your student that circle graphs are easiest to use when your data can be represented by a fraction. Show him or her that in the practice data Week 1 has a total of 100 minutes, and that on Friday the student practiced 20 minutes, or $\frac{1}{5}$ of the time. Have your student color $\frac{1}{5}$ of the circle to show Friday's practice time. Ask your student which type of graph he or she enjoyed making the most. Have your student use the following set of data to draw the graph he or she likes the most.

Colors of bicycles: 4 red, 2 blue, 2 yellow, 1 green, 1 white

GRAPHS OF ORDERED PAIRS

1 **DISCUSS** Tell your student that ordered pairs help plot specific points on a graph. Explain to him or her that points are plotted by first moving a certain number of squares to the right and then moving a certain number of squares up. Ask, *Why are there two numbers in an ordered pair?* [one number is for moving right and the other number is for moving up]

2 **PRACTICE** Show your student how to graph ordered pairs. Have him or her use a copy of the Grid found on page 357. Explain that the first number of the pair tells how many squares to move to the right, and the second number tells how many squares to move up. Help your student label the Grid with the numbers 1 to 10 horizontally and vertically. Then have him or her plot the following ordered pairs on the Grid: (4, 6), (3, 5), (1, 7), (2, 9), (2, 2), and (0, 8).

UNDERSTANDING PROBABILITY

1 **DISCUSS** Explain to your student that probability is making predictions about what will happen next. Ask, *If I flip a coin, what is the likelihood that it will land heads up?* [there is a good chance for the coin to land heads up] *What are the two possible outcomes when flipping a coin?* [it could land heads up or tails

A BRIGHT IDEA

Look through the newspaper for examples of graphs with your student, especially the business section. Help your student practice identifying and interpreting different kinds of graphs.

ENRICH THE EXPERIENCE

Your student can learn more about different types of graphs at http://nces.ed.gov/nceskids/graphing.

ENRICH THE EXPERIENCE

Your student can learn more about probability by visiting the National Center for Educational Statistics at http://nces.ed.gov/nceskids and clicking on the dice.

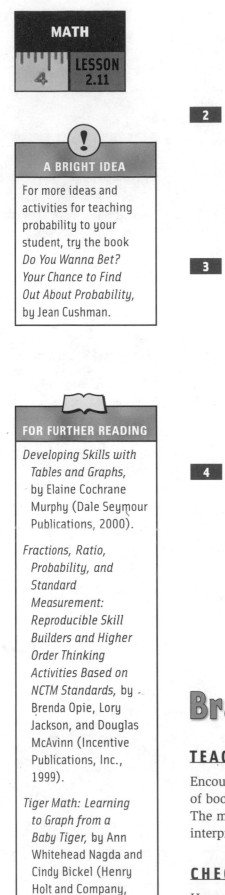

up] Ask, *There are 5 buttons in a box: 1 red, 1 blue, 1 green,
1 yellow, and 1 orange. If you pulled one out without looking,
what is the probability of pulling out the red one?* [1 in 5] *What
could I do to increase my chances of pulling out a red button?*
[take some of the other buttons out, or put more red buttons in]

2 **BUILD** Help your student make a spinner with a pencil and a
paper clip. Have him or her cut a circle out of construction paper
for the spinner's base and draw lines to divide it into 6 equal
sections. Tell your student to color each section a different color
(red, blue, green, orange, yellow, and purple). Model how to slip
a paper clip over the point of the pencil as you put the pencil
point on the center of the base. Have your student flick the paper
clip with his or her finger so that it spins around the pencil point.

3 **EXPLORE** Ask, *How many different outcomes are there if we
spin the spinner once?* [6] Have your student list the different
outcomes from one spin of the spinner. [red, blue, green, orange,
yellow, and purple] Ask, *How many times do you think we would
have to spin this spinner in order to land on each color one time?*
[6 times] Have your student spin the spinner until it lands on
each color one time. Tell him or her to keep track of the total
number of spins and to write it in his or her notebook. Ask, *Why
do you think it took that number of spins to land on each color
once?* [possible answer: because the spinner landed on one color
twice before landing on another color for the first time]

4 **EXPAND** Help your student make a new spinner base that has
2 sections colored red and the other 4 sections colored green,
orange, purple, and blue. Ask, *How many different outcomes are
there if we spin this spinner once?* [5] *What is the likelihood that
the spinner will land on the green space?* [1 in 6] *What is the
probability that the spinner will land on a red space?* [2 in 6]
Do you think this is a fair spinner? [no, because there is a better
chance that the spinner will land on red than the other colors]
Ask, *What do you think we could do to make this a fair spinner,
but keep both of the red spaces?* [only use 3 colors, and have
2 sections for each color]

Branching Out

TEACHING TIP

Encourage your student to graph a variety of data, such as the number
of books in each room of your home or the colors of his or her shirts.
The more your student organizes data, the better he or she will be at
interpreting graphs in other situations.

CHECKING IN

Have your student create two different graphs with the ages of his or her
family members.

Work with Data

73, 56, 92, 100, 60, 97, 82, 88, 69, 77

Find the average of each group.

1. 13, 16, 10, 15 _____ 13 _____

2. 70, 30, 50, 20, 40 _____ 40 _____

A+

Find the range of each group.

3. 17, 26, 24, 15, 21, 12 _____ 14 _____

4. 96, 44, 58, 77, 63, 89 _____ 52 _____

26
-12
14

96
-44
52

Plot and label the ordered pairs. Connect the points in letter order to reveal a secret animal.

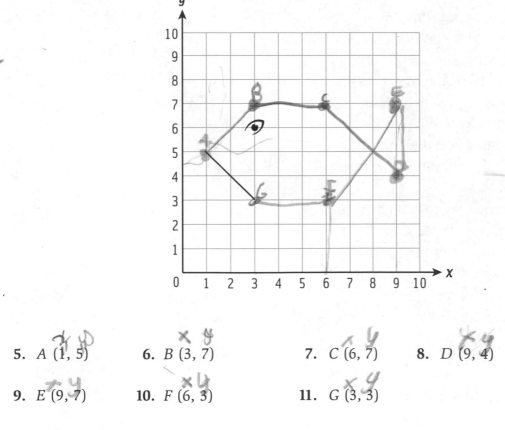

5. A (1, 5)

6. B (3, 7)

7. C (6, 7)

8. D (9, 4)

9. E (9, 7)

10. F (6, 3)

11. G (3, 3)

12. What animal did you graph? _____

What's Next? You Decide!

Now it's your turn to choose what to do next in the lesson.
Read the activities and decide which one you want to do—
you may want to try them all!

Hunt for Graphs

MATERIALS

❏ old newspapers and magazines
❏ 1 posterboard (optional)
❏ glue

STEPS

❏ Be a graph detective and hunt for graphs.
❏ Ask an adult to help you gather old newspapers and magazines.
❏ Cut out each graph you find. (Be sure to get permission first.)
❏ Spread out all your graphs where you can see them. What types of graphs do you have? What types of data are organized on the graphs?
❏ Think of ways your graphs are alike and different.
❏ Think of a good way to arrange your graphs, such as by type, size, or the kind of information in the graph.
❏ Glue each graph onto posterboard.
❏ Continue being a graph detective by adding to your collection of graphs as you find new ones.

Make a Backward Alphabet Graph

MATERIALS

❏ 1 stopwatch or clock with a second hand

STEPS

❏ Ask 10 people to say the alphabet backward. Time each person and record their times.
❏ Organize the data and make a graph.
❏ Who could say the alphabet the fastest? Who was the slowest? Find the mode, the range, and the average of the data.
❏ Arrange the data in a different way and make another type of graph.

Choose an Age

MATERIALS

❏ 1 paper bag

STEPS

❏ Cut 15 small squares from scratch paper. Write the numbers 1 to 15 on the squares of paper.
❏ Predict how many times it will take you to choose your age.
❏ Reach into the bag. Without looking, pull out one of the numbers.
❏ If the number is not the same as your age, put it back and try again.
❏ Ask family members and friends to predict how many tries it will take them to choose their age.
❏ Keep track of how many tries it takes for each person.
❏ Make a graph of the data and color it.

Exploring Geometry

Geometry shows us that math is around us everywhere.

OBJECTIVE	BACKGROUND	MATERIALS
To give your student a fundamental overview of geometry	Geometry is a branch of math that describes the world of objects and how they exist in space. In this lesson, your student will be introduced to geometry and learn how geometry allows us to compare these spaces.	■ Student Learning Pages 12.A–12.B ■ cardboard ■ 1 pair scissors ■ 1 ruler or tape measure ■ 1 box, block, or book ■ 1 photo or drawing of a pyramid

VOCABULARY

POINT a single location in space

LINE a group of points that goes on forever in both directions

ANGLE a figure formed by two rays that meet at one point

PERPENDICULAR a description for two lines that form a right angle

POLYGONS closed figures formed by line segments

CONGRUENT a description for figures that are identical in shape and size

SIMILAR a description for figures that have the same shape

SOLIDS figures that have width, height, and depth

Let's Begin

POINTS, LINES, RAYS, SEGMENTS, AND ANGLES

1 **INTRODUCE** Tell your student that geometry is the study of points, lines, shapes, and figures. Use the table on the next page as a reference, but make sure you or your student redraw each term as you discuss it. Geometry begins with the simplest element, a **point,** which is a single location in space. Show that the point in the diagram is labeled *A*. Point out that these types of labels are used throughout geometry. Explain that a group of points that continues on forever in both directions is a **line.** Show how line *BC* is labeled, and point out that the arrowheads indicate that the line continues on forever in those directions. Point to ray *DE*. Tell your student that this is a ray. Explain that point *D* is called an endpoint.

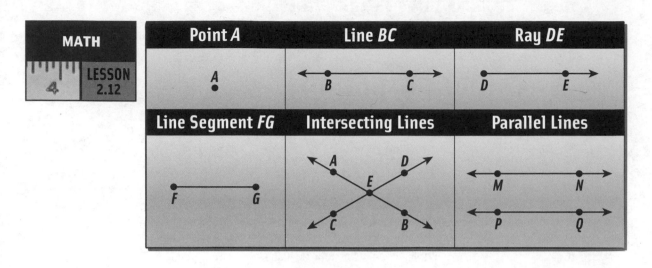

Point *A*	Line *BC*	Ray *DE*

Line Segment *FG*	Intersecting Lines	Parallel Lines

2 **EXPAND** Continue going through the other elements in the table with your student. You may take as much time as necessary. Although this lesson can be completed in a few hours, you may wish to keep returning to it throughout the week. Explain to your student that a line segment is part of a line and has two endpoints. Lines that pass through the same point are called intersecting lines. Ask, *Do all lines have to eventually intersect? Can you think of a case where two lines don't intersect?* [parallel lines] Point to the drawing and explain that lines that run alongside each other forever don't intersect and are called parallel lines.

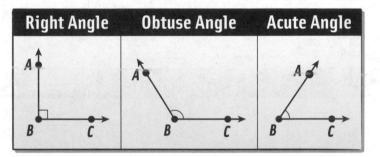

Right Angle	Obtuse Angle	Acute Angle

3 **PRESENT** Show your student that when two rays meet at the same point, the point is called a vertex and the two rays form an **angle.** The angles that are in the figure can each be called angle *ABC.* Explain that an angle that has a square corner is called a right angle. When two lines meet to form a right angle, they are called **perpendicular** lines. Mention that a right angle and perpendicular lines are always marked with a square at the vertex. Show your student that angles that are greater than a right angle are called obtuse angles and angles that are smaller than a right angle are called acute angles. Draw a right triangle (a triangle that has one right angle and two acute angles). Make sure that your drawing has the right angle marked with a square in the corner. Ask, *Can you name the types of angles that are in this drawing?* [student should point to each angle and identify one right angle and two acute angles]

POLYGONS

1 **INTRODUCE** Tell your student that he or she is probably already familiar with **polygons.** Triangles, squares, and rectangles are polygons. Explain that a polygon is a closed figure made up of line segments. Like with an angle, a point where two or more lines are connected is also called a vertex. (The plural is *vertices.*) Refer to the table below to have your student become familiar with some different types of polygons.

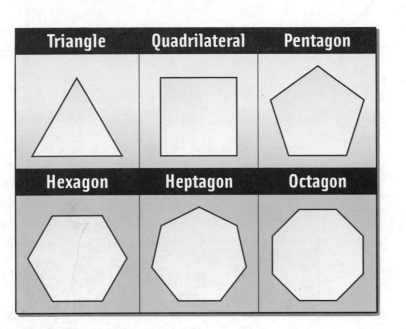

2 **MODEL** Draw a four- or five-sided figure that does *not* have all the sides connecting and show it to your student. Ask, *How is this figure different from the polygons in the table?* [not all the lines connect, so it's not a closed figure] Explain that this figure is not a polygon because it's not closed.

3 **EXPAND** Mention that the name of a polygon tells how many sides it has. The *tri–* in triangle means "three," and the *quad–* in quadrilateral means "four." Talk about the other polygon names and ask your student where he or she may have seen these shapes or names. Now have your student count the sides and vertices of a pentagon. [five sides, five vertices] Ask, *Do the number of sides and the number of vertices equal each other on every polygon?* [yes]

4 **OBSERVE** Tell your student that there are numerous ways to draw each type of polygon. Show this by drawing several odd-shaped quadrilaterals. Explain to him or her that all of these figures are quadrilaterals because they have four sides. Then make a drawing of a square and a rectangle. Be sure to mark each of the angles in your drawing as right angles. Explain that in a rectangle all the sides form right angles and the opposite sides are parallel and equal in length. Squares are like rectangles

but with all four sides equal in length. Ask, *Is every square a rectangle? Is every rectangle a square?* [every square is a rectangle, but every rectangle is not a square]

CONGRUENT AND SIMILAR FIGURES

1   **PRESENT** Explain to your student that when two figures have identical shapes and sizes they are said to be **congruent.** Figures that have the same shape and size are congruent even if one of them has been turned (see below). Show your student the four pairs of shapes below. Ask, *Which of these pairs are congruent?* [pair A and pair C] Ask your student to draw two figures that are congruent. Review his or her work.

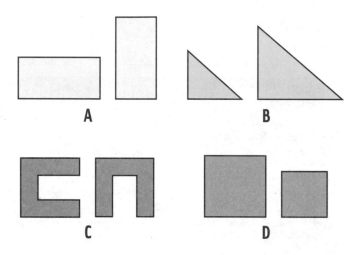

GET ORGANIZED

For answers to your questions about geometry, or for information on different approaches, go to http://mathforum. org and get geometrically organized!

2   **EXPAND** Tell your student that figures that have the same shape are said to be **similar.** Similar figures do not necessarily have the same size. Show your student the drawing again. Ask, *Which of these pairs are similar? Which are similar but not congruent?* [all of them are similar; pair B and pair D are similar but not congruent]

3   **RELATE** Ask your student if he or she thinks all rectangles are similar. Explain that all rectangles are not similar since the length relationship of their sides can vary. Draw an example of two dissimilar rectangles and point out to your student that even if the size of the smaller rectangle were increased, it wouldn't look the same as the larger one. Ask, *Are all squares similar?* [all squares are similar since the length relationship of their sides doesn't vary] Draw two different-sized squares and show that if the size of the smaller square were increased, it would look just like the larger one. Have your student draw two figures that are similar but not congruent. Review his or her work.

SLIDES, FLIPS, AND TURNS

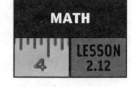
1 **INTRODUCE** Explain to your student that shapes can be moved. In geometry there are three specific types of movements, which are shown in the diagram below. A slide moves a figure in any direction. A flip is a movement that produces a mirror image of the figure. Finally, a turn is a movement that rotates the figure in one direction. Together with your student cut out two congruent triangles like the one on the previous page from a sheet of paper or cardboard. Arrange them so that they are mirror images of one another, but keep them about a foot apart. Ask, *What movements do you need to do to one figure to have it end up on top of the other figure?* [a slide and a flip] Have your student perform the two movements to test his or her answer.

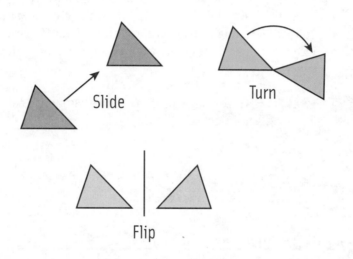

2 **PRACTICE** Have your student practice visualizing these transformations. Set up other examples and have him or her describe the movements that could make one figure end up in the position of the other. Have your student guess first ["A flip, a turn, and then a slide"] and then model his or her guess by physically moving one of the figures. Finally, have your student set up some examples for you to figure out.

SPACE FIGURES

1 **INTRODUCE** Tell your student that all the figures he or she has learned about are flat objects. These shapes have no depth. Points, lines, angles, and polygons are flat figures. Point out that geometry also deals with **solids.** A solid object has depth, width, and height. Explain that the objects around us are all solid objects. Model height, width, and depth for your student using a small box, block, or book. Have your student choose an object in the room and point to the height, width, and depth of the object.

2 **EXPAND** Tell your student that some important solid figures in geometry are the cube, rectangular prism, and pyramid. Point out that a cube is like a square that has depth and that a rectangular

DID YOU KNOW?

Geometry is a branch of mathematics that dates all the way back to ancient Egypt and Greece. A lot of the geometry that is taught today was written in books dating back to 300 B.C.

prism is like a rectangle that has depth. Examples of cubes are sugar cubes and dice. Doors, books, and many gift boxes are rectangular prisms. Explain that a pyramid is a five-sided object with one side that is square and four sides that are congruent triangles. Show your student a picture of a pyramid and mention the great pyramids in Egypt. Have your student choose an object that is a cube or rectangular prism and try drawing it. Demonstrate how to draw the object to show its depth.

3 CONTINUE Explain that three other solid geometrical figures are the sphere, cylinder, and cone. These solids are related to the circle. Point out that a sphere is a round object that is even all the way around. A tennis ball and a marble are both spheres. Cylinders are like circles with depth. A paper towel roll and a rolling pin are shaped like cylinders. Explain that a cone has a circular base and comes to a point at one end. Cones that your student might recognize are funnels and sugar cones for ice cream. Ask, *What other examples of spheres, cylinders, and cones can you think of?*

4 PRACTICE Have your student complete Student Learning Pages 12.A–12.B for practice.

Branching Out

FOR FURTHER READING

Exploring Solids and Boxes: 3-D Geometry, by Michael T. Battista; Beverly Cory and Catherine Anderson, eds. (Scott Foresman, 1998).

Geometry and Measurement: Problem Solving, Communication and Reasoning, by Carole Greenes, Linda Schulman Dacey, and Rika Spungin (Dale Seymour Publications, 1999).

TEACHING TIP

As you begin to discuss solid figures with your student, discuss the idea of dimension. Explain that solids have three dimensions, which means that they can be measured in three different directions: width, height, and depth. Thus, the phrase *3-D* (three-dimensional) is used to describe these objects. Explain that flat objects such as polygons are two-dimensional: they have only height and width. Explain that lines can be measured only in one dimension, their length. Finally, relate that points have no dimensions. Explain that a point is zero inches high, zero inches long, and zero inches deep. A point can't be measured at all!

CHECKING IN

There are many vocabulary words in this lesson. Check that your student is remembering these new words by pointing from time to time at an appropriate object and asking, *What geometrical figure does that remind you of?*

Practice Geometry

Draw an example of each.

1. Line

2. Ray

3. Acute angle

4. Obtuse angle

5. Right angle

6. Parallel lines

7. Perpendicular lines

8. Point

Read each question. Then write the answer.

9. Can you draw a triangle with three obtuse angles? Why or why not?

no, the sum of the three have to be 180° 790 × 3 = 7180

10. Can you draw a square with an acute angle? Why or why not?

no, the definition of a square is a polygon with 4 right angles and 4 same sides,

What's Next? You Decide!

Now it's your turn to choose what to do next in the lesson. Read the activities and decide which one you want to do— you may want to try them all!

Find the Lines

STEPS

❑ Look around your home for lines. In each room see how many examples you can find of parallel lines, perpendicular lines, and intersecting lines.

❑ Describe the examples in your notebook. Keep track of how many are in each room.

❑ Then look for right angles, obtuse angles, and acute angles.

❑ When you are through, look through your list. Which room in your home is the most geometric?

Model Geometrical Figures

MATERIALS

❑ 11 plastic drinking straws

STEPS

Use plastic drinking straws to model geometrical figures.

❑ Bend straws to make each of the following polygons: a pentagon, a square, a triangle with an obtuse angle, and a triangle with a right angle.

❑ Trace the outside shape of the straw models into your notebook and label them.

❑ Next, arrange the straws to model three parallel lines, two perpendicular lines, and two intersecting lines.

❑ Trace these lines into your notebook and label them.

❑ Share your creations with an adult.

Go on a Scavenger Hunt

MATERIALS

❑ 1 copy list for each player

STEPS

Ask family members and friends to participate in a scavenger hunt!

❑ Give a copy of the scavenger hunt list to each player.

❑ Decide where your scavenger hunt will be. Will it be inside your house only, in the garage, in the park?

❑ Decide on a final meeting place.

❑ The first person to return to the final meeting place with all the items on the list is the winner!

❑ Scavenger hunt list:
  - 6 rectangular prisms
  - 5 cylinders
  - 1 pyramid
  - 3 cubes
  - 5 spheres
  - 2 cones

In Your Community

To reinforce the skills and concepts taught in this section,
try one or more of these activities!

Geometric Architecture

Point out to your student that the structure he or she lives in is a bunch of geometric shapes that fit together nicely. Together with your student meet with a local architect. Have the architect show your student a set of blueprints and reveal the shapes that can be found in them. You also can look in books for examples of blueprints. Then have the architect show you how a house goes from blueprint to construction to final building. Help your student prepare for the meeting beforehand by having him or her draw a blueprint of his or her bedroom. You may have to help him or her measure.

Weighing In at the Post Office

Arrange for you and your student to take a tour of your post office. Go behind the scenes and learn how packages are weighed. Have your student find out how they weigh the really big packages. Then have your student ask what measurements they use to weigh mail (ounces? pounds?).

Tour Your Bank

Your student may have accompanied you to the bank, but does he or she really know what goes on there? Arrange for you and your student to get a tour of your bank. See if you can take a tour of the vault, the money-counting machine, and the safe-deposit box area. If possible have the tour guide show your student counterfeit money. If your student shows interest in the bank, ask your tour guide to tell you about how he or she came to work at a bank. If you haven't already, you may want to set up a savings account for your student. You can show him or her how you make deposits at the bank.

Shape-Up at the Grocery Store

The grocery store is filled with food, but did you ever notice how many shapes are there, too? Go to a grocery store with your student. Supply him or her with a pen or pencil and a clipboard and paper. Have him or her count the different geometric shapes that the food and food packages come in. How many does he or she count? Ask your student if he or she thinks certain shapes work better for packaging food.

Fractions at a Community Bake Sale

Fractions are used all the time in cooking—especially when making large quantities of food for a bake sale! The next time your community center, religious organization, or another group has a bake sale, encourage your student to help you make the food. Help him or her figure out the correct quantity of ingredients needed, which may be tricky if the batch has to be doubled, tripled, or even quadrupled. Have your student come with you to the bake sale.

Explore Statistics and Probability

Illustrate for your student how statistics and probability are used in everyday life. Arrange to have your student visit with a representative of a local marketing firm or another business that relies heavily on statistics, probability, and making graphs. Have the representative explain to your student the functions of statistics and probability as well as how they are used in his or her business. Furthermore, have the representative show your student the many ways in which his or her business presents data, such as in various graphs and charts. Then, together with the representative, think of a statistics and probability project you can do with your student.

We Have Learned

Use this checklist to summarize what you and your student have accomplished in the Math section.

❑ **Number Sense and Numeration**
☑ place value from ones to millions
☑ comparing, ordering, finding patterns, rounding
☑ estimation, number lines

❑ **Addition**
☑ addition with whole numbers and money
☑ addition of two- and three-digit numbers
☑ estimation

❑ **Subtraction**
☑ subtraction with whole numbers and money
☑ subtraction with two- and three-digit numbers
☑ estimation

❑ **Time and Measurement**
☑ telling time, temperature in degrees Celsius, and in degrees Fahrenheit
☑ customary units of length, capacity
☑ metric units of length, mass, capacity

❑ **Multiplication**
☑ multiplication by one-, two-, and three-digit numbers
☑ multiplication of multiples of 10, 100, and 1,000
☑ estimation of products

❑ **Division**
☑ division by one-, two-, and three-digit numbers
☑ divide multiples of 10, 100, 1,000
☑ estimation and adjustment of quotients

❑ **Geometry**
☑ points, lines, segments, rays, angles
☑ polygons, rectangles, squares
☑ prisms, cubes, pyramids, cylinders, cones, spheres
☑ congruency, slides, flips, turns

❑ **Fractions**
☑ fractions as parts of sets
☑ equivalent fractions
☑ comparing, ordering
☑ adding, subtracting

❑ **Decimals**
☑ understanding decimal place value
☑ estimation
☑ comparing, ordering
☑ adding, subtracting

❑ **Statistics and Probability**
☑ range, average, mode
❑ bar, line, circle, pictographs
☑ listing outcomes, evaluating fairness

We have also learned:

_____

_____

Science

Science

Key Topics

Classifying Plants and Animals

All plants and animals have characteristics that make them unique.

OBJECTIVE	BACKGROUND	MATERIALS
To teach your student about the different types of plants and animals on Earth	Learning about the characteristics animals and plants have helps us understand how they survive in various environments. In this lesson, your student will learn to classify vertebrates and invertebrates and recognize their traits. Your student will also learn to classify plants with flowers, cones, and spores.	■ Student Learning Pages 1.A–1.B ■ 1 apple

VOCABULARY

VERTEBRATES animals that have a backbone

INVERTEBRATES animals that don't have a backbone

ENDOSKELETON the supporting bony structure inside a vertebrate

EXOSKELETON a hard outer structure, such as a shell, that supports or protects an animal's body

OMNIVORES animals that eat plants and meat

CARNIVORES animals that only eat meat

HERBIVORES animals that only eat plants

SYMMETRY the way an animal's body parts are arranged

CONIFERS trees that have needles and make cones

SPORES cells that fall off a plant and grow into a new plant

Let's Begin

1 **EXPLAIN** Explain to your student that there are millions of different plant and animal species on Earth. Tell your student that this lesson will focus on the various characteristics of plants and animals that help them survive. Ask, *What is inside your body that helps you stand, helps you move, and gives you a shape?* [a skeleton] Explain that because humans have a backbone, we are classified as **vertebrates.** Animals that do not have a backbone are called **invertebrates.** Ask your student to think of some animals that are invertebrates and write them in his or her notebook. [worms, spiders, jellyfish, turtles, and so on]

2 **EXPAND** Talk more with your student about vertebrates. There are fish, amphibians, reptiles, birds, and mammals that are vertebrates. Their backbones are part of their skeletons inside their bodies. As a vertebrate's body grows, its skeleton grows along with it. Because they have skeletons to support them, vertebrates can be much larger than invertebrates. This is an advantage that invertebrates don't have. Vertebrates can also adapt more easily to their surroundings. Have your student make a five-column chart in a notebook. Have your student title the chart "Vertebrates" and use "Fish," "Amphibians," "Reptiles," "Birds," and "Mammals" as the headings for the five columns. Ask your student to list as many examples of each type of vertebrate as he or she can think of in the correct columns.

?

DID YOU KNOW?

Invertebrates make up about 98 percent of the known creatures on Earth. Vertebrates only make up about 2 percent, but they are well known because they are easier to identify than many invertebrates.

3 **RELATE** Explain that there are about 2 million species of invertebrates. Most invertebrates are small, but the giant squid can be more than 59 feet long and weigh more than 4,000 pounds. There are two body types for invertebrates. The first is circular, with their mouths in the center. Corals and sea anemones are examples of these. These invertebrates usually stay in one spot and wait for food to come to them. Other invertebrates have elongated bodies with definite front and back ends. Flatworms are an example of this body type. These invertebrates move to find their food. Ask your student to look in library books or on the Internet to find pictures of invertebrates. Have him or her decide which body shape each animal has.

+

ENRICH THE EXPERIENCE

Find a common house spider and watch it in action. How does a spider's exoskeleton help it survive?

4 **DISCUSS** Discuss with your student the difference between an **endoskeleton** and an **exoskeleton.** Endoskeletons are skeletons inside the body. Vertebrates have endoskeletons. Exoskeletons are hard coverings on the outside of the body. Insects have exoskeletons. These exoskeletons have helped make it possible for insects to survive in every habitat on Earth. Ask your student to think of other animals with exoskeletons, such as turtles and crabs. Then have him or her choose one animal to research and write a paragraph about.

GET ORGANIZED

Your student's Earthworm Olympics will go more smoothly if the earthworms are at room temperature. Earthworms are less active when they are cold.

5 **OBSERVE** Have your student observe one kind of invertebrate— worms. Dig up two earthworms from your yard or neighborhood, or buy earthworms at a bait shop. Explain that it's important to be gentle with the earthworms, so you should be careful while digging them up. Since they don't have a skeleton, their bodies can be crushed easily. Distribute Student Learning Page 1.A. Have your student conduct the Earthworm Olympics activity and complete the page.

6 **DISCUSS** Discuss with your student some of the things that people eat. Most people are **omnivores,** which means that they eat plants and meat. Examples of omnivores are grizzly bears, mockingbirds, and skunks. Some animals are **carnivores,**

meaning they only eat meat. Some examples of carnivores are red foxes and lions. Some animals are **herbivores,** meaning they only eat plants. Examples of herbivores are beavers, snails, cows, and sheep. Ask, *Are you an omnivore, a herbivore, or a carnivore?*

7 **EXPLAIN** Point out that another way that scientists classify animals is according to the way their body parts are arranged. The way a body is arranged and shaped is called **symmetry.** Most vertebrate animals have bilateral symmetry, which means that the two halves of their body mirror each other. Dogs, cats, whales, and birds all have bilateral symmetry. Some animals have bodies that are arranged around a central point, such as a starfish or jellyfish. Other animals, such as sea sponges, have an irregular shape without any pattern at all. Ask, *Why do you think most vertebrates have bilateral symmetry?* [because their backbones naturally divide their bodies into two balanced halves]

ENRICH THE EXPERIENCE

Your student can visit a virtual zoo on the Internet to learn how animals are classified at http://www. exzooberance.com.

8 **EXPLAIN** Explain to your student that scientists classify plants, too. One way to classify plants is by how they reproduce. Point out that some plants have flowers. The flower is where seeds are made. To make seeds, flowers must be pollinated first. Pollination is when the grains of pollen inside the flower are moved from one part to another. After a flower is pollinated, it's able to fertilize itself. Point out that the wind and insects, such as bees, play an important part in the process of pollination. Ask, *Why do you think some flowers have bright colors and strong scents?* [to attract insects so they can pollinate and reproduce]

9 **EXPAND** Ask your student if he or she has ever seen the seeds inside an apple or an orange. Explain that before the plant made the orange or apple, there was a flower that was pollinated, became fertilized, and grew into a fruit with the seeds inside. Some fruits, such as apples and oranges, have more than one seed. Others, such as plums and cherries, have only one seed. Point out that making fruit is a good way for a plant to distribute its seeds. Animals eat the fruit and then eliminate the seeds with their waste. This gives the plant a chance to reproduce far away from the original plant. Give your student an apple. Ask him or her to look at the apple and see if he or she can see leftover parts of its flower. Guide your student to see that at the bottom of the apple, opposite the stem, there are dried flower parts.

ENRICH THE EXPERIENCE

Check out a field guide from a local library. Take a walk around your neighborhood and help your student use the field guide to identify the different types of plants he or she finds.

10 **EXPLAIN** Explain that there are also plants that produce seeds but do not have flowers. Plants such as pine and fir trees produce seeds inside of cones. These plants are called **conifers.** Some plants don't produce seeds at all. They produce **spores.** Spores drop from the plant or are carried in the wind. Spores don't need to be pollinated or fertilized. When the spores fall onto moist ground, they grow and form new plants. Mosses and

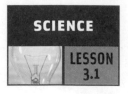
ferns produce spores. Have your student look out the window for any plants that are growing nearby. Ask him or her to decide how each plant in view might reproduce.

Conifers produce seeds inside cones.

Fruit produces seeds.

Ferns produce spores.

FOR FURTHER READING

The Kingfisher Illustrated Animal Encyclopedia, by David Burnie (Kingfisher, 2000).

The Nature and Science of Flowers, by Jane Burton and Kim Taylor (Gareth Stevens Publishing, 1998).

The Science of Animals, by Lauri Seidlitz (Gareth Stevens Publishing, 1999).

Seeds, Stems, and Stamens: The Ways Plants Fit into Their World, by Susan E. Goodman (Millbrook Press, Inc., 2001).

Trees, Leaves, and Bark, by Diane L. Burns (Gareth Stevens Publishing, 1998).

Branching Out

TEACHING TIP

Observe plants with your student at a local market. As you walk through the market, choose several different fruits and vegetables. Ask your student to consider what part of each plant we eat and how it reproduces. Have your student incorporate scientific methods when making his or her considerations: observe, hypothesize, experiment, and record results.

CHECKING IN

To assess your student's understanding of the lesson, show him or her pictures of vertebrates, such as gorillas or alligators, and invertebrates, such as jellyfish or turtles. Have your student classify each animal as vertebrate or invertebrate and as having an exoskeleton, an endoskeleton, or no skeleton.

Host the
Earthworm Olympics

Carefully dig up two earthworms from your backyard or a park. Gently place them in a cup of moist dirt until you are ready to begin. Find a warm, quiet place with dim light to hold your Olympic events. Observe the earthworms as they complete the events. Record your observations in the chart. When you're finished, return the earthworms outside to where you found them.

MATERIALS

- ❏ 1 pencil
- ❏ 2 clear plastic cups
- ❏ moist soil
- ❏ 1 clock with second hand

PENCIL LEAP

Set a pencil on a flat surface, such as a table. Set both earthworms on the table in front of the pencil. Watch how they move to get past the pencil. Be patient and observe. Record what you notice about how they move in the chart.

DIGGING COMPETITION

Place each earthworm in a clear plastic cup filled halfway with moist soil. Observe to see which earthworm digs its way down into the dirt first. Keep an eye on the clock and see how long it takes each earthworm to disappear. Record each worm's time in the chart.

	Pencil Leap	Digging Race
Worm 1		
Worm 2		

What's Next? You Decide!

Now it's your turn to choose what to do next in the lesson. Read the activities and decide which one you want to do— you may want to try them both!

Make a Neighborhood Animal Book

MATERIALS

❑ 5 sheets blank paper

❑ 1 large stapler

❑ colored pencils or crayons

❑ 1 instant camera (optional)

❑ tape

STEPS

Make a classification book of animals that live in and around your home.

❑ Fold five sheets of blank paper in half and staple them in the middle to make a book.

❑ Use colored pencils or crayons to color the cover of your book and make up a title.

❑ Look for animals inside your house and outside in your neighborhood. These can be pets, such as dogs, cats, or fish, or other creatures, such as spiders, birds, squirrels, worms, and so on.

❑ Use an instant camera to take a picture of each animal and tape the photo into your book. You can also draw a picture of each animal.

❑ Classify each animal in your book as vertebrate or invertebrate and as having an endoskeleton or an exoskeleton.

❑ Use library books or the Internet to find out whether each animal is a carnivore, an omnivore, or a herbivore. Write the classification in your book.

❑ Share your animal book with someone who lives in your neighborhood.

Identify Plants

MATERIALS

❑ 1 plant field guide

STEPS

❑ Go to a forest preserve or park with an adult.

❑ Look closely at the plants and trees that grow there. Use what you learned in this lesson to identify the plants as flowering, conifer, or having spores. Take a plant field guide with you for help.

❑ See if you can find at least one example of each type of plant.

❑ Which type of plant is most common in that area? Write your observations in a notebook.

❑ Visit a different forest preserve or park and see if you find the same or different types of plants.

Exploring Plant and Animal Life Cycles

We can learn to enjoy the cycle of life.

SCIENCE

LESSON 3.2

OBJECTIVE	BACKGROUND	MATERIALS
To help your student identify the life cycles of various plants and animals	On the journey through life, living things travel many different paths. Although the details may be different, all living things go through a series of stages called a life cycle. They are born, grow and change, have offspring, age, and eventually die. In this lesson, your student will observe how seeds germinate and grow, study animal life cycles, and learn about the major body changes known as metamorphosis.	■ Student Learning Pages 2.A–2.B ■ 1 copy Comparison Chart, page 355 ■ family photos ■ 1 plastic cup, filled with water ■ 4–5 mung bean, radish, or corn seeds ■ 1 plastic knife ■ 1 hand lens ■ dark construction paper ■ 1 glass jar ■ paper towels ■ 2 file folders ■ 1 standard ruler ■ 1 pair scissors ■ 2 paper fasteners

VOCABULARY

LIFE CYCLE all the stages and body changes in the life of a plant or animal

GROW to increase in size without necessarily changing shape or form

DEVELOPMENT a growth process that involves becoming more complex

LIFE SPAN the length of an animal or plant's natural life

GERMINATE when a living thing sprouts or forms new structures

METAMORPHOSIS major changes in body shape or form on the way to adulthood

LARVA, PUPA immature life stage

Let's Begin

1 **INTRODUCE** Explain to your student that all kinds of living things, from mushrooms to trees and from insects to mammals, go through **life cycle** changes. These include all the body changes and stages that an animal or plant goes through during its life. Encourage your student to consider the many ways he or she has grown and changed since being a baby. If you have a pet, ask your student to consider how it has changed and grown over time.

2 **REVEAL** Remind your student that people belong to the group of animals called mammals. Most mammals are born live and look like smaller forms of the adult. Over time, they **grow** bigger. Sometimes different body parts grow at different rates. Explain that human beings go through a life cycle that includes the following stages: baby, toddler, child, teenager, young adult, adult, middle age, and old age. Ask, *Which life stage are you in right now?* [child]

3 **DISTRIBUTE AND OBSERVE** Distribute Student Leaning Page 2.A. Have your student gather family photos that show him or her and other family members at various ages, from baby to adult. Ask your student to look at the photos carefully, observing the different life stages of each person. Have your student arrange and label the photos in order by life stage. Then ask your student to complete the questions.

Puppies experience much growth during their first year of life.

4 **EXPAND** Explain that most plants and some animals continue to grow throughout their lives, but that most living things also experience a series of changes in body plan at some point. This is called **development.** Ask your student to consider in which life stages people are most independent [teenage, adult, and middle age] and in which stages they are most dependent [baby, toddler, child]. Have your student consider how this relates to body changes and development. Point out that a baby or toddler needs a parent's help to eat, move, and change diapers. But the bodies of teenagers and adults are mature in that they are able to take care of their own physical needs.

5 **EXPLORE** Point out that humans and large animals live for many years. Explain that it takes a long time to observe the life cycles of living things with long lives. When we want to observe processes and learn about them, it's easier to choose living things that have a shorter **life span,** such as green plants. Have your student observe the life cycle of plants. Soak several bean seeds overnight in a cup of water. The next day, give your student a hand lens, a plastic knife, and a bean seed. Have him or her remove the tough coating from the seed and carefully separate the two halves of the seed. Have your student use the lens to identify the leaves, stem, and root of the baby plant. Ask your student to draw and label what he or she sees.

Adult dogs have well-developed senses of hearing and smell.

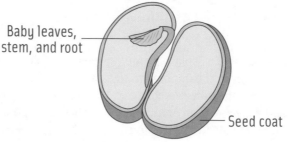

Baby leaves, stem, and root

Seed coat

6   **EXPERIMENT** Explain that the baby plant found in a seed will develop the roots, stem, and true leaves of the new plant when the seed **germinates,** or sprouts. Help your student make a seed viewer to observe seeds spouting. Together, soak some mung bean, radish, or corn seeds overnight. Line a glass jar with dark construction paper. Stuff some paper towels inside the jar to keep the paper in place. Place your seeds between the construction paper and the glass. This will make them easy to see against the dark background. Add a few inches of water. Label the jar with the type of seeds used and the date. Keep the towels damp. Over the next few days, have your student observe and describe what happens to the seedlings. Ask, *Which plant part appears first?* [the root appears first, then the shoot, stem, and leaves]

7   **RELATE** Remind your student that some animal babies, such as humans, dogs, and fish, look much like the adults they will grow into except for their size. Explain that others completely change their body shape, or form. This is called **metamorphosis.** Metamorphosis is common in the life of insects. One example of this is when a caterpillar goes into a cocoon and changes into a butterfly. A butterfly has four life stages: egg, **larva, pupa** (or cocoon), and adult. Caterpillars are in the larval stage and butterflies are in the adult stage. After metamorphosis, the habitat and lifestyle of the insect changes. Ask, *How are the habitat and lifestyle of a caterpillar different from a butterfly?* [the caterpillar crawls over a small area; butterflies fly and can live in a large area]

8   **RESEARCH** Ask your student to pick two animal life cycles to learn more about. Have one of them be an animal that experiences metamorphosis. Possible choices might include a frog, tiger, grasshopper, chicken, butterfly, horse, spider, dragonfly, or lizard. Have your student find out what each animal eats, how it moves, and how its babies are born. Your student can use Internet sources and library books. Have your student keep notes on a copy of the Comparison Chart found on page 355. Then tell your student to suppose he or she is one of the animals and write a story or journal entry describing its adventures at one stage in its life cycle.

9   **CONSTRUCT** Distribute two file folders, scissors, a pencil, paper fasteners, and a ruler. Then help your student use the file folders to make life cycle wheels for the animals he or she researched. Together, draw and cut out a circle eight inches in diameter on one of the file folders. Divide the circle into the number of parts equal to the number of stages in the animal's life cycle. Have your student draw pictures of the animal's life stages in order around the circle. Cut a wedge-shaped viewing window in the second file folder. Use a pencil to poke a hole in the center of the life wheel and in the file folder below the window. Use a paper fastener to attach the folder and circle so that the pictures turn and can be seen through the window. Compare the two animal life cycles.

? DID YOU KNOW?

The mammals of Australia and New Guinea are unique. The platypus is a member of a special branch of the mammal line that lays eggs instead of having live babies. Kangaroos are born alive but have to crawl into their mother's pouch to develop.

+ ENRICH THE EXPERIENCE

For more information on the life cycles of frogs, go to the Web site http://www.kiddyhouse.com and click on Kid's Corner and then click on All About Frogs.

A Life Cycle Wheel

1. Draw life stages on circle

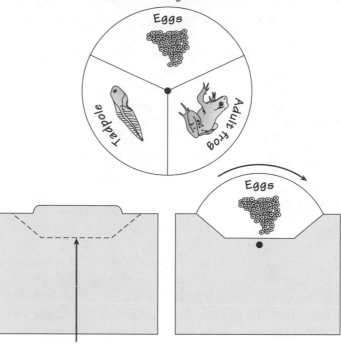

2. Cut file folder   3. Assemble life wheel

Branching Out

TEACHING TIP

To give your student more experience identifying life cycle stages, have your student look for pictures of the same animal at different stages (such as nesting birds, eggs, young birds, and adults) in some nature magazines and cut them out. Have your student arrange the pictures in life cycle order. Encourage your student to incorporate scientific methods of observation and hypothesis when reviewing life cycles.

CHECKING IN

Assess your student's understanding of life cycle changes by having him or her make a life cycle flip book that shows an animal or plant growing into an adult (such as a seed growing into a maple tree, a tadpole into a frog, or a chick into a hen). Cut sheets of paper into four equal pieces. Allow your student to choose an animal or plant. Staple the series of drawings together when completed. The flip book effect works best if your student draws the series of drawings in the same spot on each page and changes each drawing only slightly. If this becomes too challenging, have your student conduct a presentation and, using visual and oral aids, tell you about life cycles.

FOR FURTHER READING

Monarch Magic! Butterfly Activities and Nature Discoveries, by Lynn M. Rosenblatt (Williamson Publishers, 1998).

Plants, by Sally Hewitt (Copper Beech Books, 2001).

What Is a Life Cycle?, by Bobbie Kalman and Jacqueline Langille (Crabtree Publishers, 1998).

Observe Life Cycles

Tape your family photos in order from youngest to oldest on a separate sheet of paper. Complete the questions.

Human Life Stages

1. Baby
2. Toddler
3. Child
4. Teenager

5. Young adult
6. Adult
7. Middle age
8. Old age

A. Study the family photos carefully. Label each photo by the stage of human life that it shows.

B. How do human bodies change as they grow older? Which parts change the most?

_____

_____

_____

C. Write a short paragraph describing how you have grown and changed since you were a baby.

_____

_____

_____

_____

_____

_____

_____

_____

_____

What's Next? You Decide!

Now it's your turn to choose what to do next in the lesson. Read the activities and decide which one you want to do— you may want to try them both!

Raise Mealworms

MATERIALS

- ❏ 1 glass jar
- ❏ bran cereal or oatmeal
- ❏ 2–3 mealworms from a pet store or bait shop
- ❏ 1 craft stick
- ❏ paper towels
- ❏ 1 slice raw potato or carrot
- ❏ 1 piece cheesecloth
- ❏ 1 rubber band
- ❏ 1 plastic cup

STEPS

Mealworms are the larval stage of the darkling beetle. Observe this animal's life cycle up close.

- ❏ Put 1–2 inches of cereal at the bottom of the jar.
- ❏ Gently put the mealworms in the jar. Use a craft stick to move them.
- ❏ Cover the cereal with a few layers of paper towels to give them a place to hide.
- ❏ Add a piece of raw potato or a carrot for moisture. Change the veggie every few days before it gets moldy.
- ❏ Cover the jar with the cheesecloth. Fix it in place with a rubber band so the mealworms can't escape.
- ❏ Every two days, move the mealworms into a plastic cup (with high sides) and observe their size and movement. Always handle them gently and

carefully. Wash your hands after making observations.

- ❏ Observe them for four to six weeks until you see all four of their life stages. Then return the mealworms to the pet store or bait shop.

Build a Bird Feeder

MATERIALS

- ❏ $\frac{1}{2}$ gallon juice carton or 1 gallon plastic bottle
- ❏ 1 pair scissors
- ❏ 1 wooden dowel rod
- ❏ 1 bag birdseed
- ❏ 1 piece string or fishing line

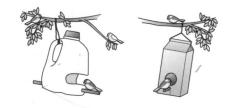

STEPS

- ❏ Wash the carton or bottle thoroughly.
- ❏ Make two small holes on opposite sides and slide a dowel rod through for a perch.
- ❏ Cut a round hole (large enough for a small bird's head) above the perch in one side of the carton or bottle.
- ❏ Fill the carton or bottle with birdseed.
- ❏ Fasten string to the top so you can hang the feeder from a tree.

Understanding Energy Flow

Producers, consumers, and decomposers work together!

OBJECTIVE	BACKGROUND	MATERIALS
To help your student see how energy flows between organisms	Organisms depend on each other for food and energy. They do this by occupying different roles. In this lesson, your student will learn how the roles of producer, consumer, and decomposer contribute to the flow of energy.	■ Student Learning Pages 3.A–3.B ■ several wildlife magazines

VOCABULARY
ORGANISMS living things **PRODUCERS** organisms that make their own food **CONSUMERS** organisms that eat other living things **DECOMPOSERS** organisms that break down the remains of other living things **FOOD CHAIN** a diagram that shows the food relationships among a group of living things

Let's Begin

1 **ASK** Ask your student to consider why he or she needs energy. [in order to live] Discuss the relationship between energy and the food we eat. Point out that we eat food in order to obtain energy. Ask your student to think about the different kinds of food that other living things eat. Have him or her make a list of six different living things with an example of a food eaten by each one. Have your student look through wildlife, nature, or oceanography magazines for photographs of living things and information about the foods they eat.

2 **EXPLAIN** Explain to your student that all living things are called **organisms.** Explain that organisms can be classified according to the way they acquire their food. **Producers** (plants) make their own food. **Consumers,** such as humans, eat other organisms for food. **Decomposers** (bacteria, mushrooms, yeast, and mold) obtain their food by breaking down the remains of other living things. Ask your student to describe a plant's relationship to producers [plants are producers], consumers [plants are eaten by consumers], and decomposers [decomposers break down plant remains].

Mushrooms are decomposers in the food chain.

3 **EXPLORE** Describe to your student the way producers, consumers, and decomposers form a **food chain.** Show your student the diagram of a simple food chain. Identify the producer and consumers in the diagram. Point out that each organism in a food chain obtains its energy by consuming the organism positioned before it. This is how energy is transferred through the food chain. Ask, *Where do plants obtain their energy?* [from the sun] *How could decomposers be included in this food chain?* [if one of the organisms died, decomposers would use the remains as energy for food]

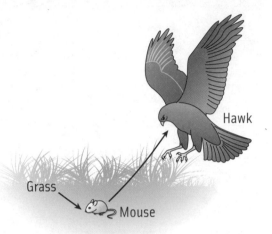

4 **RELATE** Have your student draw a simple food chain on a sheet of paper. Use a plant as the first organism in the chain. Draw an arrow from the plant to an organism that might consume it. Draw another arrow from that consumer to the next consumer. The completed food chain should have at least three organisms in it.

Branching Out

TEACHING TIP

Take a walk with your student and identify as many producers, consumers, and decomposers as possible. Encourage your student to incorporate scientific methods—such as observing, making a hypothesis, recording data, and drawing conclusions—while he or she walks, watches, and identifies.

CHECKING IN

To assess your student's understanding of this lesson, place a picture of a plant, a rabbit, and a coyote in a small box or can. Ask your student to reach into the box or can, choose one of the pictures, and identify it as a producer, a consumer, or a decomposer. Then ask your student to place the picture on a table in order to make a food chain. [plant → rabbit → coyote]

Create Food Chains

Use the list of animals below to create examples of food chains. Choose three animals from the list that might make up a food chain. In the first column, write the name of the producer in the food chain. In the second and third columns, write the names of the consumers in the food chain.

snake	robin	sunflower
horse	rabbit	grasshopper
eagle	bear	sea turtle
frog	grass	spider
bumblebee	deer	water lily
wolf	seaweed	shark

Food Chains

Producer ⟶	Consumer ⟶	Consumer

What's Next? You Decide!

Now it's your turn to choose what to do next in the lesson.
Read the activities and decide which one you want to do—
you may want to try them both!

Find the Food Chains on Your Plate

MATERIALS

- ❑ 1 posterboard
- ❑ markers or crayons
- ❑ construction paper
- ❑ 1 standard ruler
- ❑ 1–2 food and animal magazines
- ❑ glue

STEPS

Create a poster that shows the food chains from your dinner.

- ❑ On a sheet of paper, list each of the food items in your last dinner.
- ❑ Make a diagram of a food chain that includes each item.
- ❑ Make a construction paper model, or find a picture, to represent each food item.
- ❑ Find pictures of the animals or plants needed to represent the steps of the food chain.
- ❑ Glue the steps of your food chains onto the posterboard.
- ❑ Use markers or crayons to make large arrows between each step of the food chains.
- ❑ Label each part of the food chains as producer, consumer, or decomposer.

Write a Food Chain Poem

STEPS

Use the steps in a food chain to compose a poem or song.

- ❑ First, draw a four- or five-step food chain to use as a model.
- ❑ Refer to the drawing in the lesson for ideas, or take a walk in a nearby forest preserve, a park, or in your neighborhood for ideas for a food chain.
- ❑ Be sure to ask an adult's permission before taking your walk.
- ❑ Start with the producer in your food chain.
- ❑ Write a rhythmic verse to describe the producer's role in the food chain.
- ❑ Repeat for each step in the food chain.
- ❑ See if you can make your poem rhyme.
- ❑ Share your poem with your family.
- ❑ If you'd like, make it into a catchy song that others can sing to remind them how a food chain works.

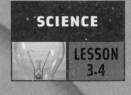

Finding Out About Nutrition

Proteins, carbohydrates, fats, and other nutrients make up your food. They also make up your body.

OBJECTIVE	BACKGROUND	MATERIALS
To teach your student about food and nutrition	Understanding basic nutrition helps us understand why we should eat a healthy diet and how to do so. In this lesson, your student will learn about the various types of nutrients, which foods they are in, and their importance for the body.	■ Student Learning Pages 4.A–4.B

VOCABULARY

NUTRIENTS substances in food that the body uses for energy, growth, and maintenance

CARBOHYDRATES nutrients that provide energy and help make cells

FATS nutrients that provide energy and are necessary for cell function

PROTEINS nutrients that are used for growth, repair, and cell maintenance

SATURATED FATS fats that are generally solid at room temperature

UNSATURATED FATS fats that are in the form of liquid oil at room temperature

CHOLESTEROL a substance found in many animal fats and also made by the liver

Let's Begin

1 **EXPLAIN** Explain to your student that all foods contain **nutrients** that are necessary for growth and survival. Invite your student to make a list in his or her notebook of the foods he or she has eaten in the past day.

2 **EXPLAIN AND GUIDE** Discuss with your student the functions of each of the three main types of nutrients—**carbohydrates, fats,** and **proteins.** Distribute Student Learning Page 4.A. Invite your student to use the illustrations to identify examples of foods that contain each type of nutrient. Encourage your student to think of other foods in addition to those in the illustrations. Have your student review the list he or she made in Step 1 and identify the types of nutrients in the foods on the list.

3 **EXPAND** Discuss with your student the possible sources of fat. Guide him or her to see that fats may be found in both animal foods, such as meats and cheeses, and in plant foods, such as

ENRICH THE EXPERIENCE

Your student can learn how to read a nutrition label at http://kidshealth.org.

peanut oil. Explain that although fats are necessary for good health, most people eat too much fat. Explain the difference between **saturated fats,** which are found primarily in animal foods, and **unsaturated fats,** which are found in plant foods. Tell students that **cholesterol** is found only in food products from animals. Too much cholesterol is thought to be a cause of heart disease. Ask your student to point out which fats shown on Student Learning Page 4.A are unsaturated fats.

4 **EXPAND** Tell your student that there are two kinds of carbohydrates: starches and sugars. Starches are found in foods such as potatoes and bread. Sugars are found in many fruits as well as in prepared foods such as cookies and ketchup. Challenge your student to point out those foods on Student Learning Page 4.A that contain starch.

5 **EXPAND** Point out to your student that foods contain other nutrients as well. Tell your student that most foods contain small amounts of vitamins and minerals that are needed for good health. By eating a variety of fruits, vegetables, dairy products, meats, and grain products, your student will probably get the vitamins and minerals he or she needs. In addition, a person should drink six to eight glasses of water a day. Ask your student to count how many glasses of water he or she has had in the past day.

6 **EXPLORE** Tell your student that some foods are not good for the body because they contain too much of one nutrient. For example, fried foods, such as french fries, are high in fat. Sweets, such as candy and desserts, contain a lot of sugar. Invite your student to suggest other foods that might fit this description.

Branching Out

TEACHING TIP

To help your student understand how to make use of the information in the lesson, have him or her create sample menus for three main meals and two snacks for one day. Instruct your student to make sure that meals contain each of the three major nutrients and plenty of water, vitamins, and minerals. Have your student plan an upcoming meal.

CHECKING IN

You can assess your student's understanding of the nutrients in foods by setting out a variety of foods on a table and having him or her identify the major nutrients found in each one and their functions.

DID YOU KNOW?

An adult's body is 50 to 65 percent water. A baby's body is 70 percent water.

FOR FURTHER READING

Body Talk: The Straight Facts on Fitness, Nutrition, and Feeling Great About Yourself, by Ann Douglas and Julie Douglas (Maple Tree Press, 2002).

Food and Nutrition for Every Kid: Easy Activities That Make Learning Science Fun, by Janice VanCleave (Wiley, 1999).

The Food Pyramid, by Joan Kalbacken and Sarah De Capua (Scholastic Library Publishing, 1998).

Explore the Big Three

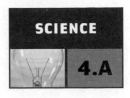

The foods listed below are high in fats, carbohydrates, or proteins.
Decide which group each food belongs in and write *F* for fat, *C* for
carbohydrate, and *P* for protein on the lines.

1. _____ tomatoes

2. _____ mashed potatoes

3. _____ tuna

4. _____ chicken breast

5. _____ corn

6. _____ cashews

7. _____ refried beans

8. _____ apples

9. _____ salad dressing

10. _____ butter

11. _____ brown rice

12. _____ flour tortillas

13. _____ bagels

14. _____ graham crackers

15. _____ low-fat mozzarella cheese

16. _____ carrots

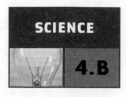
What's Next? You Decide!

Now it's your turn to choose what to do next in the lesson. Read the activities and decide which one you want to do— you may want to try them both!

Test Foods for Starch

MATERIALS

- ❑ 1 apron
- ❑ 1 pair safety goggles
- ❑ 1 teaspoon cornstarch
- ❑ 1 large plate
- ❑ 1 medicine dropper
- ❑ 1 bottle iodine
- ❑ 1 kitchen knife
- ❑ 10 foods to test

STEPS

You can test foods for starch.

- ❑ Put on the apron and safety goggles.
- ❑ To find out what happens to iodine in the presence of starch, place 1 teaspoon of cornstarch on a plate. Add three drops of iodine. Be careful with the iodine. It can stain skin and clothing. Record the change that occurs.
- ❑ Make a list of the foods you plan to test. Predict whether each food has starch in it or not. Write your prediction next to the name of the food.
- ❑ Cut off a small amount of each food. Put it on the plate. (Don't forget to ask permission before using the knife.)
- ❑ Add three drops of iodine to each food sample. Record what happens.
- ❑ Check your observations against your predictions. How often were you correct?

Test Foods for Fat

MATERIALS

- ❑ 1 brown paper bag
- ❑ 1 pair scissors
- ❑ 1 plate
- ❑ 1 kitchen knife
- ❑ 10 foods to test

STEPS

You can test foods for fat.

- ❑ Make a list of the foods you plan to test for fat.
- ❑ Predict whether each food has fat in it or not. Write your prediction next to the name of the food.
- ❑ Cut 10 small squares of paper from a brown bag. Write the name of one food on each square.
- ❑ Cut a small piece of each type of food. Rub the food on the correct square. Be sure to ask permission before using the knife.
- ❑ Scrape off any food left on the squares. Let the squares dry out.
- ❑ Observe which squares have oil stains on them.
- ❑ Check your observations against your predictions. How often were you correct?

Learning About Chemical Substances

Having accurate information about chemical substances can help your student make healthy choices.

OBJECTIVE	BACKGROUND	MATERIALS
To teach your student about a variety of helpful and harmful chemical substances	One day your student may need to make a decision about experimenting with illegal drugs, alcohol, and tobacco. Providing accurate information about the effects of these chemical substances will help your student make wise decisions. In this lesson, your student will learn about different types of chemical substances and how they can help or hurt a person.	■ Student Learning Pages 5.A–5.B ■ books about chemical substances from the library

VOCABULARY

CHEMICAL SUBSTANCE something that changes the way the body works when taken internally

STIMULANTS chemical substances that speed up the way the brain works

TOBACCO a plant that contains an addictive chemical substance called nicotine

DEPRESSANT a chemical substance that slows down the function of the brain

ALCOHOL a depressant in beer, wine, and liquor

ANTIBIOTIC a chemical substance that kills disease-causing bacteria

PRESCRIPTION an order written by a doctor for a specific medication

OVER-THE-COUNTER DRUG a drug that is available without a prescription

VACCINE a chemical substance given by a doctor to prevent a specific disease

ILLEGAL DRUGS chemical substances that are not legal to buy, sell, or use

Let's Begin

1 **INTRODUCE** Ask your student, *Do you ever drink cola or eat chocolate?* Point out that both of these foods contain a **chemical substance** called *caffeine*. A chemical substance, or drug, is something that changes the way the body works when taken internally. Some chemical substances, when used correctly, can create beneficial changes in the body. Other chemical substances can cause harm to the body when used or abused. Ask your student to name the chemical substances that he or she is aware of. Have your student share what he or she knows about each chemical substance.

2 **REVEAL** Explain that three types of chemical substances are stimulants, depressants, and antibiotics. **Stimulants** make the brain work faster. They increase alertness and decrease fatigue for short periods of time. Caffeine is a mild stimulant. Many adults drink coffee in the morning because it contains caffeine, which gives them energy. Most diet pills contain stimulants. Cigarettes and other **tobacco** products contain the stimulant nicotine. Stimulants can be dangerous because they can cause excessive behavior and sleeping problems and can have withdrawal symptoms. Some stimulants are highly addictive. Have your student read the labels on the beverages and desserts in your pantry. Ask him or her to make a list of any that contain the stimulant caffeine.

3 **EXPLAIN** A **depressant** is a chemical substance that makes the brain work slower than usual. Depressant drugs are used to make a person feel relaxed or calm. **Alcohol** is an example of a depressant drug. Other examples are valium and sleeping pills. Depressants can make a person feel sleepy. Someone who has taken depressants should never try to work a powered machine or drive a car. Depressant drugs can be very dangerous and even fatal when used incorrectly and should never be mixed with alcohol. Have your student look in library books or on the Internet to research the specific effects of depressants on the body.

4 **RELATE** Explain that an **antibiotic,** such as penicillin, is a chemical substance that can kill bacteria in the body. A doctor might give a patient an antibiotic to get rid of a bacterial infection such as strep throat. Antibiotics work by disrupting the growth of the foreign cells that have invaded the body. Mention that some strains of bacteria have adapted to resist antibiotics. For this reason, it's important to always finish an antibiotic prescription even if you don't feel sick anymore. If you don't finish, the strongest bacteria may still survive. Point out that antibiotics kill bacterial infections but not viral infections, such as the common cold. Ask, *What are some things that a person with a viral infection can do to get well?* [rest, drink lots of fluids, eat healthy foods]

5 **CHART** After you explain each type of chemical substance, help your student complete this three-column chart for stimulants, depressants, and antibiotics in his or her notebook.

Types of Chemical Substances

	Stimulants	Depressants	Antibiotics
What It Does			
Examples			

6 **EXPLAIN** Describe for your student a situation when a chemical substance helped him or her heal from an illness. You may have given your student medicine or an herbal remedy for a cold or an infection. Your doctor may have given him or her an antibiotic to treat an ear infection. Explain that many chemical substances are helpful to people when they are used correctly. A **prescription** drug is one that is only available with a doctor's recommendation to treat a specific condition. The doctor must specify the exact amount of drug to be given and provide directions for taking the drug. Prescription drugs are used to treat minor illnesses such as allergies as well as serious illnesses such as cancer. Ask, *How should people use prescription drugs?* [they should always follow the directions on the label and contact the doctor if they have any questions]

7 **DESCRIBE** Explain that an **over-the-counter drug** is a medicinal chemical substance that an adult can buy in a store. Examples are aspirin for a headache and an antibiotic salve. Point out that over-the-counter drugs are usually less potent than prescription drugs. Even so, all drugs can be harmful when used incorrectly or excessively. Tell your student that it's very important to read the labels and be aware of proper usage and warnings for over-the-counter drugs. Distribute Student Learning Page 5.A. Take your student to a local store and show him or her how to read the warning labels and directions on the packaging of over-the-counter drugs. Have your student use this information to complete the questions.

8 **REVEAL** Mention that another type of chemical substance is a **vaccine.** Vaccines are given to prevent getting serious illnesses such as measles or mumps. Mention that before there was a vaccine for polio or smallpox, many people were crippled or died from these diseases. Vaccines are given to many children in the United States. Help your student research the vaccines that he or she has received.

9 **DISCUSS** Point out that some people abuse chemical substances by using them too often or too much at one time. Alcohol is a depressant substance found in wine, beer, and liquor. It slows down the brain, and when used in excess it can make a person slur speech, have a hard time walking, and make poor decisions. When used for too long, alcohol can cause liver damage and kill brain cells. Alcohol can also be addictive. Ask, *What are the negative side effects of using alcohol?* [alcohol kills brain cells, affects decision making, can harm the liver, can be addictive]

10 **RELATE** Tobacco is a plant that is often smoked in cigarettes or pipes. Tobacco contains nicotine, which is highly addictive. Smoking is known to cause several forms of cancer. Although tobacco and alcohol are both very harmful drugs and are regulated by the government, they are legal for adults to use. Have your

DID YOU KNOW?

In 1952, there were 21,269 polio cases reported in the United States. A vaccine for polio was discovered in 1954. In 1996, there was only one case of polio reported!

FOR FURTHER READING

Drug Interactions: Protecting Yourself from Dangerous Drug, Medication, and Food Combinations, by Melanie Apel Gordon (Rosen Publishing Group, Inc., 1999).

Inhalants and Solvents, by Dr. Linda Bayer (Chelsea House Publishers, 2000).

Talking About Drugs, by Karen Bryant-Mole (Raintree Steck-Vaughn, 2000).

Tobacco and Your Mouth: The Incredibly Disgusting Story, by Michael A. Sommers (Rosen Publishing Group, Inc., 2000).

Understanding Issues: Drugs, by Gail B. Stewart (KidHaven Press, 2002).

student research the affects of tobacco and nicotine at the library or on the Internet. Ask, *Why do you think people smoke if they know it harms their bodies?* [because they are addicted; because they don't acknowledge how harmful it really is]

11 **EXPLAIN** Some drugs are not legal to buy, use, or sell. These are called **illegal drugs.** Marijuana, cocaine, crack, and heroin are examples of illegal drugs. These drugs are considered dangerous and unpredictable in their effects. Excessive marijuana use can impair brain function and learning. Cocaine and crack have caused heart attacks and death. Some of these drugs can cause a person to lose his or her sense of reality or impair his or her ability to feel pain. A person in this state can easily hurt himself or herself. Have your student read about illegal drugs in library books or on the Internet. Together discuss how each drug harms the body and the senses.

12 **REVIEW** Point out that some chemical substances are harmful and dangerous while others, when used correctly, can be beneficial and help a person heal. Remind your student that every chemical substance is potentially harmful if abused or not used correctly. Emphasize to your student the importance of exercising good judgment when making decisions about using chemical substances. Ask, *What should you always do before considering using a chemical substance?* [read the label; consult your physician; make sure it's a legal drug; find out about the negative effects and potential dangers]

Branching Out

TEACHING TIP

To help your student remember the vocabulary words and definitions, have him or her make flash cards out of index cards with the vocabulary word on one side of the index card and the definition on the other.

CHECKING IN

You can assess your student's understanding of the effects of chemical substances on the body by having him or her give an informational report about the different kinds of chemical substances, how they affect the body, how to use drugs safely, and which chemical substances are illegal and why.

Learn About
Over-the-Counter Drugs

Go to a local drug store with an adult. Together read the labels of several different types of over-the-counter drugs. Choose three and write the answers.

1. Drug name: _____

   Directions for use: _____

   _____

   _____

   _____

   Warnings: _____

2. Drug name: _____

   Directions for use: _____

   _____

   _____

   _____

   Warnings: _____

3. Drug name: _____

   Directions for use: _____

   _____

   _____

   _____

   Warnings: _____

What's Next? You Decide!

Now it's your turn to choose what to do next in the lesson. Read the activities and decide which one you want to do— you may want to try them both!

Create a Smoking Awareness Poster

MATERIALS

- ❑ old magazines
- ❑ 1 posterboard
- ❑ markers or colored pencils
- ❑ 1 pair scissors
- ❑ glue

STEPS

Cigarette advertisements try to make smoking look good. You can design a poster that educates people about the real dangers of smoking.

- ❑ Look through some old magazines for cigarette ads. Choose two or three ads and cut them out.

- ❑ Glue the ads to the posterboard and write a title such as "The Truth About Smoking."

- ❑ Study the ads. How does each ad try to make smoking look cool or glamorous? Next to each ad, write a sentence that includes a fact about the dangers of smoking. Draw a picture to illustrate your sentence.

- ❑ Display your advertisement in your home as a reminder for your family of the dangers of smoking cigarettes.

Take a Caffeine Survey

Family Member	Day	Number of Times Each Had Caffeine
Mom	Monday	|||
Dad	Monday	⊬⊦⊦⊦
Me	Monday		
Sister	Monday	||

STEPS

Caffeine is a chemical substance that stimulates the brain and nerves and can be addictive. Caffeine is in such foods as coffee, soft drinks, and chocolate.

- ❑ Make a chart like the one shown above. Include each member of your family on the chart.

- ❑ Post the chart in your family's kitchen.

- ❑ For one day, ask each member of your family to make a tally mark on the chart each time he or she eats or drinks something with caffeine in it.

- ❑ At the end of the day, discuss how much caffeine each person had.

Digging Under Your Skin

*You live in an amazing covering of tissue that
protects you from the outside world.*

OBJECTIVE	BACKGROUND	MATERIALS
To introduce your student to the properties of the skin, its different jobs, and how to protect it from hazards	The skin forms a waterproof layer over the body that protects us from injury, shock, and disease. It's the source of our nails and hair. The skin acts as an insulator against heat and cold, and it contains hundreds of tiny nerve endings and pressure sensors that respond to the most delicate touch. In this lesson, your student will learn about the layers that make up the skin and how it helps us control heat, explore our sense of touch, and discover ways to keep our skin safe.	■ Student Learning Pages 6.A–6.B ■ books about chemical substances ■ 1 hand lens ■ low-power (30X) microscope (optional) ■ collection of matched objects ■ 1 paper bag or small box ■ 1 piece card stock ■ 1 ruler ■ 2 straightpins ■ 1 large cork ■ 1 plastic container filled with lukewarm water ■ 2 paper towels ■ plastic wrap ■ 1 jar petroleum jelly ■ tape ■ 2 small thermometers ■ paper clips ■ 2 paper cups ■ 1 plastic container ■ 1 copy Web, page 356

VOCABULARY

CELLS the basic units of life

TISSUES groups of similar cells that perform a specific job in the body

ORGANS groups of similar tissues that form a structure and perform important functions

SYSTEMS groups of major organs that work together

INTEGUMENTARY SYSTEM the outer covering of the body, formed of skin, hair, and nails

DERMIS the true skin, rich in blood vessels, nerve endings, sensors, follicles, and glands

EPIDERMIS the tough outer layer of skin out of which hair and nails grow

HAIR FOLLICLES the roots from which hairs grow

MELANIN a dark-colored pigment made by special cells of the skin

Let's Begin

1   **INTRODUCE** Tell your student that the human body is made up of millions of tiny units called **cells.** Groups of similar cells called **tissues** work together to perform specific jobs in the body. For example, skin cells form a waterproof tissue that protects the body. Groups of tissues form **organs**—body parts that perform important functions. The skin is considered the largest organ in the body. Major organs are grouped together to form **systems.** Examples are the circulatory and respiratory systems. Each system has an important role. The skin, along with hair and nails, forms the outer covering of the body, known as the **integumentary system** (in-TEG-u-men-tary). Ask, *How does our skin help protect us?* [it acts as a barrier against injuries and disease]

2   **EXPLORE** Point out that the outer surface of the skin is made up of dead cells. You are constantly shedding surface skin cells and replacing them. Give your student a hand lens. Ask, *How does the skin on different parts of your body compare?* Have your student look at the skin on the back of his or her hand and then compare what he or she sees with the skin on the palm, wrist, fingers, arm, leg, and bottom of the foot. Ask, *Where is the skin the smoothest? Where do you find the most hair?* [fine, soft hair covers most parts of the body; thick, stiffer hairs are found on the head and eyebrows] *Can you find a part of the body that seems completely hairless?* [lips, palms, and the soles of the feet] Have your student draw or describe his or her discoveries in a notebook.

3   **EXPAND** Tell your student to continue his or her explorations of the outermost layer of the integumentary system. Explain that the hair and nails are made from a protein called keratin. Cut a nail clipping and a small bit of scalp hair. Have your student examine them with the hand lens. If you have access to a low-power (30X) microscope, your student will be able to see even more details. Ask, *How are your hair and nails alike or different?* [they are made from basically the same material and seem to be made in layers; hair is finer, more flexible, colored, and covered with scales; nails are white or colorless, thick, and hard]

4   **REVEAL AND GUIDE** Direct your student's attention to the diagram of the skin found on Student Learning Page 6.A. Explain that your skin is made up of two main layers: the **dermis** and the **epidermis.** The epidermis is the uppermost layer that we have been investigating. It's much thinner than the dermis and is made up of flat, interlocking cells. The thicker dermis layer contains nerve endings, the sensors responsible for touch; blood vessels; the **hair follicles** from which hairs grow; oil glands (at the base of each hair root); and tiny, coiled sweat glands, which help carry away body heat. Below the dermis is a layer of fat that helps store energy and keep in heat. Help your student label the diagram to identify the parts of the skin.

DID YOU KNOW?

Hiding in your bed or carpet may be tiny creatures too small to see with even a strong magnifier. Dust mites belong to the same family that includes spiders and scorpions. They feed on dead skin cells that rub off your body all the time. See pictures of the minibeasts at http://www.cellsalive.com/mite.htm.

A BRIGHT IDEA

Take the fingerprints of everyone in your family to show the ridges found on fingers. Together with your student compare and contrast the fingerprints. Share with your student that no two people have identical fingerprints.

5 **DISCUSS** Ask, *Do people come in one or many shades of skin?* [many shades, from pink to dark brown] Explain that all skin color comes from **melanin,** a dark coloring matter made in special cells found in the lower part of the epidermis. Point out that there are advantages to both dark and light skin colors. Dark skin protects us from too much sunlight that can lead to skin cancer (uncontrolled cell growth). Light skin is useful for making vitamin D, needed for building strong bones. Your hair color also comes from melanin deposited by cells at the bases of hair follicles. As you age, these cells begin to fail, and gray or white hairs begin to appear. Direct your student's attention to the chart found on Student Learning Page 6.A. Have your student survey his or her friends and relatives and fill in the chart with their responses.

6 **EXPLORE** Help your student test his or her sense of touch. Point out that in addition to touch, there are sensors in the skin for pressure, heat, cold, and pain. Collect a variety of objects in pairs, such as small balls, blocks, chalk, crayons, stones, erasers, and so on. Place one object from each pair inside a small box or bag. Then have your student close his or her eyes and try to match the objects using just his or her sense of touch. When you are done, count how many objects were correctly matched. Which objects were easiest to identify? Which were the most difficult? Ask, *How were you able to tell the objects apart?* [by comparing different characteristics, such as size, shape, texture, and hardness]

7 **EXPERIMENT** Explain that some parts of the skin are more sensitive than others. Make a "touch tester" to map how close together the sensors in the skin are located. Draw a line on a piece of card stock three centimeters long. Use a ruler to measure off points on that line a half centimeter apart. Put the card on top of a large cork and use two straight pins to hold the card in place. Have one person close his or her eyes and the other use the touch tester. Touch the tips of the pins to the skin lightly. Move the pins apart until the partner feels two pinpricks. Test the back of the hand, palm, fingertips, arm, knee, back of neck, and lips. Ask, *Where did the touch sensors appear to be closest together?* [at the fingertips or the lips] *Why do you think these sensors are closer together?* [they are in areas that are used for feeling objects or warning of hazards]

SCIENCE

LESSON 3.6

?
DID YOU KNOW?
The kind of hair you have depends on the shape of your hair follicles. Round follicles make straight hair, oval follicles make wavy hair, and flat follicles make curly or kinky hair.

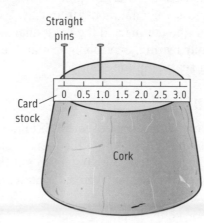

Straight pins

Card stock

0 0.5 1.0 1.5 2.0 2.5 3.0

Cork

8 **RELATE** Explain to your student that the skin helps regulate body temperature. Blood vessels in the skin narrow to conserve heat or enlarge to bring hot blood closer to the surface. Ask, *What are goose bumps?* [tiny bumps of flesh] Point out that at each bump there's a tiny hair. Explain that this helps trap air next to the body to keep it warm. Sweat glands help rid the body of excess heat. Fill a container with lukewarm water. Have your student close his or her eyes. Rub one wrist with a paper towel soaked in water, and rub the other with a dry paper towel. Ask, *Which wrist feels cooler?* [the hand with the water feels cooler; water evaporates into the air carrying heat with it]

9 **EXPERIMENT** Remind your student that underneath the dermis is a layer of fat. To show how this fat layer helps to hold in heat, spread a thick layer of petroleum jelly on a piece of plastic wrap. Cover with more plastic and seal the edges with tape. Have your student wrap the petroleum-jelly wrap around a thermometer and an equal thickness of plain plastic wrap around a second thermometer. Put both thermometers into paper cups. Use paper clips to attach the cups to the side of a plastic container and fill the container with cold water. Read and record any changes in temperature for 30 minutes. Ask, *Which thermometer showed the greatest temperature change?* [the one without the layer of petroleum jelly; the temperature difference may be as much as 20°F]

10 **CONCLUDE** Discuss some of the ways that you can protect your skin. Wear appropriate clothing at all times. When skating or bicycling, wear protective gear such as a helmet or padding to protect your skin from injuries. Daily scrubbing with mild soap and water helps remove dirt, germs, and dead skin cells. Avoid excessive exposure to the sun and wind, and use sunscreen when you are going to be outdoors for a long period of time.

Branching Out

TEACHING TIP

If your student has trouble visualizing the skin from the diagram, together make a cross-sectional model from clay. Use different colors of clay to represent the dermis and the epidermal layers. Use straws, buttons, beads, coiled string, and tubing to stand for the hair follicles, sweat glands, and sensors in the skin.

CHECKING IN

Provide your student with a copy of the Web found on page 356. Ask your student to complete the Web on the topic of skin. Have him or her refer to the skin diagram. Tell your student to put the key concept in the center and add details about the layered structure, its properties, and examples of how it protects us.

FOR FURTHER READING

101 Questions About Your Skin That Got Under Your Skin . . . Until Now, by Faith Hickman Brynie (Millbrook Press, 1999).

How Do We Feel and Touch?, by Carol Ballard (Raintree Steck-Vaughn, 1998).

Explore Your Skin, Hair, and Nails

Match the parts of the skin in the diagram with the terms listed below.

1. _____ blood vessels   5. _____ hair

2. _____ fatty layer   6. _____ sweat gland

3. _____ oil gland   7. _____ epidermis

4. _____ dermis   8. _____ hair follicle

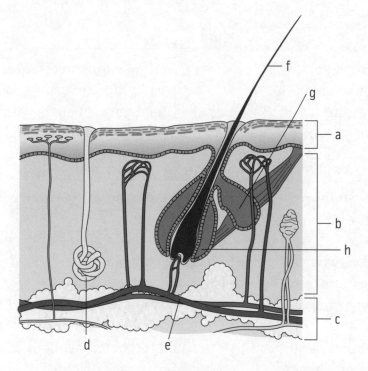

Now, survey your friends and relatives. In your notebook, make a chart that shows the skin color, eye color, and hair color and type of each person. Then answer these questions in your notebook.

9. What different types did you find among the people you surveyed?

10. What patterns did you discover?

Student Learning Page 6.A: Explore Your Skin, Hair, and Nails **191**

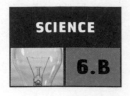

SCIENCE

6.B

What's Next? You Decide!

Now it's your turn to choose what to do next in the lesson.
Read the activities and decide which one you want to do—
you may want to try them both!

Investigate Fingerprints

MATERIALS

- ❑ 2 sheets paper
- ❑ 1 soft lead pencil
- ❑ 1 roll transparent tape
- ❑ 1 hand lens

STEPS

The swirling ridges that form your fingerprints help your fingertips grip objects. These patterns form before birth and never change. Since everyone's fingerprints are different, they are used to help identify missing persons and criminals.

- ❑ Draw around the outline of one hand with the pencil on a sheet of paper.
- ❑ With the pencil blacken a two-inch square on a second sheet of paper.
- ❑ Press the tip of one of your fingers onto the black square.
- ❑ Have someone help you press a strip of tape over the smudge on your finger. Lift the tape gently and place it on the correct finger of the hand outline.
- ❑ Repeat with each of your fingers. Examine the prints with the hand lens.

Fool Your Sense of Touch

MATERIALS

- ❑ 3 plastic containers
- ❑ water at different temperatures (hot, cold, and lukewarm)
- ❑ paper towels
- ❑ 1 rubber or plastic glove

STEPS

Try these simple tests to discover how the sensors in the skin can be fooled.

- ❑ Fill the three containers with hot (but not scalding), cold, and lukewarm water.
- ❑ Place one hand in the hot water and the other in cold water for one minute.
- ❑ Transfer each hand in turn to the lukewarm water.
- ❑ How does the hand that was in the cold water feel? What about the hand that was in hot water? How could the water feel both cold and warm at the same time?
- ❑ Dry one hand with paper towels and put on the glove. Place the gloved hand in the cold water. Describe how the hand feels now.
- ❑ Many senses, including wetness, result from several touch sensors working together. The sensation you feel seems to be a combination of the sense of cold and the pressure of the glove.

192 *Making the Grade: Everything Your 4th Grader Needs to Know*   © 2004 by Barron's Educational Series, Inc. All Rights Reserved.

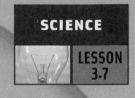

Exploring Ecosystems

Have you found your niche?

OBJECTIVE	BACKGROUND	MATERIALS
To help your student understand the nature and processes of ecosystems	There are many different types of ecosystems on our planet. Some are very large while others are microscopic. Some are simple while others are complex. Understanding how ecosystems work helps us better understand the world around us. In this lesson, your student will explore key ecosystem concepts and the changes that occur within ecosystems.	■ Student Learning Pages 7.A–7.B ■ pictures of established ecosystems (old growth forest, established lakes, deserts) ■ nature, outdoor, and wildlife magazines or books ■ 1 shoebox ■ glue ■ 1 pair scissors

VOCABULARY

ECOSYSTEM all of the interactions between living and nonliving things in an environment

NICHE an organism's role in an ecosystem

MIGRATION moving to an area that has more resources

SUCCESSION the replacement of old plant and animal populations with new ones

PIONEER STAGE the first stage of change in an ecosystem

FOOD WEB a group of food chains

Let's Begin

1 **INTRODUCE** Read the definition for the word **ecosystem** to your student. Explain that an ecosystem can be any size, and that it includes both living and nonliving things as well as the interactions that take place between these things. Show your student the picture of the fish bowl. Ask your student to name the living and nonliving things in the fish bowl ecosystem. [living things: fish, plant, bacteria; nonliving things: gravel, water, air] Ask, *What kinds of interactions take place between the living and nonliving things in the fish bowl?* [the fish takes in air and water; the plant uses air, water, and light to make food; the fish searches for food] Then have your student complete Student Learning Page 7.A.

2 **EXPLAIN** Tell your student that every living thing in an ecosystem has a role, or **niche.** Explain that what an organism does and eats in an ecosystem is its niche. Have your student

look at the fishbowl. Ask, *What is the goldfish's niche?* [the goldfish swims and eats fish food] *What is the plant's niche?* [possible answer: the plant makes its own food]

3 **DESCRIBE** Explain to your student that **migration** occurs when organisms leave one area and move into a new one. Ask your student why migration might occur. [as an ecosystem changes, supplies of food, water, and space can decrease, causing organisms to move to a new area; migration causes an ecosystem to change because when new organisms enter they create new interactions] Ask your student what organisms might migrate into the fishbowl. *How would they get into the fishbowl?* [bacteria or other microscopic organisms could enter from the air or when new water is poured into the fishbowl]

4 **DISCOVER** Tell your student that the term **succession** is used to describe the changes that occur in an ecosystem. For example, migration of new plants and animals causes succession. Ask, *How might bacteria change the fishbowl ecosystem?* [the water quality could change and become unhealthy to the fish] Since the nonliving things in an ecosystem change, they also cause succession. Ask, *What might cause nonliving things in an ecosystem to change?* [floods, storms, fire, drought, wind, or humans]

5 **EXPLORE** Help your student understand that when any part of an ecosystem changes, the whole ecosystem is affected. Ask, *Why is this so?* [a change in the ecosystem may decrease the amount of food for various organisms; organisms may then develop new ways to find food or migrate] Tell your student that natural disasters, such as fire, flood, storm, avalanche, and drought, and non-natural changes, such as pollution or destruction of land by humans, threaten ecosystems. Then ask your student to think of how a change might threaten a species. For example, a sudden drop in water temperature might kill off a group of warm water aquatic organisms.

6 **EXPAND** Tell your student that the first stage in succession is called the **pioneer stage**. Ask, *What is a pioneer?* [a person who is the first to settle in a new area] Explain that during the pioneer stage, animals and plants move into an ecosystem and establish themselves. Since they are the first organisms there, they grow rapidly. Show your student pictures of established ecosystems, such as old growth forest, established lakes, and deserts. Then show the picture on the next page of the area recovering from a forest fire. Point out that there are thousands of new plants growing from the ashes, which shows that the ecosystem is in the pioneer stage. Ask, *Why do you think the plants are able to grow rapidly?* [there are fewer animals to eat the plants and plenty of available sunlight since the old trees have been burned]

? DID YOU KNOW?

One of the major food chains in the Antarctic ecosystem is showing signs of being disrupted, which is making the whale ecosystem unbalanced. Some scientists think that because of a decrease in sea ice, the number of krill (tiny, shrimplike animals) is decreasing. Krill feed on algae that live beneath the sea ice. Penguins, albatrosses, and fur seals feed on krill.

This forest ecosystem is in the pioneer stage.

7 **APPLY** Tell your student that you will now explore an ocean ecosystem. Because the ocean is so deep, it is divided into different layers that vary according to temperature and depth (distance from the surface). Look at the diagram of the ocean layers below with your student. Say, *Name each zone and the depth at which it is found.* [sunlit zone, 0–200 meters (0–656 feet); twilight zone, 200–1,000 meters (656–3,281 feet); dark zone, 1,000–4,000 meters (3,281–13,123 feet); abyss, 4,000 meters (13,123 feet) and below] Explain to your student that most ocean animals live between the sunlit zone and the dark zone. Ask, *In which zone would most of the plant life be found?* [in the sunlit zone] *Why?* [plants need sunlight to make food]

Layers of the Ocean

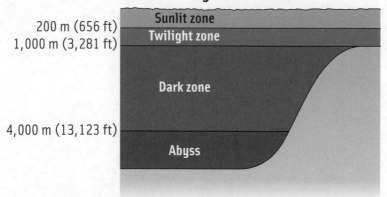

200 m (656 ft) — Sunlit zone
1,000 m (3,281 ft) — Twilight zone

Dark zone

4,000 m (13,123 ft)

Abyss

8 **DISCOVER** Explain to your student that since the ocean is so large, many different kinds of animals live there. Ask your student to name some ocean animals that he or she is familiar with. Make a list of these animals. Then challenge your student to use reference books, the Internet, or a book about oceans to find the names of less commonly known ocean animals. Add these animals to the list.

DID YOU KNOW?

Sperm whales can dive as deep as 3,200 meters (10,500 feet) into the dark zone in search of food. A dive this deep lasts about 40 minutes.

9 **EXPLORE** Explain that a group of food chains is called a **food web.** Tell your student that because the ocean is so deep, an ocean food web can include food chains that occur in different layers. For example, animals that normally swim in the sunlit zone may swim to different layers in search of food. Ask your student to use reference books or the Internet to name at least one ocean animal and its primary source of food for each ocean layer.

Branching Out

TEACHING TIP

Have your student construct a diorama (a three-dimensional scene) of an ecosystem of his or her choice. Remind your student to include pictures, models, or some other representation of both living and nonliving things. Pictures can be drawn by hand or cut out of magazines. Models can be made out of sculpting compound, clay, or other malleable materials.

CHECKING IN

To assess your student's understanding of the lesson, show him or her a large photograph of an ecosystem. Ask your student to use the photograph to identify the living and nonliving things in it and to explain how they might interact. Finally, ask your student to give one example of a change that might threaten at least one of the living things in the ecosystem.

FOR FURTHER READING

Ecosystems (Geography for Fun), by Pam Robson and Tony Kenyon (Copper Beach Books, 2001).

Ecosystems and Environment (Science Topics), by Ann Fullick (Heinemann Library, 1999).

Oceans (True Books: Ecosystems), by Darlene R. Stille (Children's Press, 2000).

Draw What's Going on in an Ecosystem

Draw an ecosystem. In the space underneath your illustration, list the living and nonliving things that are part of the ecosystem. Then think of interactions that would likely take place within the ecosystem. List at least three of these interactions.

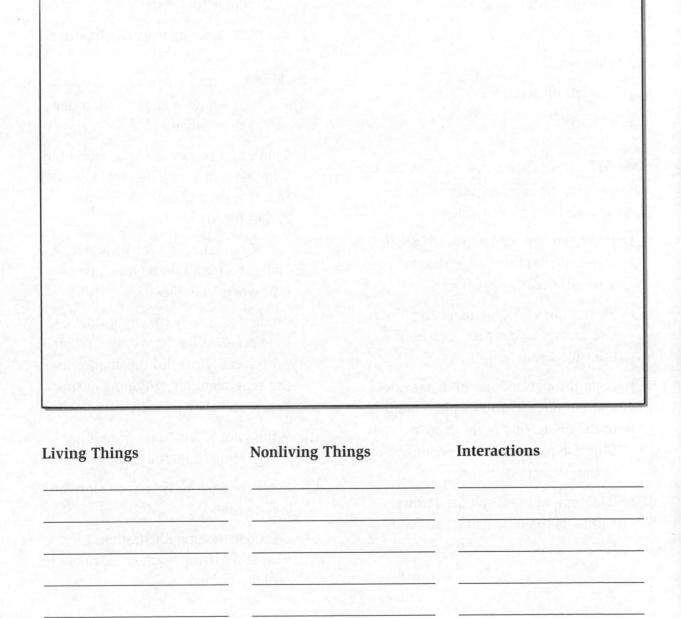

Living Things

_____

_____

_____

_____

_____

Nonliving Things

_____

_____

_____

_____

_____

Interactions

_____

_____

_____

_____

_____

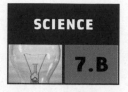

What's Next? You Decide!

Now it's your turn to choose what to do next in the lesson. Read the activities and decide which one you want to do— you may want to try them both!

Create a Food Web

MATERIALS

❑ 3–4 old nature magazines

❑ 1 pair scissors

❑ glue

❑ 1 small posterboard

❑ 1 marker

STEPS

Use pictures from magazines to create a food web from an ecosystem.

❑ Use reference books to learn about a specific food web, such as one in a forest, desert, or pond.

❑ Sketch the web on a piece of paper. Use arrows to connect organisms to their food sources.

❑ Look through old nature magazines and cut out pictures or photographs of the organisms in the food web. Glue the pictures to the posterboard in the correct positions.

❑ Use a marker to draw the arrows and label the organisms and food sources.

Write a Migration Story

MATERIALS

❑ 1 computer (optional)

❑ markers or colored pencils (optional)

STEPS

Write a story about migration from one ecosystem to another.

❑ Think of a setting for your story. In what type of ecosystem will it take place? A pine forest? The Arctic? A rain forest?

❑ Think of characters for your story. Will the organisms be humans? Carnivores? Reptiles?

❑ Think about why the organisms had to migrate. What happened to their ecosystem? How did the change in the ecosystem affect the organisms? Where did they go to?

❑ Write your story. Make sure it has a beginning, a middle, and an end.

❑ You may wish to type your story on a computer.

❑ Consider making illustrations for your story using markers or colored pencils.

Shaping and Reshaping Earth

*The planet we live on is constantly changing—
sometimes slowly, sometimes quickly.*

OBJECTIVE	BACKGROUND	MATERIALS
To teach your student about the forces of weathering and erosion and how they affect Earth's surface	Earth's surface is changing all the time. In this lesson, your student will learn about the causes of mechanical weathering of rocks and the various causes of soil and rock erosion.	■ Student Learning Pages 8.A–8.B ■ 1 smooth rock ■ 1 jagged rock ■ 1 piece sandpaper ■ pictures of Greek, Egyptian, or other ancient ruins ■ 1 small pan ■ $\frac{1}{2}$ cup cornmeal or oatmeal ■ 1 straw ■ 1 copy Venn Diagram, page 355

VOCABULARY

MECHANICAL WEATHERING   the process in which rocks are broken down into smaller pieces

EROSION   the movement of soil or rocks from one place to another

SEDIMENTS   rocks or particles of soil that are moved and deposited by erosion

GLACIER   a huge sheet of ice that moves slowly over land

AVALANCHE   the sudden movement of a large mass of ice and snow down a mountainside

LANDSLIDE   the sudden movement of rock and soil down a steep slope

Let's Begin

1   **EXPLORE** Give your student two rocks, one that's smooth and rounded and one that's sharp and jagged. Invite your student to suggest what made the two rocks different. Explain that **mechanical weathering** is the process in which rocks are broken down into smaller pieces. Point out that over long periods of time mechanical weathering can even wear down mountains. Tell your student that one factor that can cause weathering is water. Explain that flowing water in rivers and streams and along the ocean shore is filled with small particles that scrape against rock surfaces and wear them down. Ask, *Which rock might have been subjected to weathering by water? How can you tell?* [the smooth rock; the water rubbed it smooth]

DID YOU KNOW?

The Grand Canyon of Arizona is an example of the power of mechanical weathering. The canyon was formed as the rock was gradually worn away by the force of the river running through it.

ENRICH THE EXPERIENCE

Your student can take a virtual trip to the national parks in Utah to see some spectacular examples of landforms created by weathering at the Web site http://www.americansouthwest.net/utah.

2 **EXPLAIN** Explain to your student that water can also cause weathering by freezing in the cracks in rocks. As it freezes, the water expands and the cracks get larger. Eventually a piece of the rock breaks off. This process also causes cracks in sidewalks and potholes on roads. Ask your student, *Which of the two rocks might have been broken off by water freezing? How can you tell?* [the jagged one; breaking off in this way would probably create a rock with jagged edges rather than smooth edges]

3 **EXPAND** Tell your student that other factors can also cause mechanical weathering of rocks. The heating of rock by the sun or by a forest fire can cause layers of the rock to break off. Explain that the roots of trees, shrubs, and other plants can grow into rocks and cause cracks to form and grow. Eventually the rocks break apart. Small particles of sand or dirt carried by the wind or by ice scrape at rocks like sandpaper and cause bits of the rocks to break off. Give your student a piece of sandpaper and have him or her rub it on one of the rocks. Discuss how the sandpaper affects the rock and how it can be compared to sand or dirt carried by wind, water, or ice.

4 **EXPAND** Point out to your student that the rate at which weathering occurs depends on several different factors. Explain that one important factor is the type of rock. Some kinds of rock have many tiny air spaces in them. Water gets into these rocks easily and weathering occurs faster. Weather conditions also affect the rate of weathering. Areas with higher rainfall have a faster rate of weathering. In hot climates, weathering occurs faster than in cold climates. Tell your student that statues and buildings built from rocks are also subject to weathering. Show your student several pictures of ancient ruins from places such as Greece or Egypt. Have your student point out and explain the signs of weathering.

5 **EXPLAIN** Tell your student that after small particles are broken off from rocks by weathering, they are often moved from one place to another by wind, water, gravity, or ice. Explain that this movement of soil or rocks is called **erosion.** The particles that are moved by erosion are called **sediments.** Point out that sand and mud are two types of sediments. The Mississippi River delta is an example of a landform built up by the deposition of sediments carried down the river. Ask, *Do you think soil erodes faster when there are plants and trees growing or when the soil is bare? Why?* [bare soil erodes faster because there are not plant roots to hold it in place]

6 **DESCRIBE** Explain to your student that the main cause of erosion of the Earth's surface is moving water. Ask your student to describe what he or she has seen happen with water after a rainfall. Explain that erosion even happens when a single raindrop falls on soil. The raindrop can loosen soil and pick up sediment. When the water begins to move, it carries that

DID YOU KNOW?

Some raindrops are falling as fast as 30 miles per hour when they hit the ground. This is enough force to wash away a farmer's newly planted seeds.

sediment with it. Any kind of plant cover helps protect soil from eroding. Ask, *Why do you think environmentalists are concerned about clear-cutting the trees in forested areas?* [because it leaves the soil vulnerable to harmful levels of erosion]

7 **EXPLAIN** Another force of erosion is a **glacier.** Explain that a glacier is a huge sheet of ice that moves very slowly over land. Glaciers may move down valleys between high mountains. Other larger glaciers cover whole continents or large islands. Large glaciers cover Antarctica and most of Greenland. Valley glaciers are common in Alaska. Explain that as a glacier moves across land, it picks up rocks. The rocks become frozen in the ice and move along with the glacier. Some of the rocks are on the bottom of the glacier. They scratch the surface of the ground as the glacier moves along. Ask, *What do you think propels the movement of the glacier?* [gravity]

8 **MODEL** Tell your student that wind is also a power force of erosion. Wind carries lightweight particles of sand or soil. Sand dunes in deserts and on beaches are formed by wind eroding the sand and then depositing it in a new place. Put some cornmeal or oatmeal in a small pan. Have your student blow through a straw over the pan to model how wind erosion occurs. Help him or her use scientific methods—observing, making a hypothesis, recording data, and concluding—as he or she watches how wind erosion occurs.

9 **INTRODUCE** Tell your student that certain types of natural disasters cause large amounts of erosion to occur suddenly. Have your student write the names of these types of natural disasters he or she is aware of in a notebook. Ask your student to write down one thing he or she would like to learn about each one.

10 **DISCUSS** Explain that one type of natural disaster is an **avalanche.** An avalanche is the sudden movement of a large mass of ice and snow down a mountainside. Another natural disaster is a **landslide.** A landslide is the sudden movement of rock and soil down a steep slope. Large landslides occur in mountainous areas. Smaller landslides are common along the sides of roads where the land on either side of the road has been cut away. Earthquakes and volcanoes are other types of natural disasters that change the landscape by causing a sudden, violent movement of Earth's surface or by forcing material from inside Earth to the surface. Have your student research natural disasters using library books or the Internet. Ask your student to find the answers to the questions he or she wrote in Step 9.

11 **COMPARE** Have your student compare and contrast weathering and erosion using a copy of the Venn Diagram found on page 355. Together discuss the similarities and differences.

DID YOU KNOW?

One natural disaster sometimes triggers another. The volcanic eruption of Mount St. Helens in 1980 caused a massive mudflow down the Toutle River. Your student can see pictures of the landslide at http://landslides.usgs.gov. You may wish to preview the photos first and direct your student to certain images.

Branching Out

TEACHING TIPS

❑ After a rainstorm, take a walk with your student around the neighborhood. Have your student point out places where the storm has caused erosion. Discuss the reasons why erosion occurs in some places and not in others.

❑ Have your student use a sheet of paper to model mechanical weathering. Have him or her tear it, cut it, fold it, crumple it, poke holes in it, and in any way change its size or shape. Discuss the fact that what remains is still the same piece of paper but with a different size or shape. Explain that mechanical weathering changes the size or shape of rocks, but the material that made up the rocks in the first place is still there.

CHECKING IN

You can assess your student's understanding of weathering and erosion by having him or her create a science display that shows the forces of weathering and erosion. Tell your student that his or her display must show and explain the processes that weather rocks and cause erosion of the land.

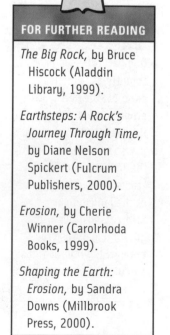

FOR FURTHER READING

The Big Rock, by Bruce Hiscock (Aladdin Library, 1999).

Earthsteps: A Rock's Journey Through Time, by Diane Nelson Spickert (Fulcrum Publishers, 2000).

Erosion, by Cherie Winner (Carolrhoda Books, 1999).

Shaping the Earth: Erosion, by Sandra Downs (Millbrook Press, 2000).

Identify Weathering and Erosion

For each picture, circle *weathering* or *erosion*. Explain what force is causing it and how the process is happening.

1. weathering   erosion

   Cause: _____

   How: _____

   _____

   _____

   _____

2. weathering   erosion

   Cause: _____

   How: _____

   _____

   _____

   _____

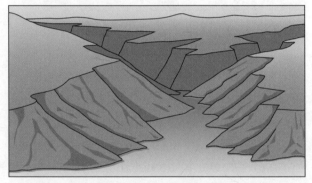

3. weathering   erosion

   Cause: _____

   How: _____

   _____

   _____

   _____

What's Next? You Decide!

Now it's your turn to choose what to do next in the lesson. Read the activities and decide which one you want to do— you may want to try them both!

Observe the Power of Plants and Water

MATERIALS

- ❏ 2 plastic cups with lids
- ❏ 1 package bean seeds
- ❏ tape
- ❏ 1 freezer
- ❏ 1 paper towel

STEPS

- ❏ Fill one plastic cup with bean seeds and water. Fill another cup with water. Place lids on both cups. Tape the lids onto the cups.
- ❏ Place the cup of water in the freezer. Place the cup with the beans on a paper towel in a cool place.
- ❏ Let them sit for one day. What do you think will happen to each cup?
- ❏ The next day, check the cups. What happened? How did it happen?
- ❏ Compare what happened in the cups to what happens to rocks due to the power of plants and freezing water.

Model a Glacier

MATERIALS

- ❏ 1 small plastic container
- ❏ 1 cup sand and small pebbles
- ❏ 1 freezer
- ❏ 2 paper towels
- ❏ 1 bar soap

STEPS

Model how a glacier causes erosion.

- ❏ Cover the bottom of a plastic container with $\frac{1}{2}$ inch of sand and pebbles.
- ❏ Fill the container halfway with water.
- ❏ Place the container in a freezer until the water has completely frozen.
- ❏ Take the ice out of the container and put it on a paper towel.
- ❏ Place a bar of soap on another paper towel.
- ❏ Hold the block of ice with the paper towel. Place the side with the sand on top of the soap bar.
- ❏ Rub and push the ice bar along the soap. What happens? How does this show what happens when a glacier moves over land?

SCIENCE

LESSON 3.9

Understanding Weather

The weather is all around us, happening and changing all the time.

OBJECTIVE	BACKGROUND	MATERIALS
To teach your student about weather and the effects of air, wind, and water	Weather affects our lives every day. It influences what we wear and even some of the activities we plan. Weather is determined by the interactions of air, wind, and water. In this lesson, your student will study the effects of air and wind on weather. He or she will also learn about the water cycle, the different types of clouds, and the different types of severe weather we experience on Earth.	■ Student Learning Pages 9.A–9.B ■ 2 balloons ■ 1 funnel ■ 1 two-liter plastic soda bottle ■ wide masking tape

VOCABULARY

ATMOSPHERE the blanket of air that surrounds Earth and makes it possible for life to exist

WATER VAPOR water that is in the form of a gas

WATER CYCLE the cyclical movement of water from the ground to the air and back to the ground again

EVAPORATE when water turns from a liquid to a gas

CUMULUS CLOUDS puffy clouds that form when large areas of warm, moist air float upward from the surface of Earth

STRATUS CLOUDS flat, gray clouds that form when a flat layer of warm, moist air rises very slowly; often bring snow or rain

CIRRUS CLOUDS thin, wispy clouds that form when the air rises high enough for ice crystals to form

Let's Begin

1 **PLAN AHEAD** You may wish to cover this lesson over the course of several days or refer to it over several weeks so that your student has time to observe many types of weather. You can begin this by talking about the different kinds of weather your region experiences.

2 **DEMONSTRATE** Have your student blow up a balloon and tie it. Ask him or her what's inside the balloon. [air] Explain that air is all the gases that make up Earth's **atmosphere.** Those gases are what we breathe. Air is a kind of matter, because it has mass and takes up space.

3 **DISCUSS** Blow up another balloon, but don't tie it. Let the air out quickly, blowing your student's hair. Ask, *When air moves*

DID YOU KNOW?

For about 40 years beginning in the 1890s, box kites were used to carry meteorologic instruments that measured wind velocity, barometric pressure, temperature, and humidity.

Understanding Weather **205**

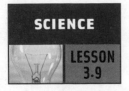

quickly from one place to another, what is it called? [wind] Explain that wind is air that moves due to differences in temperature and pressure. The air came rushing out of the balloon because the pressure outside of the balloon was greater than the pressure inside. People have come up with ways to use wind for energy. Wind-powered turbines use wind to generate electricity. Ask, *Have you ever flown a kite or seen someone fly a kite?* Ask your student to describe how the wind helps keep a kite in the air.

+ ENRICH THE EXPERIENCE

Does your student want to learn more about the water cycle? Have him or her visit the Web site http://www.epa.gov and search for water cycles.

4 **DISCUSS** Remind your student that there is a small amount of **water vapor** in the air. Tell your student that there is an interesting system that moves water from the ground into the atmosphere and back again. It's called the **water cycle.** The water cycle works like a giant circle, with no beginning and no ending. The sun **evaporates** water in the ocean and changes it to water vapor. The water vapor is carried up into the atmosphere with the warm air. As the water vapor rises, the air gets cooler. The water vapors are pressed together and form clouds. The cool air causes the clouds to release water as rain, hail, or snow. The water is absorbed by soil or plants or goes into rivers, lakes, and oceans. Ask your student to draw a picture of the water cycle.

5 **RELATE** Tell your student about the different types of clouds and how rain is created. **Cumulus clouds** are puffy and look like giant cauliflower. They are usually seen on warm, sunny days. They don't produce rain. They're usually in the sky between two and four miles up. **Stratus clouds** are flat, gray clouds that usually bring snow or rain. They are the lowest to the ground of all the clouds, less than 2,000 feet above Earth. **Cirrus clouds** are thin and wispy. Existing high in the atmosphere, they are usually found at least five miles above Earth. They can often look like a horse's tail. Invite your student to look out the window and draw a picture of the clouds he or she sees and label them.

Cumulus clouds

Stratus clouds

Cirrus clouds

6 **DISCUSS** Discuss some additional information about clouds with your student. Ask, *Why don't clouds fall from the sky?* [the water vapor in the air changes to ice crystals that are very small, so the wind currents can easily carry them along in large groups] Tell your student that clouds help keep Earth warm. On a cloudy day, some of the sun's energy penetrates the clouds and reaches the surface of Earth. Earth absorbs the energy and reradiates it up into the atmosphere. The lower parts of the clouds keep the energy from escaping. This energy is reradiated back toward Earth. So clouds help keep the warmer air close to Earth. Help your student make a drawing that shows how clouds help trap solar energy.

7 **EXPLAIN** Explain the role that rain plays in the water cycle. Rain forms when water vapor is carried up from warm bodies of water or over wet land surfaces. The moisture is carried up in the atmosphere, where it cools and condenses and forms the clouds discussed in Step 5. Then stratus clouds release the rain or snow over different areas of land. The amount of rain that falls in a particular area depends upon the temperature and trade winds. Land areas near the equator tend to get more rain. When the temperature in an area is below 32 degrees Fahrenheit or zero degrees Celsius, snow falls instead of rain. Ask your student to search the Internet to find the average yearly rainfall and/or snowfall in your town.

8 **REVEAL** Reveal to your student that weather isn't always pleasant. Severe rainstorms can cause flooding, and snowstorms can make travel dangerous. Another type of storm is a hurricane. Explain that a hurricane is a storm that starts over warm oceans and has spinning winds of at least 74 miles per hour. Hurricanes usually occur north of the equator. Their high-velocity winds move in a circular pattern around a low-pressure center, or what's called the *eye* of the storm. The strength of a hurricane is rated from one to five. Category five storms, which are very rare, have wind speeds that exceed 155 miles per hour. New technology for tracking hurricanes helps people know when to evacuate an area. Encourage your student to use library books or encyclopedias to find out why hurricanes are given names.

DID YOU KNOW?

Northeastern India has the highest annual rainfall average. That area gets about 430 inches of rain per year.

DID YOU KNOW?

Hurricanes are named after Hunracan, the Mayan storm god. Have your student choose a name for a hurricane.

Tornadoes can have wind speeds of more than 200 miles per hour.

9 **DISCUSS** Discuss with your student another type of severe storm—the tornado. A tornado is a funnel cloud that drops down from a severe thunderstorm and touches the ground. As the air in the tornado spins, it pulls in clouds and dust, making it easy to see. A tornado can occur when warm, moist air is trapped under a layer of cold, dry air and another layer of

warm, dry air. The two top layers become unstable, and the bottom layer pushes up through them. In 1971, a scientist named Theodore Fujita devised a system for classifying tornadoes based on the damage they do. The Fujita scale gives ratings from F0 to F5. An F0 tornado does little damage, and an F5 tornado can tear a house right off of its foundation. Have your student use library books or the Internet to research famous tornadoes.

10 **DISTRIBUTE** Distribute Student Learning Page 9.A. Have your student conduct the experiment and answer the questions.

Branching Out

TEACHING TIP

You may want to connect this lesson on weather with a piece of good literature. There are many novels written for students at the fourth-grade reading level that have plots related to severe weather events. Ask the librarian at your local library to help you find novels related to floods, tornadoes, or hurricanes that your student would find interesting. You can have your student read the novel independently, or you can read it together orally and discuss how the information in the novel compares to actual severe weather events.

CHECKING IN

To assess your student's understanding of this lesson, ask him or her to make an illustration with labels that includes examples of all of the vocabulary terms. Then have him or her tell you about the illustration and how the terms in the lesson are connected.

FOR FURTHER READING

Hurricanes, by Victor Gentle (Gareth Stevens Publishing, 2001).

National Audubon Society First Field Guide to Weather, by Jonathan D. W. Kahl (Scholastic, Inc., 1998).

Rain, Wind, and Storm, by Nicola Baxter (Raintree Steck-Vaughn, 1998).

The Science of Air, by Sarah Dann (Gareth Stevens Publishing, 2000).

Tornadoes, by Luke Thompson (Rosen Book Works, Inc., 2000).

The Weather Almanac, Eighth Edition, by Richard A. Wood (Gale Research, 1998).

Experiment with Air and Space

Conduct this experiment to show how air takes up space. Refer to what you've learned in the lesson before beginning. Then answer the questions.

A. Collect these materials: 1 funnel, 1 two-liter plastic soda bottle, wide masking tape.

B. Place the funnel in the mouth of an empty two-liter soda bottle. Pour some water into the funnel and observe what happens.

C. Pour the water out of the bottle. Put the funnel in the mouth of the soda bottle again. Tape the funnel to the bottle so there is no space between the funnel and the bottle. Pour some water into the funnel and observe what happens.

1. What happened when you poured the water into the funnel without the tape around it?

_____

_____

_____

2. What happened when you poured the water into the funnel with the tape around it?

_____

_____

_____

3. What do you think caused the two results? _____

_____

_____

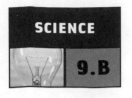

What's Next? You Decide!

Now it's your turn to choose what to do next in the lesson.
Read the activities and decide which one you want to do—
you may want to try them both!

Create Wind Power

MATERIALS

- ❑ 1 balloon
- ❑ 1 gallon-sized plastic self-closing bag
- ❑ thin string or fishing line
- ❑ 1 straw
- ❑ 2 chairs that are the same height
- ❑ tape

STEPS

You can use air to propel a balloon across the room!

- ❑ Set up two chairs at opposite ends of an open space at least 10 feet apart.
- ❑ Tie the string to the back of one chair.
- ❑ Put the other end of the string through the straw, then tie that end of the string to the back of the other chair. Make sure the string is taught and not sagging in the middle.
- ❑ Tape the plastic bag to the straw so that the open end is facing one of the chairs.
- ❑ Blow up the balloon. Hold it shut but do not tie it. Place it inside the plastic bag with the opening of the balloon facing the same way as the opening of the bag.
- ❑ Let go of the balloon, and watch it fly!

Observe Evaporation

MATERIALS

- ❑ 2 glass jars, one with a lid
- ❑ 1 measuring cup

STEPS

- ❑ Using a measuring cup, put an equal amount of water into two jars.
- ❑ Cover one jar with a lid. Leave both jars on a table for at least 24 hours.
- ❑ In your notebook, write what you think will happen to the water in the two jars.
- ❑ After 24 hours, check the amount of water in each jar. Which jar has more water? Why do you think this happened?
- ❑ Discuss what you noticed with an adult.

Examining the Rock Cycle

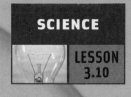
*Rocks are constantly being formed, worn down to form sediments,
and then changed back into rocks again in an endless natural cycle.*

OBJECTIVE	BACKGROUND	MATERIALS
To teach your student about the properties and formation of rocks, minerals, and soil	The raw materials for countless everyday objects come from rocks and minerals. The soil under our feet is mostly made of tiny fragments of rocks and minerals. In this lesson, your student will practice classifying rocks and learn how rocks are changed into soil and other kinds of rocks.	<ul><li>Student Learning Pages 10.A–10.B</li><li>collection of household objects</li><li>8–12 rock and mineral samples, including quartz and granite</li><li>1 hand lens</li><li>1 clear plastic bottle or jar with lid</li><li>sand, soil, and gravel</li><li>1 measuring cup</li><li>$\frac{1}{2}$ cup plaster of Paris</li><li>1 pair rubber gloves</li><li>wax paper</li><li>$\frac{1}{2}$ cup Epsom salt</li><li>1 saucepan</li><li>3–4 ice cubes</li><li>2 small paper drinking cups</li></ul>

VOCABULARY

PROPERTY a characteristic of an object that provides clues to its identity

MINERALS the building-block substances that rocks are made of

ROCK CYCLE the recycling process through which new rocks are formed

SEDIMENTARY rock formed when sediments settle out of water and harden

IGNEOUS rock formed when magma or lava cools and solidifies

METAMORPHIC rock formed when rocks are changed by heat and pressure

FOSSILS the trace remains of animal and plant life left behind in rock layers

CRYSTALS natural solids with a characteristic geometric shape or pattern

SOIL a mixture of fine grains made of weathered rock and decayed plant and animal material

Let's Begin

1 **IDENTIFY** Gather ordinary household objects such as baby powder, coins, jewelry, a ceramic cup, a mirror, a pencil, salt, and toothpaste. Tell your student to examine each item carefully. Ask, *How do you think these items might be related to rocks?* [the objects are all made from materials that are mined from Earth] Point out the objects, such as the metal coins, that are

SCIENCE

LESSON 3.10

A TIME-SAVER

To order geology kits online, go to http://www.augustana.edu and search for geology kits. Or visit http://www.geology-net.com. Click on Geology, then Rock Collections.

made from materials just as they come out of Earth. Point out the objects, such as the glass mirror, that are made indirectly from Earth materials (sand and metal). Have your student list each item in his or her notebook in a chart with these heads: "Household Object," "What It's Used For," and "What Earth Materials It's Made From." Encourage your student to look at product labels and reference books for more information. Help your student complete the chart.

2 **EXPLAIN AND CLASSIFY** Obtain a variety of rocks and minerals, about 8 to 12 samples. Inexpensive geology kits containing typical samples are available from science mail-order companies. You could also collect samples, but be sure to include examples of all three kinds of rocks listed below. Have your student arrange the samples into two or more groups based upon one **property,** or characteristic, they have in common. Give your student sufficient time to study and arrange the samples—at least five minutes. Give your student a hand lens to help identify the rock properties. Discuss what property he or she used. Possibilities include color, whether they're shiny or dull, shape, and texture. Ask your student to pick one rock and describe it in detail.

Granite   *Quartz*

3 **EXPAND** Explain to your student that **minerals** are the building blocks from which rocks are made. They are solids made from only one substance that form naturally and have unique properties. Have your student examine a piece of quartz and a piece of granite with the hand lens. Point out that the piece of quartz is made of only one substance, while the granite is composed of small grains having different shapes and colors of different substances. Ask, *Which of these two samples is the mineral?* [quartz] Give your student the samples and tell him or her to sort them into groups based on whether they appear to be made from one substance (mineral) or several different materials (rock). Discuss your student's decisions.

4 **REVEAL AND GUIDE** Direct your student's attention to the diagram of the **rock cycle** found on Student Learning Page 10.A. Explain that there are three different types of rocks. Each forms in a different way. **Sedimentary** rocks form when mud, shells, small bits of rock, and the remains of plants and animals settle out of water in layers and harden. **Igneous** rocks are formed when molten rock hardens on or below Earth's surface. Point out that **metamorphic** means "to change shape." When rocks encounter immense heat and pressure inside Earth, metamorphic rocks are formed. Emphasize that the rock cycle is a process that happens over millions of years. Using these definitions, help your student label each type of rock in the diagram.

5 **OBSERVE** Model how sedimentary rocks are formed. Explain that these rocks form in water. Have your student mix equal amounts (about two tablespoons) of sand, soil, and gravel. Pour the mixture into a clear plastic bottle or jar. Add about a cup of water. Screw on the lid and shake gently to mix the contents. Let the bottle stand undisturbed for at least an hour. Have your student watch what happens to the sediments. Discuss these observations. Ask, *In what order do the grains settle out of the water?* [the larger grains settle out first, followed by medium-sized grains, with the finer grains on top]

A BRIGHT IDEA

To support your student's comprehension of the three different rock types, provide at least one other source book where he or she can read about each type of rock and see photos. For sources online, visit http://www.bbc.co.uk or http://eduscapes.com and search for Rock Cycle.

6 **MODEL** Explain that as layers of sediment build up, tiny spaces between the grains fill with natural cement that holds them together. Use this recipe to model the process: Mix $\frac{1}{2}$ cup plaster of Paris with about $\frac{1}{4}$ cup water until it gets about as stiff as pancake batter. Mix two tablespoons each of gravel, sand, and soil into the plaster. Stir until the mixture is even. Allow the plaster to set for 10 minutes. Have your student wear rubber gloves to mold small lumps of the mixture into balls. Allow them to dry on wax paper.

ENRICH THE EXPERIENCE

Be sure to spend as much time as necessary reviewing the rock cycle and the way different types of rocks form. You may choose to spend a specific amount of time teaching about each different type of rock before moving on.

7 **CONNECT** Explain that **fossils** are the outlines of ancient animals or plants left behind in rock layers. Some fossils are formed when hard body parts, such as shells, are pressed between sedimentary rock layers. Point out that fossils are found only in sedimentary rocks. Ask, *Why do you think fossils don't form in igneous or metamorphic rock?* [because they are formed with a lot of heat; the heat would burn up the plants and animals]

8 **EXPLAIN AND MODEL** Explain that igneous rocks are made from hot liquid minerals called magma. When the hot minerals cool, they form **crystals.** Have your student grow his or her own crystals. Mix about $\frac{1}{2}$ cup of Epsom salt in a saucepan with $\frac{1}{2}$ cup of water. Heat over a low heat but do not boil. Stir until no more salt will dissolve. Remove from heat and divide the mixture between two small paper drinking cups. Write fast on one cup and place it in an ice bath. Write slow on the other and place it in a pan of warm water. Drop a few crystals of Epsom

A BRIGHT IDEA

Your student can learn more about the rock cycle, crystals, and fossils at http://www.childrensmuseum.org. Go to Kids, then Games and Activities, and click on Geo Mysteries.

SCIENCE

LESSON 3.10

salt into each cup. Shake gently. Have your student observe the two batches as they cool for 15 minutes. Let them sit overnight. Have your student use a hand lens to compare the crystals that form. Ask, *How does the cooling time of the water affect the crystals?* [slower cooling makes large crystals, faster cooling makes small crystals]

DID YOU KNOW?

Soil color provides clues as to the chemicals that make up the soil. Grey soil lacks oxygen. Red-brown, red, and yellow soil contains iron. Black and dark brown soil contains a lot of humus (organic matter).

9 **REVEAL AND DISCUSS** Explain to your student that **soil** forms when decayed plant and animal material mixes with fine grains of weathered rock. Almost the entire land surface of Earth is covered with soil, at depths varying from a few inches to many feet. Point out that without rocks and minerals, soil would not exist. Ask, *Why is soil such an important natural resource?* [without it, we would not have plants, food, or any of their products upon which we depend]

Branching Out

TEACHING TIP

To help your student connect the processes that create landforms to the study of rocks and minerals, ask your student to research how the rivers, hills, valleys, mountains, and lakes in your area were formed. Then have your student make a shoebox diorama illustrating some aspect of this history.

CHECKING IN

To assess your student's understanding of the lesson, have your student draw a series of labeled drawings showing how a sedimentary rock could change into different types of rock and eventually become soil.

FOR FURTHER READING

Geology Rocks!, by Cindy Blobaum (Williamson Publishing, 1999).

Is There a Dinosaur in Your Backyard?, by Spenser Christian (Wiley, 1998).

Learn About Rocks and Minerals, by Jack Challoner (Lorenz Books, 1998).

Investigate the Rock Cycle

Look at the drawing. It shows how rocks are formed and changed.
Three labels in the drawing are missing. Write "igneous rock,"
"sedimentary rock," and "metamorphic rock" on the correct lines.
Then answer the question at the bottom of the page.

1.

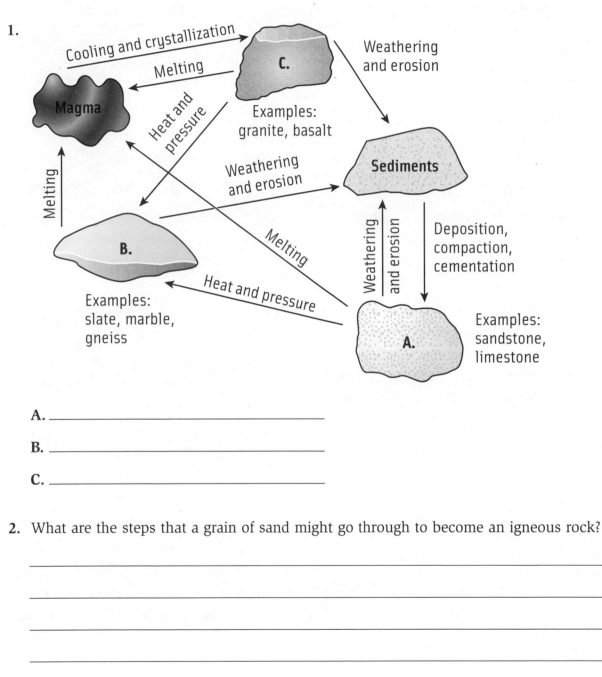

A. _____

B. _____

C. _____

2. What are the steps that a grain of sand might go through to become an igneous rock?

_____

_____

_____

_____

_____

_____

_____

What's Next? You Decide!

Now it's your turn to choose what to do next in the lesson. Read the activities and decide which one you want to do—you may want to try them both!

Become a Rockhound

MATERIALS

- ❏ 1 hammer and chisel
- ❏ 1 pair safety glasses
- ❏ 1 pair gloves
- ❏ 1 small notebook
- ❏ 1 hand lens
- ❏ 1 guidebook to rocks and minerals

STEPS

Rocks can be found around your home, in parks, or at an empty lot.

- ❏ Have an adult help you use the hammer and chisel to loosen rocks from the ground or break them into smaller samples. Wear safety glasses and gloves.

- ❏ Write a number on each rock you collect.

- ❏ Keep a notebook with the number, the place where you found each rock, the date you found it, and any other clues about it.

- ❏ Use the hand lens and guidebook to identify the rock samples.

Cast a Fossil

MATERIALS

- ❏ 1 package modeling clay
- ❏ 2 paper cups
- ❏ 1 seashell, leaf, bone, and other small object
- ❏ petroleum jelly
- ❏ $\frac{1}{2}$ cup plaster of Paris
- ❏ $\frac{1}{4}$ cup water
- ❏ 1 plastic spoon

STEPS

- ❏ Shape and flatten the clay until it fits in the bottom of one of the paper cups. Make sure the side facing up is flat.

- ❏ Press the object to be cast into the clay until it's half buried. Coating the object with petroleum jelly will make it easier to separate.

- ❏ Carefully remove the object. The clay impression is your mold.

- ❏ Mix the plaster with the water in the second paper cup. Stir and let it set for at least five minutes. When it has thickened, pour the plaster into the clay mold.

- ❏ Wait about one hour. When the plaster hardens, tear away the sides of the paper cup. Gently separate the plaster from the clay.

Exploring the Solar System

Get to know what's beyond Earth!

OBJECTIVE	BACKGROUND	MATERIALS
To help your student understand how our solar system is organized and how we humans explore it	Earth is one of the nine planets in our solar system. In this lesson, your student will learn about the other planets and how gravity affects all of the planets. Your student will also learn about the tools we use to study space.	■ Student Learning Pages 11.A–11.B

VOCABULARY
GRAVITY the force, or pull, that one object exerts on another object
ORBIT the path that a planet or other body travels on as it moves around the sun
PLANETS large objects that orbit the sun
SOLAR SYSTEM the sun, the planets, and the other objects that revolve around the sun
INNER PLANETS the group of four planets (Mercury, Venus, Earth, and Mars) that are closest to the sun
OUTER PLANETS the group of five planets (Jupiter, Saturn, Uranus, Neptune, and Pluto) that are farthest from the sun
TIDES the rising and falling of the water level in Earth's oceans
SPACE STATIONS places where humans can live and work in space for long periods of time

Let's Begin

1   **DISCOVER** Ask your student to explain what happens when we jump up off the ground. [we return to the ground] Tell him or her that it's the force of Earth's **gravity** that pulls us back to the ground when we jump. Explain that the sun's gravity is what holds Earth in **orbit.** Ask, *What do you think would happen if the sun's gravity wasn't pulling on Earth?* [Earth would move off into space]

2   **LEARN** Explain to your student that Earth and the other large objects that orbit the sun are called **planets.** Add that the planets, the sun, and all other objects orbiting the sun are collectively called the **solar system.** Show your student the diagram of the planets that illustrates their orbit positions relative to the sun.

3   **ASK** While looking at the illustration with your student, explain that the planets are divided into two groups—the **inner planets** and the **outer planets.** Point out that the four inner planets,

Mercury, Venus, Earth, and Mars, are mostly made of rock. The five outer planets are Jupiter, Saturn, Uranus, Neptune, and Pluto. Except for Pluto, which is rocky, all the outer planets are made of gases. Say the name of each planet out loud to your student and ask him or her to identify it as an inner planet or an outer planet.

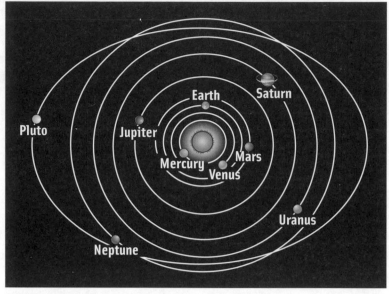

The nine planets of our solar system orbit around the sun.

4   **RELATE** Point out to your student that we call the time it takes Earth to travel once around the sun a *year*. The time it takes for Earth to spin around once on its axis is called a *day*. For other planets, a year or a day may be longer or shorter than on Earth. Look at the table of day and year lengths for each of the planets with your student. Say the name of each planet out loud to your student and ask him or her to use the table to find the day and year length for that planet. As you proceed with this exercise, refer to the solar system diagram and have your student trace the orbit of each planet with his or her finger.

5   **EXPLAIN** Explain to your student that the moon revolves around Earth. Tell your student that the gravitational pull of the moon affects Earth by causing changes in the water level of the oceans. These changes are called **tides.** Point out that the moon's gravity pulls on Earth and the water on it. This causes the parts of the oceans facing the moon to move toward it. Ask your student what he or she thinks might happen to the tides when the sun and the moon are lined up with Earth. [the combined gravitational pull causes tides that are higher and lower than normal]

Day and Year Length of the Planets

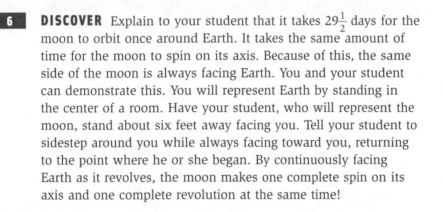

Planet	Length of Year (in Earth days)	Length of Day (in Earth hours and days)
Mercury	88	59 days
Venus	225	243 days
Earth	365	24 hours
Mars	687	24 hours 37 minutes
Jupiter	4,331	9 hours 55 minutes
Saturn	10,747	10 hours 30 minutes
Uranus	30,588	17 hours 14 minutes
Neptune	59,800	16 hours 7 minutes
Pluto	90,591	6 days 9 hours 18 minutes

6 **DISCOVER** Explain to your student that it takes $29\frac{1}{2}$ days for the moon to orbit once around Earth. It takes the same amount of time for the moon to spin on its axis. Because of this, the same side of the moon is always facing Earth. You and your student can demonstrate this. You will represent Earth by standing in the center of a room. Have your student, who will represent the moon, stand about six feet away facing you. Tell your student to sidestep around you while always facing toward you, returning to the point where he or she began. By continuously facing Earth as it revolves, the moon makes one complete spin on its axis and one complete revolution at the same time!

7 **DISCOVER** Ask your student to talk about what he or she knows about space exploration. Point out that people have traveled into space to study the moon and other planets. **Space stations** are tools that scientists use to learn about outer space. Astronauts can live on space stations. They use the space stations to observe space and do experiments. Space shuttles are spaceships that orbit Earth and can make repeated trips into space. Help your student find information on the Internet about recent space shuttle missions. The NASA Web site at http://www.nasa.gov provides descriptions and other information about space exploration projects.

ENRICH THE EXPERIENCE

If you live near the Pacific or Atlantic coast, visit the coast with your student and observe the change in tides during the day. If you don't live near a large body of water, go to http://www.hullcam.com/high_tide.html to see photos of high and low tides in Hull, Massachusetts. You can also visit http://science.howstuffworks.com and search for tides for diagrams and visual aids that show how tides happen.

DID YOU KNOW?

Certain places, such as the Mont St. Michel in France and the Bay of Fundy in Nova Scotia, experience record high and low tides. Learn more about the Bay of Fundy at http://www.bayoffundy.com.

SCIENCE
LESSON
3.11

Branching Out

TEACHING TIPS

❏ A moving solar system model is a helpful tool for understanding the lunar and planetary orbits. Usually a college or high school science lab will have one of these models. Science museums also frequently have them. Visit one of these in order to show your student how the planets revolve around the sun and how the moon revolves around Earth.

❏ One way to prepare for the lesson is to research the schedule of planetary appearances, such as for Venus, Mars, Jupiter, and Saturn (visit http://stardate.org). Then teach this lesson over a full year, marking planetary appearances on the calendar and spending a day reviewing astronomy and viewing the planets at night with binoculars.

CHECKING IN

To assess your student's understanding of the lesson, ask him or her to reteach a solar system lesson for you. Be sure your student talks about gravity and orbits, inner and outer planets, the moon, and tides.

FOR FURTHER READING

The Kingfisher Young People's Book of Space, by Martin Redfern (Kingfisher Books, 1998).

Moon (Exploring the Solar System), by Giles Sparrow (Heinemann Library, 2001).

Space: A History of Space Exploration in Photographs, by Andrew Chaikin (Carlton, 2002).

Put the Planets in Order

Order the planets from closest to the sun (1) to farthest from the sun (9). Write the numbers on the lines. Next, for each planet circle *rock* if the planet is made of rock or *gas* if it's made of gas. Then circle *inner* if it's an inner planet or *outer* if it's an outer planet.

1. _____ Jupiter

rock or gas

inner or outer

2. _____ Mercury

rock or gas

inner or outer

3. _____ Earth

rock or gas

inner or outer

4. _____ Uranus

rock or gas

inner or outer

5. _____ Saturn

rock or gas

inner or outer

6. _____ Pluto

rock or gas

inner or outer

7. _____ Mars

rock or gas

inner or outer

8. _____ Neptune

rock or gas

inner or outer

9. _____ Venus

rock or gas

inner or outer

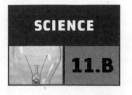
What's Next? You Decide!

Now it's your turn to choose what to do next in the lesson. Read the activities and decide which one you want to do—you may want to try them both!

Choose a Planet

MATERIALS

❑ 1 plastic ball

❑ paints

❑ 1 paintbrush

❑ 1 piece stiff wire

❑ 1 index card

❑ 1 hole puncher

❑ 1 pen or felt-tip marker

STEPS

❑ Choose one of the nine planets that you find most interesting.

❑ Make a model of it and a fact card to go with your model.

❑ Find a photograph of the planet you chose in resource books or on the Internet. Also find out more information about what the planet is like.

❑ Select a color or colors to paint your plastic ball. Make it look as much like the planet as you can.

❑ Write the name of your planet and four or five interesting facts about it on the index card. Punch a hole in the top center of the card.

❑ Push the wire through the middle of the ball so that it sticks out the opposite end. Push the end of the wire through the hole in the index card and twist it to secure. Then make a hook with the other end of the wire.

❑ Hang up your planet model where everyone can see it!

Found in Space

STEPS

Have you ever thought about what it might be like to travel trough space? Now's your chance!

❑ Suppose that you are an astronaut on a space shuttle mission.

❑ Write a story about a scientific discovery you make while aboard the space shuttle.

❑ Illustrate your story with pictures.

❑ Share your story with a friend or family member.

Examining Static Electricity and Magnetism

Two invisible forces at work around us are static electricity and magnetism.

OBJECTIVE	BACKGROUND	MATERIALS
To show your student how static electricity and magnetism work	Learning about static electricity and magnetism can help your student understand how electrically charged objects interact. In this lesson, your student will learn about positive and negative charges and how these forces relate to compasses and magnets.	■ Student Learning Pages 12.A–12.B ■ 2 balloons ■ 1 bar magnet ■ 2 small steel paper clips ■ 1 compass ■ 2 pieces string, about 2 feet long ■ 1 yardstick ■ 2 chairs

VOCABULARY

STATIC ELECTRICITY a buildup of electrical charge on an object
ATOMS tiny particles of matter
ELECTRONS negatively charged particles in an atom
PROTONS positively charged particles in an atom
MAGNETIC POLES the ends of a magnet, where the force of attraction is strongest
MAGNETIC FIELD the area around a magnet where the force of attraction is exerted

Let's Begin

1 **PREVIEW** Blow up a balloon. Rub it on your hair to make your hair stand up. Ask your student, *What do you think is making my hair stand up?*

2 **EXPLAIN** Tell your student that he or she has observed **static electricity** at work. Explain that all matter is made up of tiny particles called **atoms,** which are too small to be seen. Each atom is made up of **electrons** and **protons,** which have tiny amounts of electricity. Electrons have a negative electrical charge. Protons have a positive electrical charge. Atoms usually have the same number of positive electrical charges and negative electrical charges, so the atom has no overall electrical charge. This is called being neutral. Point out to your student items such as a book, a chair, clothing, and so on. For each one ask, *What is it made of?* [atoms] *What electrical charge does it have?* [neutral]

DID YOU KNOW?

Sometimes an electrical charge builds up in a cloud. When this static electricity moves from one cloud to another or from a cloud to the ground, a bolt of lightning results.

+

ENRICH THE EXPERIENCE

Have your student walk around your home with a magnet to find magnetic surfaces. He or she may be surprised at what attracts magnets.

FOR FURTHER READING

Eyewitness: Electricity, by Steve Parker (DK Publishing, Inc., 1999).

Sources of Forces: Science Fun with Force Fields, by Vicki Cobb (Millbrook Press, 2002).

Waves: Principles of Light, Electricity, and Magnetism, by Paul Fleisher (Lerner Publications Company, 2001).

3   **EXPAND** Tell your student that sometimes objects become electrically charged. When you rubbed the balloon on your hair, electrons moved from your hair to the balloon. As a result, the atoms in your hair had more protons than electrons, so the atoms had a positive charge. The atoms in the balloon had extra electrons, so the balloon had a negative charge. The charge on these objects is called static electricity because the charges aren't moving. With your student go to the Web site http://www. sciencemadesimple.com/static.html for more information on the basics of static electricity.

4   **APPLY** Explain that static electricity can make objects move. When two objects have different charges, they move toward each other. When they have the same charge, they move away from each other. Draw two circles to represent atoms. Put four positive signs (+) and four negative signs (–) in each. Ask your student to change the circles to show how the atoms of the balloon and your hair might look after the two were rubbed together. (One circle might have three positive signs and one negative sign, while the other would have one positive and three negative signs.)

5   **EXPLAIN** Tell your student that magnets line up in a north-south direction when allowed to swing freely. Give your student a bar magnet and point out the N and S on it. Explain that a bar magnet has two **magnetic poles.** Explain that Earth is like a giant magnet, and it also has two magnetic poles. When a bar magnet swings freely, the pole marked N is pulled toward Earth's north magnetic pole. Show your student a compass. Explain that the compass needle contains a tiny magnet, so the ends of the needle line up in a north-south direction. Have your student use the magnet to find the direction of the Earth's magnetic poles.

6   **EXPAND** Tell your student that around a magnet is a space called a **magnetic field.** Another magnet or any object that contains iron or certain other materials in this space will be pushed or pulled by the magnet. Have your student test how close a paper clip needs to be to the magnet in order to be in the magnetic field. Then have your student complete Student Learning Page 12.A.

Branching Out

TEACHING TIP

Have your student use a magnet to test various materials and find out which ones are attracted to the magnet.

CHECKING IN

Have your student rub a balloon on his or her hair and place it against a wall. Have him or her use terminology from the lesson to explain why the balloon stays there.

Watch Those Balloons!

SCIENCE

12.A

What do you think will happen if you rub two balloons on your hair and then bring them close to each other? Record your prediction. Then follow the directions to find out if you were right. This activity works best on a dry day.

1. My prediction: _____

   ❑ Blow up two balloons and tie them closed. Tie a piece of string to each one.

   ❑ Place the yardstick across the backs of two chairs.

   ❑ Rub one balloon on your hair. Tie the balloon to one end of the yardstick. Place the balloon with the side you rubbed on your hair toward the inside. Make sure the balloon doesn't touch the chair or the ground.

   ❑ Do the same thing with the other balloon. Tie it to the other end of the yardstick.

2. What happens? Why? _____

   _____

   _____

3. Was my prediction correct? _____

4. Write positive signs (+) and negative signs (−) to show the charges in the two balloons.

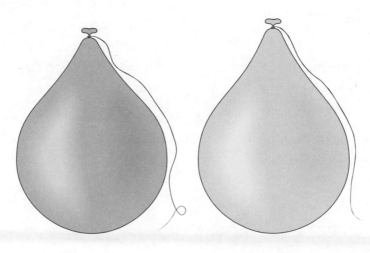

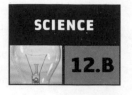

What's Next? You Decide!

Now it's your turn to choose what to do next in the lesson.
Read the activities and decide which one you want to do—
you may want to try them both!

Find the Power

MATERIALS

- ❏ 1 bar magnet
- ❏ 1 horseshoe magnet
- ❏ 1 ring magnet
- ❏ 1 box small steel paper clips

STEPS

You can find out where the power is greatest on a magnet. Do you think it will be the same on all magnets?

- ❏ Spread out the paper clips on a table.

- ❏ Place the bar magnet in the middle of the clips. Then pick up the magnet. Observe where the paper clips stick.

- ❏ Pick up paper clips with one end of the magnet. Then pick them up with the other end. Next pick them up with the middle section. Where is the magnetic power of the magnet strongest?

- ❏ Draw a picture of the magnet. Color in areas to show where the two poles are.

- ❏ Repeat these steps with each of the other magnets. How do they compare?

Make a Paper Clip Bridge

MATERIALS

- ❏ 2 bar magnets
- ❏ 1 box small steel paper clips
- ❏ 2 thick books
- ❏ transparent tape

STEPS

Can you turn a paper clip into a magnet?

- ❏ Hold the bar magnet straight up and down. Place a paper clip on the lower end.

- ❏ Touch another paper clip to the bottom of the first one. What happens?

- ❏ Touch a third paper clip to the bottom of the second one. See how many paper clips you can add to your chain. Why does this happen?

- ❏ Tape one bar magnet onto one book. Tape the second magnet onto another book. Make a paper clip bridge between the two magnets.

Learning About Energy

Discovering how to move energy helped the world use electricity, changing our lives forever.

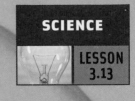

SCIENCE

LESSON
3.13

OBJECTIVE	BACKGROUND	MATERIALS
To help your student understand how electricity is used and controlled	Learning how electrical energy is transported helps us understand the importance of everything around us—even things we can't see. Harnessing the electrical energy in nature has allowed us to live much easier lives. In this lesson, your student will learn about how energy is delivered to our homes.	■ Student Learning Pages 13.A–13.B ■ 1 4.5-volt battery ■ 3 wires ■ 1 wire stripper ■ tape ■ 1 lightbulb and lightbulb stand that can be used with a 4.5-volt battery ■ several wood, plastic, and metal household items, such as a paper clip, a nail, a plastic spoon, and a pencil

VOCABULARY

CIRCUITS systems used for transporting electrical currents

CONDUCTORS substances that allow a current to pass through them with the least amount of resistance

INSULATORS substances that have a high amount of resistance so that a current cannot pass through them easily

RESISTORS substances that control the amount of current that passes through; some of that current is changed to heat

SERIES CIRCUIT a circuit that provides only one pathway for a current to travel through

PARALLEL CIRCUIT a circuit with multiple pathways for a current to travel through

SHORT CIRCUIT a circuit with no resistance so that too much current passes through; the result is an excessive amount of heat

FUSES devices that protect an electrical system against overload by breaking the current; a fuse can only be used once

CIRCUIT BREAKERS thermal elements that expand and create an open circuit to break a current

Let's Begin

1   **EXPLAIN** Explain to your student that there are complex systems for getting electricity from one place to another. Tell him or her that these systems are called **circuits.** Say that there are two basic types of circuits. Inform your student that an open circuit is one that has a break in it, so that the current cannot get through. Tell him or her that a closed circuit is one that is complete and has no breaks, so that a current can flow through.

Explain to your student that when a light switch is off an open circuit is formed, and that when the switch is on a closed circuit is formed, allowing the light to go on. Ask your student to write down other examples of open and closed circuits that he or she can find around the house. [doorbell, flashlight, toy train track]

A light switch is part of a circuit.

2 **EXPLORE** Explain to your student that every item we can see, and even those we can't, are either **conductors** or **insulators** of energy. Say, *Conductors are things that allow energy to flow through easily.* Tell your student that some good conductors are copper, gold, aluminum, silver, and water. Stress to your student the danger of using any electric appliance near water because of water's good conductivity. Say, *Insulators are things that don't allow energy to flow through easily.* Inform your student that plastic, rubber, and cement are insulators. Tell him or her that plastic is used to cover wires carrying electric currents to household appliances. Ask your student to find an example of plastic or rubber used as an insulator on an electrical appliance in his or her home.

3 **DESCRIBE** Tell your student that the exact amount of energy, or voltage, that flows through a closed circuit needs to be controlled. Then explain to him or her that **resistors** are things that control the amount of energy that can flow through a pathway. Say that some of that energy is turned to heat. If possible, show your student some examples of resistors, such as a burner on an electric stove or a lightbulb. Explain to your student that the amount of light provided by a lightbulb is dependent on the voltage of the bulb. Show your student how to see the number of volts and watts on some lightbulbs. Have him or her write the number of volts and watts for each lightbulb in his or her notebook.

4   **DESCRIBE** Tell your student that there are different ways that closed circuits can be designed. Inform him or her that one design is called a **series circuit.** Explain that in this circuit there is only one path for the current to follow. Show your student an example, such as a string of holiday lights. Inform him or her that if one light in the series goes out, the circuit is opened. Then introduce another circuit design, a **parallel circuit.** Explain that a parallel circuit allows current to flow through different parts of the circuit at the same time. Describe an example, such as how a light can be off in your bedroom while a light in the kitchen is on. Ask your student to make a list of things he or she thinks use a series circuit and a list of things he or she thinks use a parallel circuit.

5   **EXPLAIN** Explain that it's very important to be able to control an electric current. Tell your student that if an electric current is not controlled, a fire can start or a person can be badly injured. Inform him or her that when too much current gets through a pathway it's called a **short circuit.** Relate that two ways in which a short circuit can be prevented are by using **fuses** and **circuit breakers.** Explain that these things are used as safety switches. Tell your student that a fuse has a strip of metal in it that melts when too much electricity flows through it. Explain that when a fuse breaks, it needs to be replaced before the circuit can be closed again. Help your student find some items that use fuses, such as a string of holiday lights, an electric train set, and a car.

6   **EXPAND** Now give your student more information about circuit breakers. Say, *A circuit breaker has a piece of metal that expands when it gets too hot, pushing the switch open.* Explain that a circuit breaker, unlike a fuse, can be reset and used again. Tell your student that the power may go out in a room or section of a house when too many electrical appliances are turned on at once. Explain that when this happens, a circuit breaker is doing its job. Show your student the circuit breakers in the electrical panel in your house. With your supervision, have him or her draw a picture of the circuit breakers in his or her notebook and label each one. Then ask your student to determine which appliances in your home run on each circuit and to list them on a chart.

7   **CONNECT** Explain that using electricity wasn't always as easy as turning on a switch. Have your student research some inventors who worked with electricity, such as Alexander Graham Bell, Thomas Alva Edison, and Michael Faraday. Together explore what they invented and how their inventions paved the way for products and services we use today. A good place to begin looking for inventors and their inventions is at http://inventors.about.com.

ENRICH THE EXPERIENCE

Does your student want to learn about how electricity is formed? Encourage him or her to visit the Web site http://www.surfnetkids.com/electric.htm.

8 **DISTRIBUTE** Distribute Student Learning Page 13.A to your student and have him or her complete the activity.

Thomas Alva Edison patented more than 1,000 inventions—many of which used electricity.

FOR FURTHER READING

Awesome Experiments in Electricity and Magnetism, by Michael DiSpezio (Sterling Publishing Company, Inc., 1998).

Electricity and Magnetism, by Chris Oxlade (Heinemann Library, 2000).

Physics Matters: Volume 7 Electric Current, by Christopher Cooper (Grolier Educational, 2001).

Physics Matters: Volume 8 Magnetism, by Christopher Cooper (Grolier Educational, 2001).

Branching Out

TEACHING TIPS

❑ Most of the materials needed to teach this lesson can be purchased at a hobby shop or an electrical supply shop. You may find it safer to do all of the wire stripping yourself before your student works on the Student Learning Pages. If you've never created a closed circuit before, you may want to practice the experiment on Student Learning Page 13.A ahead of time.

❑ The content in this lesson may be difficult for your student to grasp. Take as much time as needed with each step, and let your student be a guide for pacing.

CHECKING IN

The next time you ask your student to turn off the lights, ask him or her if an open or a closed circuit is created when the switch is flipped. [open] Also, after completing Student Learning Page 13.A, go for a walk around your neighborhood. Point out different items to your student and ask him or her to tell you whether those items are conductors or insulators. Finally, after teaching this lesson, have your student help you do an electrical safety check in your home. As you find wires in good condition, have your student explain why they are safe. Have your student explain as well why wires in poor condition are not safe.

Create a Circuit and Discover Conductors and Insulators

Follow the steps to create an electrical circuit. Then use that circuit to test things around the house to see if they are conductors or insulators.

1. First, use the 4.5-volt battery, three wires, the tape, the lightbulb, and the lightbulb holder to create a circuit.

2. Strip about a half inch of the plastic coating off each end of all wires with a wire stripper. Get an adult to help you with this.

3. Using two wires, connect one end of each wire to the battery by wrapping them as shown in the picture.

4. Connect the third wire to one end of one of the wires by wrapping the stripped sections together.

5. Connect the two remaining wire ends to the screws on the lightbulb stand by wrapping them. Your lightbulb should go on. You have created a circuit!

6. Now gather some small items made of plastic, metal, or wood. You will use your circuit to test whether these items are conductors or insulators.

7. In your notebook, write these headings above two columns: "Conductor" and "Insulator."

8. Attach one of your items to the stripped wires as shown in the picture. Does your lightbulb work? If it does, the item you used is a conductor. Write the item under the Conductor heading. If the lightbulb doesn't work, the item you used is an insulator. Write the item under the Insulator heading in your notebook. Repeat this activity with the other items you gathered.

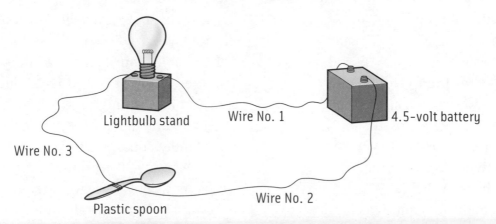

Lightbulb stand   Wire No. 1   4.5-volt battery

Wire No. 3

Plastic spoon   Wire No. 2

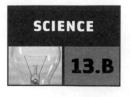
What's Next? You Decide!

Now it's your turn to choose what to do next in the lesson. Read the activities and decide which one you want to do—you may want to try them both!

Test Food Power

MATERIALS

- ❏ the closed circuit you made for Student Learning Page 13.A
- ❏ 1 lemon
- ❏ 1 copper penny
- ❏ 1 strip zinc
- ❏ 1 small current meter
- ❏ 1 knife
- ❏ steel wool

STEPS

Can foods produce electricity? Not really. But some foods are good conductors of electrical currents!

- ❏ Take the lightbulb stand out of your circuit and replace it with the current meter.
- ❏ Use the steel wool to shine the surfaces of the penny and zinc strip.
- ❏ Have an adult use the knife to cut two slits in the lemon's peel.
- ❏ Insert the penny into one slit. Insert the zinc strip into the other slit. Make sure the penny and the zinc strip don't touch.
- ❏ Touch the wires from your circuit to the penny and the zinc strip at the same time to make a closed circuit.
- ❏ Watch the meter! What do you see?
- ❏ Try this activity again with other foods you have available. Which foods are conductors and which are insulators?

Survey Your Electricity

STEPS

Some things in your home need electricity to work, some don't. Find out what items need electricity to work in your home and how often you use them.

- ❏ Walk through each room in your home. Look around for light switches, lamps, appliances, and any other items.

- ❏ Write each item that needs electricity in your notebook.
- ❏ Then write approximately how long each item is used on a weekly basis. For example, your bedside reading lamp might only be used for about a half hour each night.
- ❏ Are there any items that you and your family could use less to help save electricity? For example, turning off lights when you leave a room.
- ❏ Talk with your family about how you could use those items.

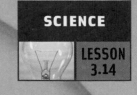

Investigating Heat

Heat isn't just a warm, fuzzy feeling. It's the energy of moving matter.

OBJECTIVE	BACKGROUND	MATERIALS
To help your student understand how heat is produced and transferred	Heat fuels our bodies and keeps us warm. Heat supplies the energy to run machines and produces electricity. In this lesson, your student will learn what heat is, how heat is produced, how heat moves, and how heat provides the energy we need.	■ Student Learning Pages 14.A–14.B ■ 2 plastic cups ■ 1 shaker salt ■ 2 drops food coloring ■ 2 ice cubes ■ 2 paper towels ■ 1 sheet dark construction paper or 1 dark cloth ■ 1 hand lens ■ 1 copy Web, page 356

VOCABULARY

HEAT the energy of moving particles of matter

COMBUSTION a chemical reaction that combines oxygen and fuel to produce heat

CONDUCTION heat transfer by direct physical contact

CONVECTION heat transfer by the motion of circulating gases or liquids

RADIATION heat transfer by waves of energy

Let's Begin

1 **INTRODUCE** Explain to your student that **heat** is energy produced by the motion of matter. To show how motion produces heat, have your student rub his or her hands together. Now fill one plastic cup with hot water and the other with cold water. Add a drop of food coloring to each cup and tell your student to watch carefully. Ask, *In which cup did the food coloring spread faster?* [the cup with the hot water] Explain to your student that the motion of the water particles bumping into each other helps spread the food coloring. Ask him or her to start a chart that lists heat sources in a notebook. Your student might list a candle flame, hot stove, fireplace, toaster, campfire, and so on. Have your student add to the list throughout the lesson.

2 **DISCUSS** Explain to your student that energy sources that are burned to produce heat are called fuels. Ask him or her to speculate about what might have been the first fuel people in

ENRICH THE EXPERIENCE

Invite your student to learn about the history of the thermometer and the invention of temperature scales at http://inventors.about.com/library/inventors/blthermometer.htm.

FOR FURTHER READING

Experiments with Heat (True Books), by Salvatore Tocci, Robert Gardner, and Nanci R. Vargus (Scholastic Library Publishing, 2003).

Heat and Energy, by Bobbi Searle (Copper Beech Books, 2001).

Hot and Cold, by Sally Hewitt (Children's Press, 2000).

the past used. [people learned very early to burn wood and used it to keep warm, frighten predators, and cook food] Point out that the main source of heat on Earth is the sun. Tell your student that wood comes from plants, which get their energy from sunlight. Explain to him or her that another name for the reaction that combines the gas oxygen with a fuel to make heat is **combustion.** Inform your student that our bodies use a slow form of this reaction to make energy from food.

3 **EXPLORE** Distribute Student Learning Page 14.A to your student. Challenge your student to use any method he or she can think of to speed the melting of the ice cube. Tell him or her to describe his or her plan to you and then try it out.

4 **REVEAL** Explain to your student that temperature controls the direction in which heat flows. Tell him or her that heat always moves from a warmer material to a cooler one. Explain that heat can move by touch or by contact. This is called **conduction.** Tell your student that warming your hands around a warm cup is an example of conduction. Explain that **convection** is the transfer of heat by moving liquids or gases. Say, *Heated gases rise and cooled gases sink.* A space heater warms the air in a room by convection. Tell your student to hold his or her hand under a lamp. Explain that the heat he or she feels is **radiation,** which travels in waves. Radiation is the way that heat travels across space. Now invite your student to explain how heat was transferred to the ice cube during the experiment for Step 3.

5 **DISCUSS** Heat is an important source of energy. Explain to your student that coal, oil, and natural gas are called fossil fuels. These fuels come from the energy in plants and animals that were buried long ago. When the fuels are burned, the stored energy is released. Most of the energy used to produce the electricity that runs machines comes from fossil fuels. These fuels are used to boil water. The resulting steam turns turbines that generate electricity. Discuss with your student some of the advantages and disadvantages of using fossil fuels. Then have your student complete Student Learning Page 14.B.

Branching Out

TEACHING TIP

Use food coloring to make convection currents visible in moving liquids. Start with a cup of cold water. Fill a medicine vial with hot water and food color. Use a dropper to add the colored warm water to the cup.

CHECKING IN

Give your student a copy of the Web found on page 356. Ask your student to write a key concept about heat in the center. Then have him or her include details about how heat is produced and transferred and examples of how it is used.

Race Ice Cubes

Conduct this experiment to find a way to melt one ice cube faster than another ice cube. Refer to what you've learned in the lesson before beginning. Then answer the questions.

A. Collect these materials: 2 ice cubes, 1 hand lens, salt, 1 sheet dark construction paper or 1 dark cloth, 2 paper towels

B. Take two ice cubes. Put the first cube on a paper towel. Don't touch it during the test. Find a way to melt the second cube faster. For safety, don't use matches or put the ice in your mouth.

1. Write your plan on how to melt the second cube faster in the form of a series of numbered steps. Have an adult check your plan. Make any changes to your plan the adult suggests. Then try it out!

_____

_____

_____

2. Were you successful? Which ice cube melted first?

_____

3. Did your plan involve adding heat in some way? What was the heat source?

_____

4. Which method of heat transfer did you use? Explain.

_____

_____

Use Heat Energy

Keep track of how you use heat or other energy sources that use heat (such as electricity) for one day. List four uses of energy in the chart. Check your notebook for ideas. Name the energy source. Tell how it is produced. Explain why each use is an important part of your daily life. Ask an adult for help if you can't figure out how the energy is produced. The first one is completed for you.

Energy Use

Heat Use	Heat Source	How the Energy Is Produced	Why This Use of Heat Is Important to You
(a) Driving in car	Gasoline (fossil fuel)	Fuel runs combustion engine	Transportation
(b)			
(c)			
(d)			
(e)			

Now review your list. Do you think people living in other parts of the country or the world would have different uses for the energy listed? Explain.

_____

_____

_____

_____

_____

_____

Understanding Matter, Motion, and Machines

Matter and motion are related to the forces acting on them.
Machines make it easier to move matter!

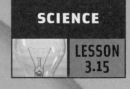

SCIENCE

LESSON
3.15

OBJECTIVE	BACKGROUND	MATERIALS
To help your student learn about the relationship between matter and motion and understand how machines make work easier	Almost everything around us is made of matter. All matter has mass, so matter with a lot of mass can be hard to move. Machines make it easier to move matter. In this lesson, your student will study different properties of matter and the six simple machines that make it easier to move matter from one place to another.	■ Student Learning Pages 15.A–15.B ■ 2 identical brown bags ■ enough sand to fill 1 bag halfway ■ enough feathers or paper wads to fill 1 bag halfway ■ 1 table-tennis ball ■ 1 golf ball ■ 1 glass filled with water ■ 1 paring knife

VOCABULARY

MATTER   anything that has mass and takes up space

MASS   the amount of matter an object has

VOLUME   the amount of space taken up by something

DENSITY   the amount of mass something has compared to its volume

FORCE   a push or pull that acts on something

WEIGHT   the measure of the amount of gravity acting on something

BUOYANCY   the property something has to rise or float in water

INERTIA   the property something has to resist any change in motion

FRICTION   a force that resists motion

SIMPLE MACHINES   devices that make work easier

Let's Begin

1   **OBSERVE** Tell your student that **matter** is anything that has **mass** and takes up space. Explain to him or her that the amount of matter that something is made of is called its mass. Inform your student that mass is measured by the metric units grams and kilograms. Add that matter can be observed, described, and measured. Ask him or her to look around and name things that he or she can observe, describe, and measure. Point out that there is matter everywhere around us. Have your student distinguish between matter that has a lot of mass and matter

that has a small amount of mass. For example, a table has a lot of mass, and a newspaper has a small amount of mass.

2 **COMPARE** Point out to your student that the amount of space that can be taken up by matter is called **volume.** Explain that a thing that's made up of a lot of matter has a higher **density** than a thing that takes up the same amount of space but is made up of less matter. To demonstrate this, have your student fill one brown bag halfway with sand and fold the top closed. Then instruct him or her to fill a second identical brown bag halfway with feathers or paper wads and to fold the top closed. Make sure that the two bags are indistinguishable from the outside. Ask your student to lift each bag but not to open it. Ask, *Which bag has more mass, volume, and density?* [the bag with the sand has more mass and more density; the bags have equal volumes]

3 **EXPLAIN** Tell your student that a **force** is any push or pull that acts on something. Explain that gravity is a force that pulls on objects. Inform your student that gravity and weight are related: The **weight** of an object is determined by both its mass and the amount of gravity pulling on it. Explain that the weight of an object is generally the same anywhere on Earth. Tell your student that on the moon, which has a gravitational pull less than Earth's, the weight of that same object would be different. Ask your student, *Is the weight of a 60-pound child on Earth less or more on the moon? Why?* [less, because the force of gravity pulling the child toward the surface would be weaker]

4 **OBSERVE** Ask, *Why do some objects sink in water while others float?* Explain to your student that **buoyancy** is the property that describes how well an object floats in water. Have your student fill a glass with water and set a golf ball on the surface of the water. Ask, *Does the golf ball float or sink?* [sink] Then have him or her do the same with a table-tennis ball. Ask, *Does this float or sink?* [float] Ask your student to think about why one ball is buoyant and the other is not. Tell your student that buoyancy is determined by an object's density. Explain that objects that are denser than water don't float and objects that are less dense than water do float. Have your student find other objects to test for buoyancy. Ask him or her to predict whether each item will float or sink in the water.

5 **RELATE** Ask your student to imagine what happens when a boulder starts rolling down a hill. [it rolls slowly at first, then speeds up until it reaches the bottom and eventually stops] Ask, *What would make the boulder change its path once it's in motion?* [some outside force] Explain to your student that **inertia** is an object's tendency to resist a change in motion. The boulder has a lot of inertia as it's rolling down the hill, so a large force would be necessary to change its path of motion. Ask your student to describe the relationship between inertia and mass. [the more mass an object has, the more inertia it has]

ENRICH THE EXPERIENCE

Fill a large, clear container with water. Have your student carefully place an egg into the water. Ask, *What happens? Why?* [the egg sinks to the bottom because it is denser than the water] Tell your student to remove the egg. Have him or her dissolve several spoonfuls of salt in the water. Ask him or her to place the egg into the water again. Ask, *Now what happens?* [the egg floats] Explain to your student that the salt makes the water denser!

6 **OBSERVE** Ask your student if he or she has ever been ice skating or tried walking on ice. Ask, *Is it easy or difficult to walk on ice?* [difficult, because it's slippery] Explain to your student that an example of a force that resists motion is **friction.** This force is produced between a moving object and the things around it. Explain that when we walk on ice, there's very little friction between our shoes and the ice, so movement isn't resisted and it becomes difficult to walk. Ask your student to think of a surface that would produce a lot of friction when you walk on it. [sand, gravel, cement, and so on]

7 **OBSERVE** Explain to your student that a machine is a device that makes work easier. Tell him or her that there are six kinds of **simple machines**—the inclined plane, the wedge, the lever, the wheel and axle, the screw, and the pulley. Show your student the images below representing each of the six simple machines. In order, clockwise starting at the top photo, they are: inclined plane, lever, pulley, screw, wheel and axle, and wedge. Discuss with him or her why using these machines makes work easier.

8 **RELATE** Ask your student if he or she has ever used a knife to cut something. Show him or her a paring knife and how the knife is used to cut something. Be sure to demonstrate (without saying so) how the knife works both like a wedge and a lever. Explain to your student that two kinds of simple machines are represented by a paring knife. Ask, *What two simple machines are they?* [a wedge and a lever]

9 **RELATE** Discuss with your student another example of a simple machine that is used every day. Ask, *How does a person open or close a door?* [with a door knob] Ask your student what kind of simple machine is used to open and close a door. [a wheel and axle]

?

DID YOU KNOW?

The most slippery substance in the world is a compound known as Teflon. This nonsticky chemical was discovered by accident by Dr. Roy Plunkett in 1938 when he was trying to produce a nontoxic gas that could be used as a coolant. Today, Teflon is used to make nonstick pots and pans, equipment for space travel, and even artificial body parts.

10 **IDENTIFY** Have your student find other examples of simple machines around the house. Point out to your student that, as you've demonstrated, many household appliances are really a combination of one or more simple machines. Explain that these are called compound machines. Encourage your student to find as many examples around your home as possible.

11 **DISTRIBUTE** Distribute Student Learning Page 15.A to your student and have him or her complete the page.

Branching Out

TEACHING TIPS

❑ Motion and machines are part of our everyday lives. There are objects all around us (including ourselves!) that move in response to other forces. We use machines all the time to help make work easier. Have a collection of items handy while teaching this lesson—such as small toys with wheels, different types of balls, a hammer, a screwdriver, a can opener, and a pencil sharpener—to help demonstrate how forces make things move and to show how much easier certain tasks are when a machine is used to perform them.

❑ Although this lesson could be completed in a few hours, you may wish to spend more time as your student shows interest. For more activities related to the lesson, go to http://www.funology.com.

FOR FURTHER READING

Magnificent Machines, by Doug Sylvester (Rainbow Horizons Publishing, 1999).

Science Experiments with Simple Machines (Science Experiments), by Sally Nankivein-Aston and Dorothy Jackson (Franklin Watts, Inc., 2000).

Simple Machines, by Adrienne Mason and Deborah Hodge of the Ontario Science Centre (Kids Can Press, 2000).

CHECKING IN

To assess your student's understanding of the lesson, give him or her a table-tennis ball, a glass of water, an ice cube, foil, newspaper, and a hammer. Ask your student to be creative and to use these items to demonstrate force, motion, friction, inertia, buoyancy, and simple machines. (The glass of water and the ping pong ball can be used to demonstrate buoyancy. The ice cube can be slid along the foil and the newspaper to demonstrate motion, friction, and inertia. The hammer can be used to show how much easier it is to smash an ice cube with a simple machine such as a lever than it is with your hand or fist.)

Name That Machine

Look at the pictures on page 239. Then draw an example of each simple machine.

Now explore mass and matter. Read questions 1–3. Next to each question write the correct description(s) of the ball:

❑   has the most mass.

❑   would be buoyant in water.

❑   would have the most inertia.

❑   has the highest volume.

❑   is the densest.

1. An inflatable beach ball that measures 30 inches across:

   _____

2. A ball made of clay that measures 20 inches across:

   _____

3. A rubber ball that measures 24 inches across:

   _____

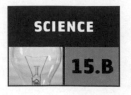

What's Next? You Decide!

Now it's your turn to choose what to do next in the lesson.
Read the activities and decide which one you want to do—
you may want to try them both!

Explore Friction and Motion

MATERIALS

- ❑ 1 length stiff cardboard or thin wood, about 6 inches long by 3 inches wide
- ❑ 1 small toy car with free-moving wheels
- ❑ aluminum foil
- ❑ wax paper
- ❑ 1 cotton cloth
- ❑ 1 stopwatch or clock with a second hand
- ❑ table for recording seconds

STEPS

Discover what kinds of materials decrease friction.

- ❑ Make a ramp by setting one end of the cardboard on a small stack of two or three books.
- ❑ Hold the car at the top of the ramp and let go. Use a stopwatch or clock to time how long it takes the car to reach the bottom of the ramp. Record the time in seconds in your notebook.
- ❑ Cover the ramp with the foil and test the car again. Record the time in seconds in your notebook.

- ❑ Repeat using the wax paper and the cotton cloth. Which surface created the least friction? Which surface created the most friction? How do you know?

Describe a Day in the Life of a Machine

MATERIALS

- ❑ markers or colored pencils

STEPS

How would a simple machine describe its day? Write a short story that shows what one day would be like for a simple machine.

- ❑ Put yourself in the machine's place! Come up with a title for your story such as "A Day in the Life of Donald the Doorknob" or "Sammy the Screwdriver's Day."
- ❑ Answer these questions in your story: How does your machine begin its day? Where is it found in a house? Is your machine happy or sad? How does the day end?
- ❑ Make your story one page long and draw pictures with the markers or colored pencils.
- ❑ Give your story to an adult to read.

In Your Community

To reinforce the skills and concepts taught in this section,
try one or more of these activities!

Different Kinds of Telescopes

Is your student interested in astronomy? Find out if there's an exhibit that shows the evolution of the telescope at a museum of science and industry or a planetarium in your town. Take a visit to see the telescopes firsthand. If you aren't near a planetarium or museum, you may be able to find an astronomy group that meets in your area. Many astronomy groups have Web sites. Arrange for a time when you and your student could attend a gathering and look at the sky through telescopes!

Soil in Your Neighborhood

There are thousands of different kinds of soil on Earth. Have your student examine the soil around your home. He or she will need a magnifying lens, a small spatula, and a surface to work on that has good lighting. Ask your student to collect a handful of soil from several inches under the surface of the ground. Show him or her how to use the spatula and magnifying glass to examine the color and texture of the soil. Arrange to have him or her meet with a local landscaper to find out what types of vegetation grow best in this type of soil.

Community Recycling

Does your community have a recycling program? Together with your student find out how your recycling program works. What is recycled? Where do they recycle it? How long does it take? What is made from the recycled material? If you can, visit the recycling center in your area. See if you can arrange a guided tour or an interview with a manager for your student. If there isn't a recycling program in your community, have your student find out why not. See if you can create a plan to start a recycling program together and propose it to your city hall.

Endangered Animals Close to Home

There are hundreds of animals in the United States that are on the endangered species list. Together with your student use the Internet or contact a local ecology center to find out about the animals that live in or close to your community that are endangered. Have your student choose one animal to learn more about. Ask him or her to find out how the people in your community can help protect this animal. Then have your student make a poster that teaches people about the animal and how they can help. After getting permission, have your student display the poster at your local library or another public place.

Local Life Science

Do you live close to a forest preserve? If so, your student can learn a great deal about the plants and animals in your area by paying it a visit. Try to make an appointment with a naturalist at the forest preserve to show your student different plants and animals that are native to your area. Have your student prepare a list of questions to ask the naturalist about how plants and animals are classified and any adaptations they have to help them survive. It may be useful for your student if you go to the local library beforehand to find a field guide containing information about the various plants and animals you may encounter. The field guide can be used as a supplement to the information supplied by the naturalist.

We Have Learned

Use this checklist to summarize what you and your student
have accomplished in the Science section.

❑ **Animal and Plant Kingdoms**
❑ animal and plant characteristics
❑ animal life cycles: growth and development
❑ plant life cycles: germination, growth, reproduction
❑ food chains, producers, consumers, decomposers

❑ **Skin**
❑ integumentary system, melanin, epidermis
❑ protection of skin

❑ **Chemical Substances**
❑ stimulants, depressants, antibiotics
❑ chemical abuse, alcohol, tobacco, illegal drugs

❑ **Nutrition**
❑ carbohydrates, fats, proteins
❑ water, vitamins, minerals

❑ **Ecosystems**
❑ limited resources, migration, niche
❑ food web, changing ecosystems, ecosystem stages

❑ **Weather**
❑ air, wind, water cycle, clouds
❑ storms, hurricanes, tornadoes

❑ **Shaping and Reshaping Earth**
❑ weathering, erosion
❑ catastrophic events

❑ **Rocks, Minerals, and Soils**
❑ rock types, formation
❑ Earth's minerals, soil preservation

❑ **Static Electricity and Magnets**
❑ atoms, electrons, protons
❑ magnetic poles, magnetic fields

❑ **Energy Pathways**
❑ flow of electricity, electromagnetism, electric current
❑ series circuits, parallel circuits

❑ **Heat**
❑ measuring heat, producing heat, using heat
❑ heat transfer

❑ **Matter, Motion, and Machines**
❑ volume, mass, weight, density, buoyancy
❑ inertia, force, motion, friction
❑ lever, wheel and axle, pulley, inclined plane, wedge, screw

❑ **Solar System**
❑ gravity, space exploration
❑ sun, moon, Earth

We have also learned:

_____

_____

_____

Social Studies

Social Studies

Key Topics

U.S. Climate and Geography

Natural Resources

Northeast Region

Southeast Region

Midwest Region

Southwest Region

West Region

Your State and Town

U.S. Civics and Citizenship

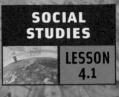

SOCIAL
STUDIES

LESSON
4.1

Discovering the Climate and Geography of the United States

Taking good care of our Earth is a gift for future generations.

OBJECTIVE	BACKGROUND	MATERIALS
To help your student learn about the geography and climate of the United States	The climate and geography of the United States is quite diverse. The various parts of the United States have different types of land, water, plants, animals, and climates. In this lesson, your student will learn more about the diverse environments of the United States.	■ Student Learning Pages 1.A–1.B ■ 1 U.S. map ■ 1 copy national newspaper

VOCABULARY

ENVIRONMENT the surroundings where people, animals, and plants live

GEOGRAPHY the study of Earth and the life on it

LANDFORMS the different kinds of shapes on Earth's surface

ELEVATION MAP a kind of map that shows the heights of the land's surface

CLIMATE the average weather in a place over many years

PRECIPITATION falling water in the form of rain, hail, snow, or sleet

Let's Begin

1 **EXPLAIN** Explain to your student that the United States is one country under a common government, but the land and weather in different areas of the country are different. Look at the pictures of a beach in Florida and a landscape in Alaska with your student. Ask him or her to compare and describe each picture. Show your student that the shape of the surface of Earth in these places is different. Emphasize to your student that each of these pictures shows a different **environment.** Ask your student to explain how the weather in each of these places is different.

Oceanside beaches make up parts of Florida's landscape.

2 **EXPLAIN AND DISCUSS** Consider the definition of the words **geography** and geographer with your student. Tell your student that *geo* is a Greek word that means "earth," "ground," or "soil." Explain that geography is the study of Earth and the plant, animal, and human life on it. A geographer is a person

Mountainous terrain can be found in Alaska.

Discovering the Climate and Geography of the United States   247

SOCIAL STUDIES

LESSON 4.1

who studies Earth. Discuss with your student that the study of geography is important because it helps us better understand our environment. Have your student tell you at least five things that he or she already knows about the geography of the United States. [where there are mountains, where it is flat, where the rivers and oceans are] Then discuss with your student at least three things he or she would like to learn about U.S. geography during this lesson.

Plains are located in the central part of the United States.

Mountains are found in different regions of the United States.

3 DESCRIBE Explain that **landforms** are the different kinds of shapes on Earth's surface. The United States is a large country and has many different types of landforms. Some landforms of the United States are plains, plateaus, mountains, basins, swamps, deserts, and coasts. Have your student look at the pictures of the plains and the mountains. Then invite him or her to write a descriptive sentence about each of those landforms and locate on a map of the United States one or two places where the landform can be found.

4 EXPAND Tell your student that there are many different kinds of maps. An **elevation map** is a map that illustrates the heights of the land on Earth's surface. Have your student use the Internet or geography books from the library to find an elevation map. Look at the map with your student and identify which colors represent which heights. Then help your student locate the Great Plains of North Dakota, South Dakota, and Montana and the Rocky Mountains in Colorado on the map. Ask your student to compare the heights of these two landforms. Ask, *Which landform is higher?* [Rocky Mountains] Then help your student find the area where he or she lives on the map. Ask, *What is the elevation where you live?* Note how the elevation where he or she lives compares to other parts of the United States.

5 EXPLAIN Explain to your student that bodies of water are another important part of the environment in many parts of the United States. Point out the Atlantic Ocean, Lake Michigan, and the Mississippi River on the map. Explain that an ocean is a body of saltwater while a lake is a body of freshwater surrounded by land. A river is a large stream of water. Invite your student to identify other bodies of water he or she sees on the map. [Pacific Ocean, Lake Erie, Rio Grande] Ask your student to brainstorm some of the things people who live close to the water do for fun. [go fishing, swimming, boating, go to the beach]

6 ASK Explain that **climate** is the average weather conditions in a certain area. Different parts of the United States have different climates. Tell your student that the climate in Arizona is hot and dry, while the climate in Wisconsin is cooler. Both Arizona and Wisconsin are part of the United States, but their climates are very different. Guide your student to think about the climate in which he or she lives. Ask, *Is it usually hot or cold here? Does it rain or snow a lot or a little? What kind of climate do you enjoy the most?*

SOCIAL STUDIES

LESSON 4.1

7   **DESCRIBE AND RESEARCH** Tell your student that the climate of a region refers to its average temperature and **precipitation.** Because of the seasons, in some parts of the country temperatures vary a great deal. For example, during January the average temperature in Chicago, Illinois, is around 20 degrees Fahrenheit, but in July the average temperature is around 85 degrees Fahrenheit. Have your student find the average high and low temperatures for each month of the year in his or her town or the closest large city. Ask your student to record the information in a chart in his or her notebook. This information can be found in an encyclopedia or on the Internet.

8   **RELATE** Explain that precipitation is falling water that can take the form of rain, snow, hail, or sleet. In places such as Seattle, Washington, where it rains a lot, the average precipitation for the whole year is much greater than the average precipitation in a dry climate such as that of Tempe, Arizona, where it rarely rains or snows. Have your student add the average precipitation in his or her town to the chart.

9   **DEFINE** Tell your student that the words *weather* and *climate* are related, but they don't have the same meaning. Weather is the condition of the air or atmosphere at a particular time and place. Climate has to do with the weather over a longer period of time. If the weather is going to be rainy for the next few days, you need to carry an umbrella or wear your raincoat. If you live in a colder climate, you need to own a heavy winter jacket. If you live in a warmer climate, your winter jacket may not need to be very thick and heavy. Weather affects our plans on a daily basis while climate affects our long-term plans. Ask your student, *What is the weather like today? What is the climate like in our part of the United States?*

10   **DISTRIBUTE AND IDENTIFY** Distribute Student Learning Page 1.A. Look at the climate map together with your student. Explain that this climate map shows the average temperature throughout the United States for the year 2002. Then direct your student to use the map to answer the questions on the page.

11   **COMPARE** Tell your student that because the geography and climate of the United States is so diverse, different types of animals and plants live and grow in different places. For example, palm trees grow in warmer climates such as Florida's but not in colder climates such as Alaska's. Lake Erie is filled with various kinds of fish, such as bluegills, while the Sonoran Desert in Arizona is home to the kangaroo rat. Ask your student to choose one specific area of the United States to learn more about. Have him or her use books from the library, encyclopedias, or the Internet to learn about the climate and the animals that live there.

SOCIAL STUDIES

LESSON 4.1

12 **RELATE** Illustrate the importance of our environment in our daily lives. Explain that geography and climate affect the kinds of clothes we wear, food we eat, and jobs we work. In Minnesota during the winter, people need to wear warm jackets, gloves, and boots to protect themselves from the cold air. In Georgia, the warm climate is good for growing peaches. On the coast of Maine close to the Atlantic Ocean, many people have jobs fishing for lobsters and other seafood. Ask, *During the winter, what type of clothes do people wear where you live?*

13 **LIST** Remind your student that he or she has learned a lot about the importance and diversity of our environment in the United States. Tell him or her that we need to help protect our environment. Some of the ways we can help protect our environment include planting a tree, recycling newspapers, turning off lights, and walking, riding, or taking a bus instead of driving a car. Challenge your student to create a list of five things people can do to help protect the environment. Then invite him or her to pick one of these things to do for at least one week.

Branching Out

TEACHING TIP

As you talk about the different climates throughout the United States, spend some time with your student watching the weather segment of the news or reading the weather section of the newspaper. Guide your student to note how the temperatures vary in different places in the United States.

CHECKING IN

You can assess your student's understanding of the diverse geography and climates in our country by asking him or her to describe how various parts of the United States are different from each other. [different landforms, climates, jobs, food, clothing]

FOR FURTHER READING

Atlas of Geology and Landforms (Watts Reference), by Cally Oldershaw (Franklin Watts, 2001).

Climate and Environment (21st Century Science), by Sergio D. Amico, ed. (World Almanac Education, 2002).

Global Warming: The Threat of Earth's Changing Climates, by Laurence Pringle (Seastar Publishing, 2001).

Read a Climate Map

Look at the climate map. Then answer the questions.

Average Temperature (°F)
January–December 2002

LEGEND

100
90
80
70
60
50
40
30
20
10
0
−10
−20
−30

1. What does this map tell you about? _____

2. Which colors represent warmer average temperatures on the map? _____

3. Which colors represent colder average temperatures on the map? _____

4. Name three states with the same average temperature. _____

_____

5. Describe the difference in the types of clothes people wear in North Dakota and Texas.

_____

_____

_____

What's Next? You Decide!

Now it's your turn to choose what to do next in the lesson.
Read the activities and decide which one you want to do—
you may want to try them both!

Be a Television Weatherperson

MATERIALS

- ❏ 1 large U.S. map
- ❏ 1 copy national newspaper
- ❏ 4 self-stick notes
- ❏ 1 videocassette recorder (optional)
- ❏ 1 videocassette tape (optional)

STEPS

- ❏ Watch a television weather report that shows the weather around the United States. Pay attention to how the weatherperson describes the weather.
- ❏ Look at the weather page in your newspaper. Write the temperatures or type of precipitation (rain, snow, sleet, hail) of four different places around the United States on the notes.
- ❏ Affix the notes to the places on a large map of the United States.
- ❏ Write a script for your weather report explaining what the weather is like in the four places.
- ❏ Practice your weather report using your map and any other charts you would like to create.
- ❏ Give your weather report to someone in your family. If you have a videocassette recorder, tape yourself and then play the tape for others.

Create a Mini Mountain Range

MATERIALS

- ❏ 1 shoebox
- ❏ construction paper
- ❏ clay
- ❏ colored pencils or markers
- ❏ 1 pair scissors
- ❏ tape

STEPS

Create your own model of a mountain range.

- ❏ Choose a mountain range in the United States. Find a picture of it in a book to use as a model.
- ❏ Use a shoebox as your background. Take the top off and stand it longways on its side.
- ❏ Use construction paper and colored pencils or markers to make the sky and the ground in the shoebox.
- ❏ Form the clay into mountains and place them in the shoebox.
- ❏ Display your model mountain range somewhere in your house where your family can see it.

Appreciating Our Country's Resources

Our survival depends on the resources of the land.

OBJECTIVE	BACKGROUND	MATERIALS
To help your student understand natural resources and the importance of conserving them for the future	The people in the United States are very fortunate. Our country has a rich variety of natural resources. In this lesson, your student will learn about natural resources in the United States and how to use them wisely.	▪ Student Learning Pages 2.A–2.B ▪ 1 U.S. road map

VOCABULARY

NATURAL RESOURCES things in the environment that people can use
CONSERVATION the careful use of our natural resources
RECYCLING changing a thing into something else so it can be used again
RENEWABLE RESOURCES resources that can re-create themselves over time
NONRENEWABLE RESOURCES resources that can be used up
FUEL a nonrenewable resource such as oil, natural gas, and coal used to make heat or energy

Let's Begin

1 **EXPLAIN** Explain that people use **natural resources** every day. An example is cutting down trees to build houses. Unfortunately, we know that some natural resources can be used up, so we need to try to preserve them as much as possible. Ask your student, *What are some things that could happen if we ran out of trees one day?* [we would have to find other materials to take the place of wood, air would be more polluted, less fruit]

2 **DISCUSS AND RESEARCH** Explain to your student that while some natural resources could be used up one day, some people have shown their support for **conservation,** or the careful use of resources. One way to do this is by **recycling** such things as plastic and glass. Some factories even recycle items by making them into other useful things. Have your student call your city hall and ask about your town's recycling program. Ask him or her to find out what items are recyclable [plastic, glass, paper] and how they are collected and processed.

Aluminum cans can be recycled and used again.

3 **EXPLAIN AND DISCUSS** Reveal that some natural resources are **renewable resources.** This means that they are able to re-create themselves over time. Renewable resources include forests, soil, and water. Forests can be renewed by planting new trees. Soil can be renewed when farmers take care to add special nutrients. Point out that even though these resources are renewable, they need time to re-create themselves. Ask your student, *How can water become renewed?* [rain renews water supply]

4 **EXPAND** Explain that there are also **nonrenewable resources.** These resources, such as oil and precious minerals, take thousands or millions of years to be created inside Earth. Minerals found inside Earth include silver, iron, and copper. We use many nonrenewable resources as **fuel.** Fuels include coal, oil, and natural gas. These fuels are for heat and energy. Ask your student, *What are some ways we could conserve gasoline and heat?* [walking or riding bikes instead of driving, carpooling, keeping heat lower when no one is home]

5 **RELATE** Tell your student that people are the most important resource. They do the work and use our natural resources to meet our needs. Have your student list reasons why people are an important resource. [farmers grow food, miners produce fuels, factory workers make goods] The best way to develop better human resources is education. This will help prepare people for the future. Ask, *How could education help a farmer?* [he or she could learn new ways to care for crops, keep the soil healthy, or provide improved nutrition for his or her animals]

6 **SHOW** Show your student a U.S. road map. Practice reading the map together. Have your student find the highways that stretch across the entire country. Ask, *What major highways are close to your town?* Take turns selecting different cities in the country and have your student find the most direct roads there from his or her town.

7 **DISTRIBUTE** Distribute Student Learning Page 2.A. Show your student a globe. Point out the lines of latitude, or parallels, and the lines of longitude, or meridians. Explain that these are imagined lines that help us measure distance.

FOR FURTHER READING

Soil (True Books: Natural Resources), by Christin Ditchfield (Scholastic Library Publishing, 2001).

Water (True Books: Natural Resources), by Christin Ditchfield (Scholastic Library Publishing, 2001).

Branching Out

TEACHING TIP

Ask your student to give a recycling presentation to his or her family, pointing out the household items that can be recycled and the importance of recycling.

CHECKING IN

To assess your student's understanding of our country's resources and their importance, have him or her list natural resources used at home.

Find Latitude and Longitude

Use a globe to answer the questions.

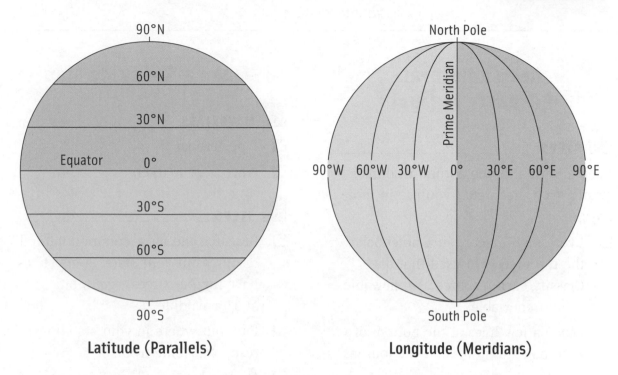

Latitude (Parallels)

Longitude (Meridians)

1. Find the prime meridian, or 0° longitude, on the globe. Name one country in Europe that is on the prime meridian. _____

2. What happens to the distance between the lines of longitude as they get closer to the North and South Poles? _____

3. Find the equator, or 0° latitude, on the globe. What large country in South America is located on the equator? _____

4. Find your state on the globe. What latitude line is closest to where you live? _____

5. What longitude line is closest to where you live? _____

What's Next? You Decide!

Now it's your turn to choose what to do next in the lesson. Read the activities and decide which one you want to do— you may want to try them both!

Keep a Natural Resource Journal

STEPS

Keep a journal of the natural resources (water, fruit, heat, etc.) you use in three days.

❏ Every night, record in a notebook the resources you used that day. Classify each resource as renewable or nonrenewable.

❏ Leave a few lines at the bottom of each page to fill in after the journal is done.

❏ After three days, look back at each page. At the bottom, write ways you could have used the natural resources in a better or less wasteful way.

❏ Share what you learned with an adult.

Make a Resource Map

MATERIALS

❏ 1 posterboard
❏ crayons or markers

STEPS

❏ Research the most common natural resources in your state. Some states have lumber (trees), gold, oil, and/or wildlife.

❏ Find out where in your state these resources come from.

❏ Draw a large outline of your state on the posterboard.

❏ Give your poster the title "Natural Resources of (name of your state)."

❏ Use crayons or markers to show the areas where each natural resource is found.

❏ You can draw pictures to represent natural resources.

❏ Once your poster is complete, share it with an adult. Then find a place to hang it in your home.

Understanding the Northeast

When you visit the Northeast, you might want to bring your hiking boots.

OBJECTIVE	BACKGROUND	MATERIALS
To help your student identify important features and people that have influenced the development of the Northeast region	The Northeast region is rich with American history. The features of the land, which include the Appalachian Mountains, have influenced the region's development. In this lesson, your student will learn about the environment, history, and people of the Northeastern United States.	<ul><li>Student Learning Pages 3.A–3.B</li><li>1 U.S. map</li><li>self-stick notes</li></ul>

VOCABULARY

GLACIERS large masses of ice that slowly move across land

ELEVATION the height of something

INDUSTRIAL REVOLUTION a major change in the U.S. economy due to the growth of industry

LONGHOUSES long, rectangular houses made from elm trees

LEAGUE a group of people who unite together for a common goal

SACHEMS council members

IMMIGRANTS people who leave their homeland to live in a new place

POPULATION the number of people who live in a place

URBAN a city environment

RURAL a country or farm environment

SUBURBS communities that lie just outside a city

Let's Begin

1   **EXPLAIN AND DISTRIBUTE** Explain to your student that the region you will focus on now is called the Northeast region. Show your student the map of the Northeast region on Student Learning Page 3.A and a map of the United States. Looking at the map, have your student identify which states make up the Northeast region by pointing them out and reading their names. [Delaware, Maryland, Pennsylvania, New York, Vermont, New Hampshire, New Jersey, Connecticut, Massachusetts, Maine, Rhode Island] Ask, *Why do you think this region is called the Northeast?* [because the states that make up this region are in the northeastern part of the United States]

The Iroquois lived in longhouses.

2 **INFORM** Ask, *From looking at the map, can you figure out what is the largest mountain chain in the Northeast region?* [the Appalachian Mountains, which are made up of smaller mountain groups such as the Green Mountains and the Allegheny Mountains] Tell your student that the Appalachian Mountains are one of the oldest mountain ranges in the whole world. Although they used to be very tall, they are much smaller now. Over time water, wind, and ice have caused them to slowly break down. Explain that for thousands of years large blocks of ice called **glaciers** moved very slowly over the mountains and wore them down. Ask, *What recreational activities do you think are popular in the mountains in the Northeast?* [hiking, skiing, camping]

3 **PRACTICE** Before having your student complete Student Learning Page 3.A, discuss the map and how to read it. Ask, *What information is this map showing us?* [the **elevation** of the Northeast] Ask, *What do you think elevation is? Here is a clue: think of what an "elevator" does.* [elevation is the height of something] Then have your student complete the page.

4 **EXPAND** Tell your student that the Northeast region has many rivers and waterfalls. This was very important to the growth of the region because the power produced by the running water made it possible for people to build mills, or factories. By using water-driven power, people could run machines and make things such as cloth from cotton at a much faster pace than people could at home by hand. This led to the **Industrial Revolution,** a time when products began being made using machines operated by people on assembly lines. Today factories use other sources of power in the form of electricity, but the Northeast continues to be an important manufacturing center in the United States. Ask your student, *What happened in the Northeast during the Industrial Revolution?* [machines powered by water replaced manual labor and industry grew quickly]

5 **EXPLAIN** Explain that the Iroquois and other Native American tribes had lived in the Northeast region for hundreds of years before European settlers arrived. They lived in villages and built **longhouses** for shelter that could be as large as 300 feet long! Show your student the picture of a longhouse. Many families lived together. The Iroquois and the other tribes (the Seneca, Cayuga, Onondaga, Mohawk, and Tuscarora) shared the region's rich natural resources by hunting deer, duck, and other animals; farming the soil; and fishing in the lakes and rivers. However, by the 1500s, the region became more and more crowded and the resources and land became less accessible. Ask your student, *What do you think happened between the Native American tribes?* [they began to fight for the resources]

6 **INTRODUCE** Introduce two great Native American leaders, Deganawida of the Huron tribe and Hiawatha of the Mohawk tribe. They realized that if their tribes were going to survive, they had to stop fighting. In fact, they wanted the tribes to unite. Together they began the Iroquois **League,** a union of six groups whose goal was peace and to help each other. It was ruled by a Grand Council that was made up of **sachems,** or council members from each tribe. Sachems were Native American men who were chosen by respected Native American women. Ask, *How is this selection process different from the way Americans elect a president?* [the U.S. president has to campaign and all the people vote; the sachems were chosen by the elder women of the tribe]

7   **EXPAND AND BRAINSTORM** Explain that the Iroquois League still exists today. About 60,000 Iroquois live in the Northeast and the Grand Council meets once a year to vote on decisions. Ask, *Do you think the Iroquois League was a success?* [yes, they kept the peace between the tribes for hundreds of years and still exist today, 400 years later] Ask your student to brainstorm ideas that could help his or her family become more united and peaceful. Have your student write his or her ideas in a notebook and present them to the family at a "Grand Council" meeting.

8   **INTRODUCE** Remind your student that the United States became a country in 1776. Point out that the Declaration of Independence was signed in the Northeast in Philadelphia, Pennsylvania. Important historical leaders such as Benjamin Franklin and George Washington were there. Explain that much of the history of the founding of the United States can be traced to the Northeast. The first national capital was Philadelphia. The current capital is Washington, D.C. Both are in the Northeast. Have your student find Philadelphia and Washington, D.C. on the map.

9   **RELATE** Point out that America was a new country that offered people a chance for a different life. When the United States was a new country, many people came to live here from European countries, such as Ireland, Poland, Russia, Italy, and Greece. People also came from China and Japan. Between 1890 and 1914, more than 12 million people moved to America! Explain that people who leave their home country and move to another country are called **immigrants.** Ask, *What do you think it would have been like to leave your home country and move so far away?* Have your student write a journal entry about his or her feelings, hopes, and fears.

10   **LOCATE** Share with your student that the boat ride across the Atlantic Ocean from Europe to the United States took about three weeks. Although the immigrants moved to many different cities, they all had to stop at Ellis Island first. Ellis Island is located about a mile off the coast of New York City. Ask, *Can you find Ellis Island on the map?*

DID YOU KNOW?

Ellis Island closed in 1954 and is now a museum. Today, the majority of new immigrants coming to the United States are from Mexico and Central and South America.

11 **EXPAND** Tell your student that Ellis Island was like an admission office for new immigrants. Some immigrants had a difficult time at Ellis Island. They were tagged with numbers and shown to the registry room. A doctor examined them, and if they weren't healthy they were sent home. After being questioned by an officer, an immigrant was finally able to enter the country. Ask your student, *Where were most of the first immigrants from?* [European countries, China, Japan] *Where was the first place the European immigrants stopped?* [Ellis Island]

12 **EXPLAIN AND DISCUSS** Explain that as more and more immigrants moved to America, the **population** rose. Many people found work in factories in **urban** areas. Some immigrants wanted to farm, so they lived in **rural** areas. Ask, *What are some differences between life in urban areas and life in rural areas?* [in urban areas people live close together, there's public transportation, and people work in factories or businesses; in rural areas people live far apart and work on farms or in small towns]

13 **EXPAND** Point out that by 1920 people began moving to the **suburbs** because they wanted more space, bigger houses, yards, and so on; yet they also wanted to be able to work in the city. Transportation had improved so much that people could live farther away from where they worked. Ask, *What are some types of transportation that help people travel quickly between home and work?* [cars, buses, trains, subways]

Branching Out

TEACHING TIP

Have your student consider whether any of the immigrants who came through Ellis Island might have been his or her ancestors. Talk about how his or her ancestors got here and where they settled.

FOR FURTHER READING

A Century of Immigration, by Christopher Collier (Benchmark Books, 2000).

The Color of Home, by Mary Hoffman (Phyllis Fogelman Books, 2002).

Thomas in Danger, by Bonnie Pryor (Morrow Junior Books, 1999).

CHECKING IN

You can assess your student's learning by asking him or her for a summary of the important features and people of the Northeast. Write the names of important features and people on sticky notes. Without looking at the notes, have your student stick the paper onto his or her head so that you can see the word but your student can't. Your student will then ask yes or no questions until he or she figures out what is written on the paper.

Read Elevation Maps

Look at the map. Then answer the questions.

Elevation of the Northeast

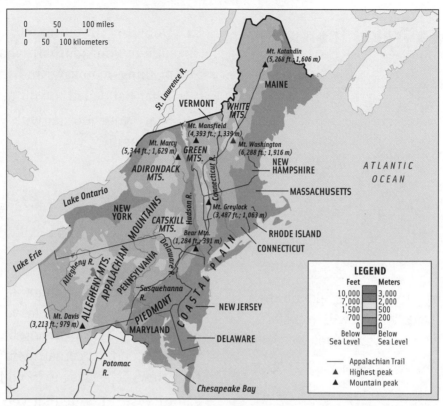

1. What is the elevation of the land in Connecticut? _____

2. Which mountain peak is higher, Mt. Marcy or Mt. Washington? _____

3. Which state does not include part of the Appalachian Trail: New York, Delaware, or New Hampshire? _____

4. Which two states have elevations between zero and 700 feet above sea level?

_____

5. If you were a farmer, do you think it would be better to live in the western or eastern part of the Northeast region? Why? _____

_____

What's Next? You Decide!

Now it's your turn to choose what to do next in the lesson. Read the activities and decide which one you want to do—you may want to try them both!

Create a Travel Journal

MATERIALS

- ❑ white paper
- ❑ markers
- ❑ old magazines
- ❑ glue
- ❑ 1 hole puncher
- ❑ string or yarn

STEPS

Suppose you are planning a hike on the Appalachian Trail. Where will you start? How far will you go? What will you see?

- ❑ Decide how many days your hike will be.
- ❑ Make a small journal with one page for each day, plus one more for the book cover.
- ❑ Use a hole punch and string or yarn to tie the pages together into a book.
- ❑ Decorate the cover of your journal.
- ❑ Find a library book or Internet site that has information about hikes on the Appalachian Trail. Read a few stories about people who have hiked there.
- ❑ Then make up your own story in your journal. On each page write the date, where you started the day, where you ended the day, and how many miles you traveled. Also write about the weather.
- ❑ Draw (or cut out of old magazines to glue in your journal) what animals or things you saw, and write about what happened to you that day.
- ❑ Share your journal with your friends and family.

Put on a Play

STEPS

Suppose you're a member of the Iroquois League. Write a play about an issue you're facing. For example, you may be experiencing a drought and have little water or food, or perhaps you're looking for a new, faster way to build longhouses.

- ❑ Choose an issue that you and the rest of the Iroquois League are facing. It could be serious, funny, or a little of both. You decide!
- ❑ Choose characters who will be in your play. For example, you could choose a whole family or tribe or just a few characters.
- ❑ Decide what your characters will say and do.
- ❑ Don't forget about costumes and props. Ask an adult to help you find clothing and items around the house for your play.
- ❑ Write your play and invite friends and family to be in it with you.
- ❑ Then put on your play!

Learning About the Southeast

The people are the true heart of a country.

OBJECTIVE	BACKGROUND	MATERIALS
To help your student learn more about the Southeast region of the United States	The Southeast region of the United States has a rich history. The land and the people of the Southeast are important to our entire country. In this lesson, your student will learn about the environment, people, and heritage of the Southeast.	■ Student Learning Pages 4.A–4.B ■ 1 copy national newspaper ■ markers or colored pencils ■ 1 globe ■ 1 U.S. map

VOCABULARY

WETLANDS subtropical swamp areas in low, flat places along the coast of a body of water

EQUATOR an imaginary line that goes around Earth halfway between the North Pole and the South Pole

CORAL REEFS colorful underwater gardens formed by the skeletons of tiny sea animals

SEGREGATION the separation of groups of people

Let's Begin

1   **INTRODUCE** Explain to your student that he or she will be learning more about the Southeast region of the United States. Explain that the Southeast region is made up of 12 states: Arkansas, Louisiana, Kentucky, Tennessee, Mississippi, Alabama, Florida, Georgia, South Carolina, North Carolina, Virginia, and West Virginia. Show your student a map of the United States, and identify the location of each of these states on the map. Then distribute Student Learning Page 4.A. Ask your student to label each of the 12 states by writing its name and then highlight them as a group by drawing an outline around them with a marker or colored pencil.

2   **LABEL** Tell your student that the Southeast is a region with many different kinds of landforms. The landforms of the Southeast include mountains, **wetlands,** and rivers. Have your student tell you what he or she knows about mountains and rivers. Explain that wetlands are subtropical swamp areas in low, flat places along the coast of a body of water. Help your student find the Appalachian Mountains, the wetlands (called the Everglades)

in Florida, and the Coastal Plain (along the Atlantic coast) on the map. Then have your student use markers or colored pencils to label these landforms on the map on Student Learning Page 4.A.

3 **EXPAND** Explain to your student that another important landform found in the Southeast is rivers. Rivers are streams of water that flow into larger rivers, lakes, or oceans. The majority of the rivers in the Southeast begin in the Appalachian Mountains. These rivers flow into the Atlantic Ocean, the Gulf of Mexico, and the Mississippi River. The rivers are important to the people, animals, and plants that live in the Southeast. The rivers allow people to travel and provide good soil for growing crops. On the map of the United States, have your student locate three rivers in the Southeast.

4 **EXPLAIN** Tell your student that part of the Mississippi River is in the Southeast. It's the second largest river in the United States. It takes its name from the Native Americans who called the mighty river *Misi Sipi*, which means "big water." The Mississippi River is an important route for transportation and trade. Farmers from the north can transport their crops on boats traveling on the Mississippi. Have your student find the Mississippi River on the map of the United States and follow it from its starting point in Minnesota down to its ending point in Louisiana at the Gulf of Mexico. Then have him or her use a blue pencil or marker to draw and label the Mississippi River on the map on Student Learning Page 4.A.

5 **INVESTIGATE** Show your student the weather section of a national newspaper. Ask, *How would you describe the temperatures in the Southeast?* [warm or hot] Explain that the climate in the Southeast is warm with moderate amounts of precipitation. Show your student a globe, and guide him or her to notice the location of the United States in relation to the **equator.** Explain that the equator is an imaginary line around Earth that is halfway between the North Pole and the South Pole. Have your student pick one state that is closer to the equator and one state that is farther away from the equator. Then have your student look at the weather page to find the temperatures in these two states. Ask, *Which state has warmer temperatures?* [the state closer to the equator has warmer temperatures]

6 **EXPAND** Explain that agriculture is the growing of crops and the raising of animals. Agriculture is a major source of jobs in the Southeast. The warm temperatures and moderate level of precipitation make the Southeast a good place to grow crops and raise animals. Tobacco, rice, peanuts, beans, peas, and oranges are all crops that are grown in the Southeast. Have your student look around the kitchen for products from these crops.

7 **RELATE** Tell your student that many people like to travel to the Southeast. Ask, *Why do you think people want to travel to the*

?

DID YOU KNOW?

The busiest port in the country is the Port of South Louisiana, which is near the mouth of the Mississippi River. About 200 million tons of cargo pass through the port each year.

The Mississippi River is 2,340 miles in length and extends from Minnesota to the Gulf of Mexico.

Southeast? [because of the warm climate and beaches] Tourism, the business of travel for fun and pleasure, is an important source of jobs in many parts of the Southeast. In the winter months, many people from northern states travel to the Southeast for a break from the cold weather. Have your student make a list of some fun things to do on vacation in the Southeast. [fishing, swimming, boating, golfing]

8 **ASK** Tell your student that one special place tourists like to travel to is the **coral reefs** of Florida. Coral reefs are colorful underwater gardens of hard stony substances. Coral is made from the skeletons of tiny sea animals. The coral reefs offer shelter and food to many underwater plants and animals. Water pollution and damage from divers and boats can destroy the coral reefs. Our government has made laws to protect the reefs. Ask, *Why do you think it is important to protect the coral reefs?* [they are fragile and can be damaged easily; many animals and plants depend on them to survive]

DID YOU KNOW?

The word *Arkansas* means "south wind" in Algonquin. It was the name for the Quapaw Native Americans.

9 **DISCUSS** Explain to your student that there are people from the Southeast who are important to the history of the United States. One of these individuals is Dr. Martin Luther King Jr. Dr. King was a minister in Atlanta, Georgia. He recognized that all people, regardless of color, religion, race, or gender, deserved the same rights. He organized peaceful protests and helped bring change to the United States. Dr. King gave a famous speech in which he stated his dream. Have your student research Dr. King's life and the famous "I Have a Dream" speech. Read and discuss the speech together.

10 **EXPAND** Point out that one of the things Dr. King fought against was **segregation.** Segregation occurs when a certain group of people is kept apart from another group of people by law and may receive unequal treatment. In the United States, segregation occurred when African-Americans were prevented from using the same facilities—such as schools, stores, restaurants, or drinking fountains—as white Americans. The Civil Rights Movement is the name given to the work done to make sure that all people are treated equally under the law. Have your student find out more about the history of segregation and the Civil Rights Movement at the library or on the Internet.

11 **EXPLAIN** Tell your student that an important group in the history of the Southeast is the Native American Cherokee. The Cherokee settled in the area that is now Georgia, Tennessee, North Carolina, and Alabama. Explain that the government forced many Cherokee and other Native Americans to leave their homes in the 1830s to make room for white settlers. The Cherokee were made to travel hundreds of miles in harsh conditions. More than 4,000 people died on the journey. This journey is known as the Trail of Tears. Invite your student to read about the Trail of Tears in books or on the Internet. Ask, *Where were the Cherokee forced to go?* [west to Arkansas and Oklahoma]

DID YOU KNOW?

The Cherokee called themselves *Aniyunwiya,* which means "first people."

12 **TELL** Tell your student that one important Cherokee was Sequoyah. Sequoyah loved listening to stories in his Cherokee language. As he got older, he saw that the white people wrote their stories down on paper. The Cherokee language was only spoken, not written, and Sequoyah worried that the history and the stories he loved so much would be lost. So between 1809 and 1821 Sequoyah developed an alphabet with 86 symbols to record the Cherokee language. The alphabet is still used by the Cherokee today. Ask, *How could an alphabet help preserve the history and culture of the Cherokee?* [the alphabet allowed the Cherokee language to be written so that their stories and history could be recorded and saved]

Branching Out

TEACHING TIP

You can emphasize the importance of the written word when you read a story or book with your student. Explain that by having the story written down, it is preserved for many people to read. It was important to Sequoyah and to the Cherokee people to ensure that their history and stories were recorded for future generations.

CHECKING IN

Invite your student to review the map that he or she created on Student Learning Page 4.A. Ask your student to tell you about the different landforms and states he or she has marked on the map. Ask your student to tell about the crops that are grown in the Southeast and the region's climate.

FOR FURTHER READING

Cherokee Sister, by Debbie Dadey (Random House Children's, 2001).

Christy: The Young Reader's Edition, by Anna Wilson Fishel and Catherine Marshall (Chosen Books Publishing Company, 2001).

Mark Twain and the Queens of the Mississippi, by Cheryl Harness (Simon and Schuster, 1998).

Mississippi River: A Journey Down the Father of Waters, by Peter Lourie (Boyds Mills Press, 2000).

Map the Southeast

Look at the map. Label the states and landforms of the Southeast.

What's Next? You Decide!

Now it's your turn to choose what to do next in the lesson. Read the activities and decide which one you want to do—you may want to try them both!

Plan a Trip to the Southeast

MATERIALS

- ❏ 2–3 envelopes
- ❏ 2–3 first-class stamps

STEPS

Plan a trip to see some of the important sites in the Southeast! Would you like to visit the Everglades in Florida, the Appalachian Mountains, the Coastal Plains along the Atlantic Ocean?

- ❏ Choose two or three states in the Southeast that you would like to visit.
- ❏ Use library books or the Internet to find the addresses of tourism offices in those states.
- ❏ Write letters asking the tourism offices to send you some information about things to do in their state. Remember to include your address in the letter so the offices know where to send the information.
- ❏ Together with an adult, mail your letters.
- ❏ Suppose that you will be traveling the Southeast for a week. Make a list of some fun and interesting things you would like to do each day. Use the information from the tourism offices to plan your trip.

Make a Kentucky Treat

MATERIALS

- ❏ 1 tablespoon vegetable oil
- ❏ 5 cups miniature marshmallows
- ❏ $\frac{1}{2}$ cup butter
- ❏ $\frac{1}{2}$ cup popping corn
- ❏ 1 greased 9-by-12-inch baking dish
- ❏ 1 4-quart saucepan with lid

STEPS

Corn used for popping grows in Kentucky. Ask an adult to help you make popcorn balls.

- ❏ Pour vegetable oil into the saucepan and heat on high.
- ❏ When the oil is hot, add popping corn and cover with a lid. Move pan constantly.
- ❏ When the popcorn is finished popping, pour the popcorn into the greased dish.
- ❏ Melt the butter on low heat and stir until melted.
- ❏ Add marshmallows to the butter and stir until melted.
- ❏ Pour the marshmallow mixture over the popcorn and mix with a spoon. Make sure all the popcorn is covered with the marshmallows.
- ❏ When the popcorn is cool enough to touch, use your hands to form the popcorn into balls.

Studying the Plains of the Midwest

The Plains states lie at the heart of America.

OBJECTIVE	BACKGROUND	MATERIALS
To help your student learn about the area of the United States called the Plains	The Midwest region of the United States consists of an area called the Interior Plains. In this lesson, your student will learn that this area is made up of very unique land, people, and history.	■ Student Learning Pages 5.A–5.B ■ 1 copy Venn Diagram, page 355 ■ 1 agricultural map

VOCABULARY

PLAINS areas of flat land

LIVESTOCK animals that are raised on a farm, such as cattle, pigs, and chickens

DROUGHT a period of little or no rain

FRONTIER the edge of a settled area

PIONEERS the people who are the first to settle a new land

LAKOTA a Native American group who lived in the Midwest region

TEEPEES cone-shaped dwellings made of poles and animal hides

RESERVATION land set aside by the government for Native Americans

Let's Begin

1 **EXPLAIN** Explain that the Midwest can be divided into different groups of states. The states around the Great Lakes are called the Great Lakes states. The other states in this area are called the Plains states. Most of the landforms that make up the Midwest are **plains.** Ask, *What are plains?* [areas of flat land]

2 **COMPARE** Explain that the land between the Appalachian Mountains and the Rocky Mountains is called the Interior Plains. This land is divided into two parts: the Central Plains in the eastern part and the Great Plains in the western part. The Central Plains are low, but this area's land rises slowly west of the Mississippi River. The Great Plains are much higher and reach as high as 5,000 feet at their western edge. The Great Plains mainly consist of dry grassland with few trees. Distribute a copy of the Venn Diagram found on page 355. Have your

SOCIAL STUDIES

LESSON 4.5

?

DID YOU KNOW?

Long ago, when most people lived near the east coast, any land west of the Appalachian Mountains was called the West. Only later, when that land was settled, did people consider land between the Appalachians and the Rocky Mountains the Middle West, or as most people call it today, the Midwest. The land west of the Rockies became known as the West.

student compare the Central Plains and the Great Plains. You may lead your student to reference books and the Internet to extend this activity and provide your student with more background.

3 SUMMARIZE Tell your student that the Plains are an important agricultural center in the United States. The Plains states have very fertile soil because many wild plants used to grow there. The flatness of the land also makes it great for farming. The main crop of the Central Plains is corn. The major crop of the Great Plains is wheat, which grows best in dry climates. The Plains also are good for raising **livestock.** Livestock animals graze on the grass in the dry areas. Have your student summarize how and why the resources of the Plains are important to the country.

4 EXPLAIN Explain that farmers often face difficulties in their work. First, they can have a short growing season. Farmers must be sure to plant only when they know there will be no frost. Next, they may encounter a **drought,** which could destroy crops. Finally, dangerous tornadoes moving at high speeds can tear up land and crops. Ask, *What are three problems farmers in the Midwest might face?* [cold weather, drought, tornadoes]

5 WRITE Tell your student that in the 1800s people started to move west of the Appalachian Mountains in search of new land. This area was called the **frontier.** Native Americans lived on the frontier hundreds of years before, however. Even though the Native Americans lived there, traders founded trading posts. Many American **pioneers** decided to follow and settle the new land. Have your student write a journal entry describing how he or she would feel living as a Native American during the 1800s.

6 RELATE Explain that many pioneer families built shelters called cabins. Settlers also cleared the land for planting crops. They had to make almost everything they needed to survive. This included tools, furniture, clothing, and food. Crops were planted in grooves dug slowly into the ground by hand. In the 1830s, a blacksmith named John Deere invented a machine used for digging the ground. Ask, *Can you give two reasons why John Deere's invention was important to the settlers?* [it saved time and dug large areas of land more easily]

7 WRITE Tell your student that the Midwest region was home to many groups of Native Americans, including the **Lakota.** Traveling was slow, but by the 1700s Europeans had moved to North America and brought horses. Soon Native Americans learned to catch stray horses. Have your student suppose that he or she is from the Lakota tribe. Invite your student to draw three pictures that show how having horses changed life for the Lakota people.

270   *Making the Grade: Everything Your 4th Grader Needs to Know*

8 **EXPAND** Tell your student that the Lakota moved often and built temporary homes called **teepees.** The group moved to follow buffalo herds. Point out the picture of the buffalo. Invite your student to notice its sturdy frame and thick coat. Tell your student that buffaloes were an important part of Lakota daily life. They were used to make food, clothes, teepees, spoons, headdresses, ropes, arrowheads, and needles. Their tails were even used to swat flies!

The buffalo was integral to the Native Americans of the Midwest.

9 **EXPLAIN** Explain to your student that settlers began killing buffaloes as they moved to the Lakota land. By 1885, there were very few buffalo left in the Midwest region and the Lakota found it difficult to survive. The Native Americans began fighting the settlers. The government forced the Lakota onto a **reservation.** Most of the Lakota were very angry about this because they were not free to travel and were dependent on the government for food. The Lakota were also treated unfairly by many government workers. Ask, *Why do you think the government put the Lakota on a reservation?* [to stop the fighting; to get them out of the settlers' way]

10 **DISCUSS** Tell your student that in 1874 gold was found in the Black Hills, an area that was very important to the Lakota. Soon settlers traveled to the Black Hills in search of gold. The Lakota began fighting these settlers. They, along with their leader, Sitting Bull, refused to give the Black Hills to the government. Finally, in May 1877 the Lakota surrendered and moved to the reservation where they lived unhappily and under difficult conditions. Today, more than 60,000 Lakota live on reservations or in cities in the Midwest. Ask, *Do you think the Lakota had good reasons to fight? Explain.* [their land was stolen; they were forced to live in one place; the government treated them unfairly; they could not live as they used to]

11 **APPLY** Distribute Student Learning Page 5.A. Invite your student to reinforce what he or she has learned in this lesson so far.

12 **EXPLAIN** Explain to your student that agriculture is still very much a part of life in the Midwest today. However, farming has changed greatly. Today, computers and improved machines are used for many jobs. Machines such as combines help cut and thresh wheat as well as remove grain from the stalk. Computers help farmers keep track of profits and expenses. Although farming has changed, farmers still worry that droughts or storms will destroy their crops just as they did years ago. Ask, *How has farming changed?* [improved machines make is easier to harvest crops; computers can be used to manage money]

13 **ANALYZE** Tell your student that there are many types of maps. An agricultural map generally shows important farming areas and the crops that are grown there. Find an agricultural map of the Midwest or of the entire United States. Look in an

encyclopedia or search for one on the Internet. Invite your student to identify major crops grown in different areas of the region. Be sure your student understands how symbols on the map legend correspond to the areas on the map.

14 **CONNECT** Point out some uses of natural resources that come from the Midwest to help your student make real-world connections. For example, identify some products used at home that contain wheat and/or corn. If there are meat eaters in your household, point out that much of the livestock from the meat industry is raised in the Midwest.

15 **EXPLORE** As your student shows interest in the Midwest, direct him or her to Lesson 1.1 to read *Little House on the Prairie* by Laura Ingalls Wilder. Ask your student how he or she thinks living in the Midwest in the 1800s would compare to living there now. Discuss.

Branching Out

TEACHING TIP

Your library may have videos available showing the Midwest to give your student a fuller picture of the area's characteristics.

CHECKING IN

To assess your student's understanding of the lesson, have your student compare the Interior Plains to another region of the United States that he or she has studied or visited. Identifying similarities and differences often builds context in which your student can apply what he or she has learned.

FOR FURTHER READING

A Blossom from a Barnyard, by Judith Lynn Sanson (iUniverse.com, 2001).

The Lakota Sioux (True Books: American Indians), by Andrew Santella (Children's Press, 2000).

You Wouldn't Want to Be an American Pioneer!: A Wilderness You'd Rather Not Tame (You Wouldn't Want to . . .), by Jacqueline Morley and David Salariya (Franklin Watts, Inc., 2002).

Complete a Vocabulary Crossword

Read the crossword puzzle clues. Then complete the puzzle to see how well you know the vocabulary words.

Across

1. land set aside for Native Americans
2. the edge of unsettled land
3. flat land

Down

1. lived in the Midwest before pioneers
2. settles new land

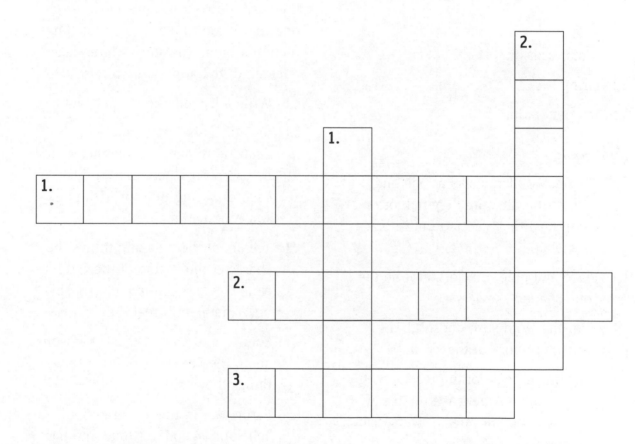

Now suppose you're a Lakota Native American. You're about to move to a reservation. In your notebook, write a letter to a friend describing your experiences. Use as many of the vocabulary words in your letter as you can!

SOCIAL STUDIES
5.B

What's Next? You Decide!

Now it's your turn to choose what to do next in the lesson.
Read the activities and decide which one you want to do—
you may want to try them both!

Build a Teepee

MATERIALS

- ❏ 8 wooden meat skewers
- ❏ 1 piece solid-colored cloth
- ❏ glue
- ❏ 1 pair scissors
- ❏ string
- ❏ tempera paint

STEPS

- ❏ Tie the wooden sticks at one end with string. Be sure they're loose enough so they can fan out into a cone shape!

- ❏ Place and glue the cloth around the cone-shaped skewers.

- ❏ Trim the cloth so it doesn't hang past the bottom of the skewers.

- ❏ Paint the outside of the teepee with things Native Americans often saw and used (buffalo, trees, rivers, fish, and so on).

Write a Lakota Legend

STEPS

Many Native Americans have an interesting oral tradition. This means they pass down the same stories from one generation to another by retelling them out loud. The stories often teach a lesson or tell about a culture's history.

- ❏ Write a legend about the Lakota.

- ❏ Include a character who does amazing things. The character may be based on a person from real life, such as Sitting Bull, or it can be someone fictional.

- ❏ Tell about the amazing things the character did. Some of these things can be events that could probably never happen in real life.

- ❏ Your legend should teach a lesson about the Lakota people and the things they valued.

- ❏ Participate in the oral tradition. Tell your legend out loud and pass it down!

- ❏ When telling your legend aloud, be sure to use hand gestures and facial expressions.

Revealing the Southwest

Get ready to visit the environment and cultures that have influenced the Southwest. You might need some sunglasses!

OBJECTIVE	BACKGROUND	MATERIALS
To help your student study the environment and people of the Southwest region	Many people connect the desert to their images of the Southwest region. However, this diverse area of the United States has a variety of landforms, including vast plains, spectacular canyons, and colorful plateaus. Its variety is also reflected in its heritage, which includes a blend of Native American, Mexican, and Spanish cultures. In this lesson, your student will learn about the land and people of the Southwest region.	■ Student Learning Pages 6.A–6.B ■ 1 U.S. map ■ 1 globe or world map

VOCABULARY

PLAINS areas of flatland

PLATEAUS raised areas of flatland with steep sides

MESAS raised areas of flatland; are smaller than plateaus

CANYONS deep, narrow valleys with steep sides

EROSION the wearing away of rock and soil from wind, water, or ice

DESERT an area that receives very little rainfall and is dry and hot

DROUGHT a period of little or no rain

AQUEDUCTS pipes that connect large bodies of water to other places

AQUIFERS water trapped between layers of rock under Earth's surface

RESERVATIONS land set aside by the government for Native Americans

HOGANS houses made from stacking short logs

MISSIONS settlements where people learn about the Christian religion

Let's Begin

1 **DISCUSS** Tell your student that he or she is going to learn about the Southwest region. With your finger, circle this region on a map of the United States. Ask your student to name at least one state that is in the Southwest region. [Texas, Oklahoma, Arizona, or New Mexico]

2 **EXPLAIN** Point out to your student that even though the Southwest covers a large amount of land, it has the smallest number of states compared to other regions. Much of the land in

The Southwest is home to the
Grand Canyon.

DID YOU KNOW?

Did you know that Grand
Canyon National Park is
bigger than the state of
Rhode Island? Wow, that
is grand!

Oklahoma and Texas is made up of **plains,** which are areas of
flatland. Then point out the Rocky Mountains on the map. Tell
your student that these mountains stretch across New Mexico
and Arizona. The Rocky Mountains have peaks, **plateaus,** and
mesas. Explain to your student that plateaus are raised areas
of flatland with steep sides. Mesas are similar to plateaus, but
they are smaller. Ask your student to compare a plateau to a
mountain or plain.

3 Tell your student that the Grand Canyon is another important
landform in the Southwest. It runs through 217 miles of Arizona.
Explain to your student that **canyons** are deep, narrow valleys
with steep sides. Parts of the Grand Canyon are a mile deep and
18 miles wide. Then show your student the picture of the Grand
Canyon. Invite him or her to say three words that describe the
Grand Canyon.

4 **EXPAND** Tell your student that the Grand Canyon is made up
of layers of rock. The bottom layers are more than a billion years
old! At the bottom of the canyon is the Colorado River. This river
has been flowing from the Rocky Mountains for millions of years
and has caused the walls of the canyon to wear away over time.
This wearing away of rock is called **erosion;** it is the reason why
the Grand Canyon is so deep. Tell your student that many people
today enjoy Grand Canyon National Park by hiking, riding mules
on trails, rafting on the Colorado River, or simply looking at the
beautiful landforms! Ask, *Why do you think many people like
exploring the Grand Canyon?*

5 **PRACTICE** Distribute Student Learning Page 6.A to your
student. Read the directions together and make sure your student
understands how to read the elevation map. Review that elevation
is the height of land above sea level. Point out the areas on the
map that your student studied in the lesson, such as the Rocky
Mountains. Then have your student complete the worksheet.

6 **DISCUSS** Tell your student that much of the Southwest is
desert, so it has a hot and dry climate. The eastern parts of
Oklahoma and Texas get enough rain to grow crops, but water
must still be used carefully. When it doesn't rain for a long
time, a **drought** can occur. Droughts can cause serious problems
because they can hurt crops. Ask your student to share what
can happen when a drought hurts crops.

7 **EXAMINE** Tell your student that one way to get water in the
Southwest is to build dams that trap river water. **Aqueducts** are
then used to carry the trapped water to farms and other places
that need it. Tell your student that many people in the Southwest
also get their water from layers of underground rock called
aquifers. Aquifers are being used more frequently as the
population of the Southwest grows. Ask your student to share
his or her ideas on what could happen if the aquifers are used
too much.

INTRODUCE Explain that Native Americans have lived in the Southwest region for thousands of years. Tell your student that many Native Americans today live on **reservations,** land that the government has set aside for them. Now direct your student to the map below that shows reservations in the Southwest. Ask, *Which reservation is in northeast Arizona and northwest New Mexico?* [the Navajo reservation]

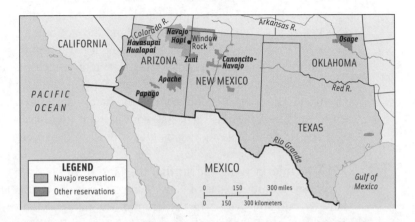

9 **EXPLAIN** Tell your student that many people believe the Navajo moved to the Southwest from Canada. Many years ago, they hunted animals and grew maize, or corn, for food. Next, show your student the location of Spain on a globe or world map. Tell him or her that when Spanish settlers came to the region in the 1500s they introduced the Navajo to sheep and horses. As a result, many Navajo began herding these animals. Say, *Sheep supplied the Navajo with two very important things. Can you think of what these things were?* [wool to make clothes and meat for food]

10 **DESCRIBE** Tell your student that the Navajo lived in houses called **hogans.** These houses were made out of short, stacked logs. Navajo girls and boys had many chores to do that began early in the morning. Girls learned how to weave colorful blankets, clothing, and moccasins (shoes). Boys protected and guarded the village while the older men were away. The Navajo had the freedom to travel and hunt wherever they wanted. However, by the 1600s more Spanish settlers came to the Southwest. Ask, *What do you think happened as more settlers from other countries came to the Southwest?* [the Navajo lost some of their land]

ENRICH THE EXPERIENCE

Weaving is a fun activity that you may want to try with your student. You can purchase kits at craft stores or toy stores and create your own designs.

11 **COMPARE** Explain that as the Spaniards settled more of the land they tried to teach the Native Americans their Christian religion. To accomplish this goal, the Spaniards built settlements called **missions.** The missions included farmland, small houses, and a church. At a mission, the Native Americans learned about Christianity. They also worked for the Spaniards in exchange for food and housing. Many of the Native Americans were treated badly at the missions. They were forced to work hard and to become Christians. However, some of the mission priests were kind to the Native Americans. For example, a Spanish priest named Eusebio Francisco Kino helped the Native Americans

learn how to farm better. He also taught them how to raise cattle and new crops. Challenge your student to compare life on a mission to life on a reservation.

12 **DISCUSS** Tell your students that American settlers moved west in the 1800s as the United States claimed more of the land of the Southwest region. In 1855, the U.S. government decided to move the Navajo to a reservation. Many of the Navajo refused to move from the land because they had lived there for generations. However, the U.S. government said the land did not belong to the Native Americans anymore. This disagreement led to fighting between the Navajo and the government. A man named Manuelito led the Navajo, while the government sent Kit Carson to lead the U.S. Army. The Navajo eventually lost the battle, and they were sent to the reservation in 1868. Ask your student to describe how he or she thinks the Navajo felt as they moved to the reservation.

13 **EXPLAIN** Inform your student that the land of the Navajo reservation includes parts of New Mexico, Arizona, and Utah. Many Navajo still live on this reservation, which is often called *Dinetah*. Its land is about the size of the state of West Virginia. It has many natural resources, such as oil and minerals. Many of the Navajo who live there still follow some of their Native American traditions, while others have a more modern lifestyle. Some people live in modern homes, while others live in hogans. Some Navajos still herd sheep and cattle, while others have learned technical skills.

14 **CONCLUDE** Tell your student that the number of people living in the Southwest has grown greatly. Although people started moving to the Southwest in the 1800s, many people did not want to live in the region because of the hot climate. However, after the automobile and air conditioner were invented, the Southwest's population grew quickly. Some big cities in the region are Phoenix, Dallas, and Houston. These cities have many businesses, especially technology companies. Ask your student to name some reasons why people would want to move to the Southwest.

Branching Out

TEACHING TIP

Help your student make real-world connections to the lesson. If possible, have pictures and artifacts available for your student to observe.

CHECKING IN

To assess your student's understanding of the lesson, have your student compare and contrast the Southwest to another region he or she has studied.

?

DID YOU KNOW?

Did you know that many astronomers work in the Southwest? The largest solar telescope in the world is found in Kitt Peak, Arizona. It is 36 feet long! Now that's a "stellar" fact!

FOR FURTHER READING

Brighty of the Grand Canyon, by Marguerite Henry and Wesley Dennis, ill. (Aladdin Paperbacks, 2001).

The Girl Who Chased Away Sorrow, by Ann Warren Turner (Scholastic, Inc., 1998).

Navajo Summer, by Jennifer Dewey (Boyds Mill Press, 1998).

That's Good! That's Bad! in the Grand Canyon, by Margery Cuyler (Henry Holt, 2002).

Look How High!

Look at the elevation map. Then answer the questions.

Elevation is how high land is above sea level. Sea level is always at zero feet (or zero meters). A hill that is 200 feet high has an elevation of 200 feet. That means the hill is 200 feet above the level of the sea.

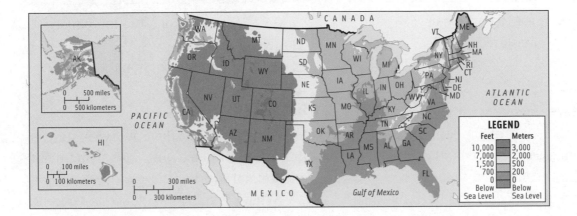

1. Name three states that have land with an elevation of 10,000 feet or higher.

   _____

2. Which part of the United States do you think is best for farming?

   _____

3. Which mountains are higher, the Rocky Mountains or the Appalachian Mountains?

   _____

4. Find your state on the map. What is the elevation where you live?

   _____

5. Do you think Florida is a good place for skiing? Why or why not?

   _____

What's Next? You Decide!

Now it's your turn to choose what to do next in the lesson.
Read the activities and decide which one you want to do—
you may want to try them both!

Create a Travel Brochure

MATERIALS

❏ 1 sheet construction paper
❏ markers or colored pencils

STEPS

Make a travel brochure for the Southwest.

❏ Fold one sheet of paper into three columns. Fold the paper horizontally.

❏ Unfold the paper so you can see the creases. In each column, draw pictures of things to see in the Southwest. Then write captions for the pictures.

❏ List facts about the land of the Southwest region. Write only one or two sentences for each fact. You may write about the region's land, people, and heritage. Also list some fun things to do in the Southwest.

❏ Research on the Internet, in encyclopedias, or at your local library if you want to find more information to include in your brochure.

❏ Refold the sheet of construction paper. Then decorate the cover of your brochure. Add a title in colorful letters and draw a picture that shows something interesting about the Southwest region.

❏ Show your brochure to family and friends. Ask them to share their opinions. Would your brochure make them want to visit the Southwest?

Paint a Desert Scene

MATERIALS

❏ 1 sheet heavy construction paper
❏ tempera paints
❏ 1 picture frame (optional)

STEPS

Many people think the Southwest desert is a beautiful place with interesting plant and animal life.

❏ What pictures do you see in your mind when you think of the desert? Do you see a blazing sun and stretches of sand? Do you see prickly cactuses, snakes, and lizards? Brainstorm images and note them on a sheet of paper.

❏ If you need more background about the desert, use the Internet or encyclopedias for research.

❏ Paint a picture that shows what you see when you think of the desert. Work from your imagination and use any colors you like.

❏ When you're done, show your painting to your family. You may want to frame your painting. If you can't find a frame, make your own out of construction paper.

❏ Hang your painting in a place where everyone can enjoy it.

Discovering the West

The diversity of the United States is what makes our country special.

OBJECTIVE	BACKGROUND	MATERIALS
To help your student discover more about the West	The West is the largest region of the United States. The landforms, climate, and people of this area of our country are diverse and unique. In this lesson, your student will learn more about the West and why it is such an interesting region.	■ Student Learning Pages 7.A–7.B ■ 1 U.S. map ■ 20 index cards ■ 1 dictionary ■ 1 copy national newspaper

VOCABULARY

ISLAND a body of land that is completely surrounded by water

BASIN a large depression in the surface of the land

CENTRAL VALLEY a flat, oval shaped landform in California that is found between the Sierra Nevada and the Coastal Ranges

FERTILE describes land that is rich in nutrients and suitable for growing crops and plants

CROPS plants that are grown to be used for food or to make other products

KINGDOM a country that is ruled by a king or queen

HOUSE OF REPRESENTATIVES a government group; one of the two houses of the U.S. Congress

POLYNESIANS a group of people from Asia who are thought to be the early settlers of Hawaii

INUIT a group of people who settled in Alaska

IMMIGRANTS people who leave their homeland to live in a new place

Let's Begin

1 **INTRODUCE** Tell your student that the West is the largest region in the United States. The West has various types of landforms and different climates. Also, many important events in U.S. history took place in the West. Give your student an index card and ask him or her to write two or three questions he or she may have about the West. Refer to the questions as they are answered throughout the lesson.

2 **IDENTIFY** Explain to your student that the West includes 11 states. These 11 states are divided into two groups: the mountain states and the Pacific states. The mountain states are Montana, Wyoming, Colorado, Utah, Nevada, and Idaho. The Pacific states consist of California, Oregon, Washington, Alaska, and Hawaii.

Show your student a map of the United States. Together with your student identify the 11 states of the West. Ask, *Why do you think the states are called "mountain" and "Pacific"?* [the mountain states have mountainous landforms and the Pacific states are close to the Pacific Ocean] Point out Alaska and Hawaii on the map. Ask, *How are Alaska and Hawaii different from other states?* [Alaska and Hawaii don't border any other states in the United States]

3 **EXPLORE** Remind your student that the West has many different types of landforms such as the Rocky Mountains, the Hawaiian Islands, and the Great Basin. Explain that an **island** is land surrounded by water on all sides. A **basin** is a large depression of land. Use the map of the United States to point out the Hawaiian Islands as well as the Great Basin surrounded by the Sierra Nevada and the Rocky Mountains.

4 **DESCRIBE** Tell your student that one important landform of the West is the **Central Valley.** The Central Valley is a flat, oval-shaped landform that lies between the Sierra Nevada and the Coastal Ranges. The San Joaquin River and the Sacramento River both travel through the Central Valley. The climate of the Central Valley is warm. Help your student find the Central Valley, the Sierra Nevada, and the Coastal Range on the map of the United States. Distribute Student Learning Page 7.A. Invite your student to use this page to express his or her images of landforms.

5 **ASK** Explain to your student that the land of the Central Valley is very **fertile.** Fertile land is rich in nutrients and suitable for growing **crops** and plants. Crops are plants that are grown for food or to make other products. Crops produced in the Central Valley of California are very important to the food supply of the United States. These crops are sent to stores across the United States. They include strawberries, cabbage, tomatoes, lettuce, grapes, olives, oranges, grapefruits, plums, peaches, artichokes, and cotton. Tell your student that in 1995 there were terrible floods in southern California. Ask, *How would floods in the Central Valley affect other people in the United States?* [if the floods destroyed the crops, there would not be as much food to eat]

6 **OBSERVE** Explain to your student that just as the West consists of different landforms, the climate of the West also varies from place to place. The region extends from Hawaii, which is close to the equator, to northern Alaska in the Arctic Circle. This large area of land experiences many different climates. Have your student look at the weather page in a national newspaper. Ask, *What is the temperature in Alaska and Hawaii? How are the temperatures different?* [the temperatures in Hawaii are warmer than the temperatures in Alaska]

ENRICH THE EXPERIENCE

Your library may have videocassettes showing aspects of the West. Or, if a friend or family member has traveled to the West, ask him or her to share with your student photos or travel stories about the region.

A BRIGHT IDEA

Go grocery shopping with your student. While you're at the store, point out some of the foods that are grown in the Central Valley. Examine the labels on the foods to see where they came from. Guide your student to see that much of the food we buy at the grocery store comes from places all over the United States.

7 **COMPARE** Explain that precipitation levels also vary throughout the West. Every year almost 500 inches of rain fall in Mount Walaleale, Hawaii, the wettest place in the world! Death Valley in California receives less than 2 inches of rain each year, making it the driest place in the United States. Tell your student that the plants and animals in Death Valley are different from those in Mount Walaleale. Ask, *What must plants and animals in Death Valley live without?* [they must live without a lot of water]

8 **EXPLAIN** There are a number of individuals who are an important part of the history of the West. One prominent figure is Chief Kamehameha. Look at the different islands of Hawaii on the map of the United States. Tell your student that a different chief ruled each island. In the late 1700s, Chief Kamehameha fought a war and by 1810 all of the islands were united under his control. The islands of Hawaii became one **kingdom** under the rule of Chief Kamehameha. Ask, *What is a kingdom?* [a region under the rule of a king or queen]

9 **DISCUSS** Explain that Jeannette Rankin is another important person in the history of the West. Rankin was the first woman ever elected to Congress. She was from Montana and was elected in 1916 to the **House of Representatives.** Rankin was elected again as a representative in 1940. Tell your student that the House of Representatives is one of the two houses of the U.S. Congress that makes laws for our country. Ask, *Can you name some important women who work as leaders in government today?* [answers may include Hillary Rodham Clinton, Elizabeth Dole, Madeline Albright]

Jeannette Rankin was from Montana and was the first woman elected to Congress.

10 **EXPLORE** Tell your student that there are many groups of people who are important to the West. Experts think that the first people to settle Hawaii came from Asia. They are known as **Polynesians.** The Polynesians are said to have cleared the land to grow foods such as bananas and sweet potatoes. The influence of the Polynesians can still be heard today. Have your student practice saying hello (aloha) and thank you (mahalo) in Hawaiian.

11 **ASK** Explain to your student that the **Inuit,** also known as Eskimos, are a group of people who settled in Alaska. The land was low, flat, and treeless with permanently frozen ground. Some groups of Inuit people settled near rivers and depended on fishing, while others lived as hunters. Traditional Inuit clothing was made from the skins of birds and animals. There are about 40,000 Inuit in Alaska today. Ask, *What skills did the Inuit need to survive as early settlers of Alaska?* [they had to find ways to survive in the frozen land by being good hunters and fishers and by using what they could find, such as animal skins, to stay warm]

The Inuit have survived harsh Alaskan weather.

DID YOU KNOW?

The word *Eskimo* means "eater of raw meat." Non-Inuit people used this term to criticize their Inuit neighbors.

12 **EXPLAIN** Tell your student that many people move to the United States to live and work. People who are born in one

country and move to a new country to live and work are called **immigrants.** There have been many immigrants who moved to San Francisco, California. They came from countries such as Russia, Mexico, Italy, France, and Japan. The greatest number of immigrants came from China. The immigrants helped San Francisco grow into a great city. Discuss with your student what it might be like to move to a new country. Encourage your student to consider things that immigrants might leave behind and things that immigrants might have to learn in a new country.

13 **RELATE** Explain to your student that there are a variety of different jobs in the West. Gold was discovered in California in 1848. People rushed to California in search of gold and many people came to the West to work in the gold mines. Today, people in the West still work in the mines of Nevada, Wyoming, and Colorado. Many people work as farmers in the fertile land of the Central Valley. The forests of the Rocky Mountains provide many people with jobs in logging and lumbering. The entertainment industry is also a source of many jobs in the West. Many people in California work in film and television. They may have jobs as directors, actors, actresses, camera operators, set designers, costume designers, and makeup artists. Ask, *What jobs of the West would you like to try? Why?*

Branching Out

TEACHING TIP

Ask your student to think about why immigrants are so important to our country. Guide your student to see that immigrants bring with them the languages, customs, foods, and art forms of their native land. No other country in the world displays the cultural diversity of the United States.

CHECKING IN

Write the names of various people, landforms, and jobs on index cards. On the back of each card, write a question about the thing listed. Invite your student to draw some of the index cards. Ask the questions to assess his or her knowledge of the lesson. Be sure your student arrives at the correct answers.

FOR FURTHER READING

Arctic Crossing: A Journey Through the Northwest Passage and Inuit Culture, by Jonathan Waterman (Lyons Press, 2002).

High Tide in Hawaii, by Mary Pope Osborne (Random House, 2003).

The Life of a Miner (Life in the Old West), by Bobbie Kalman and Kate Calder (Crabtree Publishing, 2000).

Seaman: The Dog Who Explored the West with Lewis and Clark, by Gail Karwoski and James Watling, ill. (Peachtree Publisher, Ltd., 2003).

Celebrate the Landforms of the West

The West has many different types of landforms: Rocky Mountains, Hawaiian Islands, Great Basin, Central Valley, Sierra Nevada, and Coastal Range. Draw a landform in the box. Write a poem about the landform on the lines.

_____
(Name of Landform)

_____

_____

_____

_____

_____

_____

_____

_____

_____

What's Next? You Decide!

Now it's your turn to choose what to do next in the lesson. Read the activities and decide which one you want to do—you may want to try them both!

Make a Special Meal

◼ MATERIALS

❑ lettuce

❑ tomatoes

❑ salad dressing

❑ bowls

❑ forks

◼ STEPS

Have you ever wanted to be a chef? Try making a meal with some of the foods that are grown in the Central Valley of California, such as strawberries, cabbage, olives, and so on.

❑ Use lettuce, tomatoes, any other vegetables you like, and salad dressing to make a salad. Be sure to wash the vegetables before putting them in the salad. Ask an adult to help you cut the vegetables.

❑ Invite members of your family to eat the salad together. Maybe you could eat it together at dinner or lunch.

❑ While you're eating together, tell your family about the Central Valley of California. Explain that many important crops are grown there, including lettuce and tomatoes—just like the ones they're eating together in the salad you made!

Make Your Own Lei

◼ MATERIALS

❑ 1 long piece yarn or string

❑ different colored tissue paper

❑ 1 pair scissors

❑ 1 pencil

◼ STEPS

A lei is a necklace made of flowers that many Hawaiians wear. Use some materials you have at home to make your own lei!

❑ Cut different colored tissue paper into small squares (about the size of a CD case).

❑ Use your pencil to punch a hole into the middle of the tissue squares.

❑ String the tissue squares onto the yarn or string.

❑ Tie the ends of the string into a knot.

❑ Wear your lei around your neck just like the people of Hawaii.

Investigating Your State

Knowing where we come from helps us discover where we are going.

OBJECTIVE	BACKGROUND	MATERIALS
To help your student learn more about his or her own state	Every state in the United States is unique. A state's land features, environment, and people make it special. In this lesson, your student will learn what makes his or her own state like no other state in the country.	■ Student Learning Pages 8.A–8.B ■ 1 map of your student's state ■ 1 U.S. map ■ colored pencils or markers

VOCABULARY

CAPITAL a city that serves as a state's or country's main government center
LANDFORMS the different kinds of shapes on Earth's surface
CLIMATE the average weather in a place over many years
BAR GRAPH a graph that shows information with bars of different heights

Let's Begin

1 **INTRODUCE** Invite your student to talk about his or her state. Ask your student what he or she likes and dislikes about the state. Explain that every state is unique. Ask your student to name some things that make his or her state special.

2 **SHOW** Together with your student, find your state on a U.S. map. Ask him or her to name the state's **capital.** Explain that a capital is a city that serves as a state's or country's main government center. Then find the capital of your state on the map. Ask, *What happens in a state capital?* [possible answers: politicians meet with each other, laws are made, and so on]

3 **LABEL** Look at a map of your state with your student. Then remind your student that **landforms** are natural structures of Earth's surface. Use the map to point out landforms such as mountains, plains, hills, and plateaus. Also identify important bodies of water, such as lakes, rivers, and oceans. Provide your student with a blank outline map of your state. If you'd like, go to http://www.50states.com for a map on the Internet. Invite your student to use colored pencils or markers to label the state capital, landforms, and bodies of water.

ENRICH THE EXPERIENCE

Help your student enjoy his or her own state! Show your student some of the features that make his or her state unique. Take him or her on a trip to a site of interest, such as a beach, a museum, or a park.

What's Next? You Decide!

Now it's your turn to choose what to do next in the lesson. Read the activities and decide which one you want to do— you may want to try them both!

Design a State Collage

MATERIALS

- ❏ old magazines and/or newspapers
- ❏ 1 sheet construction paper
- ❏ glue
- ❏ 1 pair scissors

STEPS

A collage is a piece of art made up of different pictures and words assembled together. Create a collage all about your state!

- ❏ Look through some old magazines and newspapers.
- ❏ Find pictures and words that remind you of your state.
- ❏ Glue the different pictures and words onto a sheet of construction paper to create your state collage.
- ❏ Now you have a special collage that shows what makes your state so great!
- ❏ Show it to your friends and family— especially to guests who visit you from out of town.
- ❏ If you'd like, make a collage of your home town. You may have to look for pictures in your local newspaper, too.

Create a State Postcard

MATERIALS

- ❏ 1 3-by-5-inch sheet heavy white construction paper
- ❏ markers

STEPS

Create your own state postcard to send to a family member or friend.

- ❏ Think about some of your favorite things from your state.
- ❏ Write some of these things down in your notebook.
- ❏ Draw a picture of a favorite thing on one side of a 3-by-5-inch sheet of construction paper. This picture will be on the front of your postcard.
- ❏ Write a neat or funny greeting on your picture.
- ❏ Use interesting and creative letters to write the words.
- ❏ Send your postcard to someone who might enjoy it!
- ❏ On the back of the postcard, write the name and address of the person you are sending it to. Use half of the space—just how you would on a real postcard.
- ❏ On the other half of the back side, write a friendly message. Tell about the picture on your postcard and share why you like your state.
- ❏ Ask someone to help you mail the postcard.

Exploring Your Town

There are thousands of towns all across the country.
What makes yours special?

OBJECTIVE	BACKGROUND	MATERIALS
To help your student learn about maps and globes as well as about his or her own town	Each town is unique for its people, resources, history, and much more. Studying one's town can help your student gain a greater understanding of what comprises a town and why each town is unique. In this lesson, your student will practice using maps and discover new facts about his or her town.	■ Student Learning Pages 9.A–9.B ■ 1 U.S. political map ■ 1 U.S. landform map ■ 1 globe ■ reference books about your town ■ local newspaper ■ 1 posterboard ■ 1 copy Venn Diagram, page 355

Let's Begin

1 **EXPLORE** Show your student a political map of the United States. Tell your student that this is called a political map because it shows city, state, and national boundaries. Ask, *Does this map show where mountains are located?* [no] Explain that to learn about the terrain of an area, such as where mountains and cliffs are located, you would use a landform map. Show your student a landform map of the United States and ask him or her to identify features such as mountains. Then ask, *Which type of map would you use to find the boundary between two states?* [political map] *Which type of map would you use to find the elevation or landforms of an area?* [landform map]

2 **EXPLAIN** Then show your student a globe. Explain that some globes show both terrain and boundaries. Ask, *When might you use a globe rather than a map?* [when trying to find out where one country, continent, ocean, or other feature is in relation to another] Challenge your student to locate various places of interest on the globe, such as Antarctica, the Indian Ocean, and the Panama Canal.

3 **CONNECT** Ask your student to locate the general area of your town on the globe. Then ask him or her to think about how your town is similar to and different from other towns and cities shown on the globe. Have your student make a list of these characteristics, such as differences in climate, people, and culture.

A BRIGHT IDEA

For more information about different types of maps, go to http://www.enchantedlearning.com and search for maps.

DID YOU KNOW?

The Langlois Globe is considered to be the largest globe in the world. The globe was made in France in 1824 and is 128 feet (39 meters) in diameter.

4 **EXAMINE** Discuss how a town is shaped by its natural environment. Offer the example of Los Angeles, California. The city has a warm, sunny climate, so it's a good place for making films. As a result, most films in the United States are filmed in Los Angeles. Then ask, *How does your town's environment affect the way people live there?*

5 **CONSIDER** Explain that the people of a town play a huge part in making the town unique. While all members of a town are important, there are always people who make important contributions or serve as important leaders. These people may include politicians, clergymen, school workers, and so on. Have your student use local newspapers and the Internet to identify people from the town who have done helpful or important work there either recently or in the past. You can also have your student visit the library or local chamber of commerce to find out more about prominent community members. Have your student take notes on what he or she learns.

6 **RESEARCH** Distribute Student Learning Page 9.A. Read the directions with your student. Make arrangements, if necessary, for your student to visit the library, village hall, or local historical society to learn more about your town. Your student may not be able to answer all the questions on the page. Encourage him or her to find as much interesting and relevant information as possible. Once your student has obtained the information, have him or her organize it on a posterboard. You may wish to have your student make a brief presentation to a family member or your homeschooling group. After the project has been completed, ask, *What information about your town surprised or interested you? What else would you like to learn about your town?*

Branching Out

TEACHING TIP

Have your student use the Internet or reference books to learn about other kinds of maps, such as topographic maps. Have your student print out and label each new type of map he or she finds.

CHECKING IN

To assess your student's understanding of the lesson, have your student compare the characteristics of his or her town to another town. Consider having your student complete a copy of the Venn Diagram found on page 355 to compare his or her town to another town.

Become an Expert on Your Town!

Find answers to the questions listed. Use the Internet, reference books, and a local newspaper to find information. You can also visit your town's historical society, or meet with town leaders.

History

❑ When was your town founded?

❑ Which individual or group of people founded it?

❑ What important events have taken place in your town?

❑ Who are some of the important people or groups in your town's history? What did they do?

Environment

❑ What is the climate of your town like?

❑ How do the climate and environment affect the way of life of people in your town?

Culture

❑ What cultural groups stand out in your town?

❑ What cultural events or celebrations does your town have?

Economy and Resources

❑ What large industries are in your town?

❑ What types of jobs do people have?

❑ What products are made in your town?

❑ What natural resources does your town have?

People

❑ Who are some important people in your town today? What do they do?

❑ What is the population of your town?

Now present your information on posterboard. Summarize the key points using brief sentences or lists. Include at least one visual aid, such as a map or photograph.

What's Next? You Decide!

Now it's your turn to choose what to do next in the lesson.
Read the activities and decide which one you want to do—
you may want to try them both!

Make a Papier-Mâché Globe

MATERIALS

- ❏ 1 round 12-inch balloon
- ❏ 1 newspaper
- ❏ 1 small pan
- ❏ 2–3 cups flour
- ❏ 1 thick marker
- ❏ paints
- ❏ 1 paintbrush

STEPS

- ❏ Cut newspaper into 15 to 20 strips. Each strip should be about 12 inches long and 2 inches wide.

- ❏ Fill the small pan with water. Slowly add flour and stir. Continue adding and stirring until you have a thin paste.

- ❏ Inflate the balloon. Dip a strip of newspaper in the paste. Then place the strip on the balloon. Repeat until the entire balloon is covered.

- ❏ Let the balloon dry for one day.

- ❏ Use a thick marker to draw all the continents on your globe.

- ❏ Paint the globe and then label the continents and oceans. You may wish to use a thin marker to draw and label several countries.

Write About Your Changing Town

STEPS

Write a creative story about the future of your town. How might your town grow or change over time? What event or events might make it grow or change? What type of leader might influence the town?

- ❏ On a sheet of scratch paper, brainstorm a list of ideas for your story. Then choose one.

- ❏ Begin your story in an interesting way that will make someone want to read the story.

- ❏ Make sure your story has a beginning, a middle, and an end.

Learning to Be a Good Citizen

A good citizen enjoys both the rights and responsibilities of his or her country.

OBJECTIVE	BACKGROUND	MATERIALS
To help your student learn more about being a citizen of the United States	The United States is a country where citizens enjoy tremendous freedom. The United States guarantees its citizens many important rights. Citizens also have many important responsibilities. In this lesson, your student will discover more about what it means to be a citizen of the United States.	■ Student Learning Pages 10.A–10.B. ■ 1 dictionary ■ 1 U.S. map ■ 1 sheet each blue and yellow construction paper ■ blue and yellow markers ■ game pieces, such as coins

VOCABULARY

GOODS things that are made to be sold

SERVICES jobs that people do to help others

AGRICULTURE the business of growing crops and raising animals

INDUSTRY the business of manufacturing or making goods to sell

CITIZEN a member of a country

CONSTITUTION a plan for how a government should work

IMMIGRANTS people who leave their homeland to live in a new place

NATURALIZATION the process where an immigrant becomes a U.S. citizen

Let's Begin

1 **TELL** Tell your student that an economy is a system of buying and selling goods and services. The economy of the United States is helped by the hard work of Americans. Our economy involves both **goods** and **services.** Goods are things that are made to be sold, such as clothes, appliances, and food. Services are jobs that people do to help others, such as the work of a barber, a travel agent, or a carpet cleaner. People sell goods and provide services in exchange for money. Explain to your student that in the United States people are able to own their own businesses. Ask, *What are some goods and services that you or your family members have purchased recently?* [groceries, car wash, and so on]

2 **ASK** Tell your student that **agriculture,** the business of growing crops and raising animals, is an important part of the U.S. economy. The business of agriculture provides jobs for many Americans and also provides crops for people to use. Corn is an important part of the economy in Iowa, while in Wisconsin raising cows provides many jobs. Ask, *What kinds of jobs might there be in the agriculture business?* [farmers, cattle ranchers, fruit and vegetable pickers, producers of farm machinery] Ask, *How do you think a drought would affect the economy?* [it would be difficult to grow crops and so food prices might increase]

3 **EXPLAIN** Explain that **industry** is another important part of the U.S. economy. Challenge your student to find a definition for *industry* in a dictionary. Tell your student that industry is the business of manufacturing or making things to sell. For example, in Florida the production of aerospace and aircraft equipment is an important industry. Other important industries in the United States include the production of automobiles, computer equipment, and steel. Ask your student to name some other industries. [logging, furniture, oil] Ask, *What is the difference between agriculture and industry?* [agriculture is the business of growing crops and raising animals; industry is the business of manufacturing or making things]

4 **DISCUSS** Tell your student that a **citizen** is a member of a country. Emphasize to your student that being a citizen in the United States means that he or she has certain responsibilities and rights. A responsibility is something that a person is expected to do. A right is something that the law says you can have or do. Ask, *What do you think some of the responsibilities of U.S. citizens are?* [voting, recycling, following the law, and so on]

5 **RELATE** Tell your student that one responsibility of a good citizen is voting. To vote means to make a choice in an election. The United States is a democracy, which means that the people have the right to vote for the people who lead them, represent them, and make their laws. We make this choice by voting. Tell your student that in the United States you can vote when you are 18 years old. Ask, *Why is voting an important responsibility of a good citizen?* [because it's when we say whom we want to make our laws and represent us]

6 **EXPLAIN** Tell your student that the United States has a **constitution,** which is a plan for how the government should work. The Constitution of the United States was written in 1787. It defines our most important laws and establishes and protects the rights of the people. Ask, *What might happen if the Constitution didn't protect the rights of the people?* [if people were treated unfairly, they would have no legal way to pursue justice]

7 **REVIEW** Review with your student what he or she knows about early American history, such as the Declaration of Independence,

---

ENRICH THE EXPERIENCE

Don't be afraid to take as long as you need with the topics covered in this lesson—let your student be the guide.

GET ORGANIZED

You may wish to preview http://memory.loc.gov before beginning Step 7.

---

the 13 colonies, George Washington, Thomas Jefferson, and so on. Together with your student go to the library and look for books about this time period and then discuss. If you'd like, go to http://memory.loc.gov and click on "Learning Page" for activities and information about this time period. Click on "Collection Finder" to search for first-person documents, such as letters, diary entries, and photos of the time period.

8 **EXPAND** Explain to your student that anyone who was born in the United States is a citizen of the United States. But there are also many people who were born in other countries who come to live and work in the United States. These people are called **immigrants.** Many immigrants want to become citizens of the United States. The process of becoming a U.S. citizen is called **naturalization.** Usually, immigrants have to have been living in the United States for five years to become a citizen. They have to make a promise to be loyal to the United States and to obey its laws and take a test about U.S. history and government. Ask, *Can you name some countries where immigrants to the United States come from?* [China, Mexico, Japan, Ireland, Cuba, Vietnam, Italy, India, and so on]

DID YOU KNOW?

Other general requirements for naturalization include good moral character, a favorable disposition toward the United States, and the ability to read, write, and speak English.

9 **SHOW** Ask, *How are communities in the United States different from one another?* [they are different sizes, are in different regions, and have different resources] Explain that one reason communities vary from place to place is because of their geography. The landforms and climates of a community influence the lives of the people who live there. For example, many parts of the state of Washington are covered with thick forests, so many citizens there work in the logging industry. From the information you researched in Step 7, have your student compare his or her community to one found in the 13 colonies. Discuss how they are alike and different.

Washington's forests and mountains contribute to the uniqueness of the state's communities.

10 **ASK** Tell your student that some communities in the United States are rural and others are urban. Rural communities are areas far from a city where there is a lot of open land. Urban communities are areas made up of a city and of the area around the city. Many people in rural communities have jobs in agriculture and farming, while many people in urban communities have jobs in factories and offices. Ask, *How are urban and rural communities different?* [an urban area includes a city and the places close to a city; a rural area is not near a city and has more open spaces]

11 **DISCUSS** Discuss with your student some of the new things he or she learned in this lesson. Give your student Student Learning Page 10.A. Tell your student that he or she can use the page to create a game about what he or she learned in this lesson. Read the directions with your student and help him or her develop appropriate questions and answers.

Branching Out

TEACHING TIP

As your student learns about the economy of the United States, guide him or her to notice the many different kinds of jobs there are in the United States. When you are out in the community with your student point out the many different types of jobs people have. Encourage your student to brainstorm the many different jobs people in the United States have.

CHECKING IN

Ask your student to explain to you what a citizen is. Then challenge your student to name three to five things a good citizen does.

FOR FURTHER READING

America: A Patriotic Primer, by Lynne V. Cheney (Simon and Schuster, 2002).

Becoming a Citizen (True Books), by Sarah De Capua (Children's Press, 2002).

Landmark Events in American History: Arriving at Ellis Island, the Battle of Little Bighorn, the California Missions, the Plymouth Colony, the Settling of Jamestown, the Siege of the Alamo (Gareth Stevens Audio, 2002).

Paying Taxes (True Books), by Sarah De Capua (Children's Press, 2002).

Create Your Own Game

Follow the steps to make and play a game about what you've learned.

1. Take one sheet of blue and one sheet of yellow construction paper. Cut eight squares from each sheet of paper.

2. On the blue squares, write questions about the U.S. economy.

3. On the yellow squares, write questions about the rights and responsibilities of U.S. citizens.

4. Color the squares numbered 1, 3, 5, and 7 on the game board blue.

5. Color the squares numbered 2, 4, 6, and 8 on the game board yellow.

6. Ask one other person to play the game with you.

7. Use coins as your game pieces.

8. Each player begins by putting his or her piece at Start.

9. Take turns picking a question card and asking the question of the other player. If your piece is on a blue square, ask a blue-card question. If your piece is on a yellow square, ask a yellow-card question.

10. When a player knows the answer, he or she can move his or her game piece to the next square.

11. The first player to reach Finish wins the game.

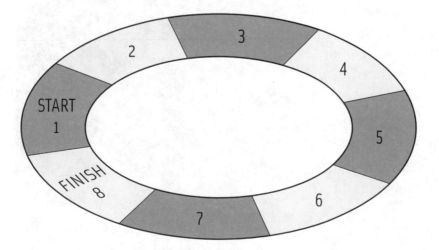

What's Next? You Decide!

Now it's your turn to choose what to do next in the lesson. Read the activities and decide which one you want to do—you may want to try them both!

Research and Report

STEPS

Learn more about how immigrants have made our country great.

❏ Choose one immigrant group that you would like to learn more about. For example, you could choose Chinese, Irish, Japanese, Italian, Korean, Mexican, Puerto Rican, or Cuban people.

❏ Use the library or the Internet to learn more about the group. Research what parts of the United States the group immigrated to and what they did to help make our country special.

❏ Then visit a neighborhood, cook a food, or practice a custom of the immigrant group with an adult.

Interview and Learn More

STEPS

There are many different jobs you can have in the United States.

❏ Choose one job that you're interested in.

❏ Write three to five questions you would like to ask someone who has that job. For example, maybe you want to know what that person likes the most about his or her job.

❏ Then ask an adult for help in using the phone book to call someone who has that job. When you call, tell the person that you want to know more about his or her job and ask if it would be okay to ask them a few questions.

❏ After you have interviewed the person, think about their answers. What new things did you learn about the job?

In Your Community

To reinforce the skills and concepts taught in this section,
try one or more of these activities!

Help Wanted: Cartographers

Have your student use the map skills learned in the lessons by making a map. Find an area in your town that you and your student can explore. Note the important landmarks—human-made or natural—that your student can incorporate into the map. The map should include all the features of a map, such as a key or legend, a compass rose, and geographic features. Then go to your town hall or police department and look at a map of that same area of town. Have your student compare the two maps and see how they are the same and different.

Explore the Origins of Your Town

Your student has learned that the United States has an eclectic group of citizens. People from many different countries have come to America seeking a new beginning. With your student, research the history of your community. Go to the library and learn the origins of the first settlers who came to your area and their reasons for coming. Also, find early historical figures who had a major impact in making your community what it is today. Use the information to locate and visit historical landmarks in your community. For example, you could visit the first schoolhouse, church, or other historic building if still in existence. Arrange for your student to meet with a local historian. Have your student think of questions ahead of time to ask.

Your Town's Resources

The environmental characteristics and resources of a town often provide a major source of economic stability and success. For example, farms, factories, or tourism may contribute a large percentage of income and employment in a particular area if its environmental characteristics and resources can support them. Research with your student how your town uses its physical characteristics and resources to provide employment. Then have your student choose an occupation that relies on the environment and arrange an interview with someone in that particular field (for example, a park ranger). Have your student ask questions about the job and its importance to the employee and the community. Is this a job your student would want to do?

The Role of Municipalities

Municipalities, or city governments, generally provide police and fire protection, city maintenance, and other services to their respective cities. They also make and enforce laws that affect the citizens of the cities. Arrange a tour of your city hall so your student can see the role of a municipality in a town's everyday life. Try to meet with a local official who will explain the activities your local government is involved in. If possible, attend a town meeting so your student can see government in action.

Become the Town's Historian

Work with your student to select a festival or celebration that's about to occur in your town. Have him or her research the event to see how long your town has been celebrating it and what's involved in the celebration. Then, at the celebration have your student interview people in attendance or those involved with its planning. Encourage your student to take photographs or draw pictures of what's happening. Have him or her collect artifacts from the celebration, such as a flyer or ticket stub. If possible, have him or her record parts of the celebration using a tape recorder or video camera. Then help him or her put together a display complete with photos, quotes, and artifacts. Arrange to have your student display it in the library, community center, town hall, or local museum.

We Have Learned

Use this checklist to summarize what you and your student
have accomplished in the Social Studies section.

❏ **United States—Environment**
❏ geography, climate of the United
States
❏ resources of the United States

❏ **United States—Southeast Region**
❏ characteristics of Southeast,
Mississippi River
❏ important individuals, important
groups
❏ heritage of region

❏ **United States—Northeast Region**
❏ characteristics of Northeast,
Appalachian Mountains
❏ important individuals, important
groups
❏ heritage of region

❏ **United States—Midwest Region**
❏ characteristics of Midwest, Interior
Plains
❏ important individuals, important
groups
❏ heritage of region

❏ **United States—Southwest Region**
❏ characteristics of Southwest, dry
landscape
❏ important individuals, important
groups
❏ heritage of region

❏ **United States—West Region**
❏ characteristics of West, Central Valley
❏ important individuals, important
groups
❏ heritage of region

❏ **Student's Own State**
❏ identity
❏ cultural characteristics, environmental
characteristics
❏ important individuals, important
groups

❏ **Student's Own Town**
❏ identity
❏ cultural characteristics, environmental
characteristics
❏ important individuals, important
groups

❏ **Civics and Citizenship**
❏ rights of citizens, citizenship
❏ attributes of good citizenship
❏ differences of communities
❏ economy of United States

We have also learned:

_____

_____

_____

_____

> Read each question and the answer choices that follow. Circle the letter of the correct answer.

1. Writing that is written about someone by someone else is a(n)—

   A autobiography.

   B biography.

   C play.

   D poem.

2. Which of the following is an important part of a story?

   A a character

   B a fun title

   C a pretty picture

   D a page number

3. The plot of a story is the—

   A name of the setting.

   B place where characters live.

   C events that occur in the story.

   D talent the author has.

4. Which of the following is an example of historical fiction?

   A a story about a girl flying to the moon on a fork

   B a fictional story taking place during the Civil War

   C a poem about bears

   D a play about three talking mice

5. Which of these compares two unlike things?

   A cause

   B effect

   C summary

   D metaphor

6. A comparison using *like* or *as* is—

   A a simile.

   B a viewpoint.

   C realism.

   D fantasy.

7. Which of these is the correct location of a main idea?

   A as the title of an essay

   B in the first paragraph of an essay

   C at the end of an essay

   D beside the pictures used in an essay

8. Which of these supports a main idea?

   A details

   B photos

   C punctuation

   D setting

Read the sentences in the box.
Decide which type of writing it is.
Circle the letter of the correct answer.

9.

New Year's Day is on January 1st. This holiday brings in each new year. A calendar year has 365 days.

A play

B biography

C nonfiction

D fiction

10.

George W. Bush has an important title: President of the United States. He is married to Laura Bush. They have twin daughters.

A fable

B fiction

C play

D biography

11.

(Kimberly and Lawrence enter stage right)
Kimberly: Let's go to the store to get ice cream.
Lawrence: I can't. I have to study.
Kimberly (sighing): I guess I should study too.
Lawrence: Well, a little ice cream break won't hurt.
(Kimberly and Lawrence exit the stage)

A interview

B play

C legend

D poem

12.

A winter storm hit the Northeast region of the United States in December. It was the largest storm in years. Many people were without power for days.

A news article

B fable

C poem

D autobiography

PROMOTING LITERACY

> Read each selection. Read the questions and answer choices that go with each selection. Circle the letter of the correct answer.

Use for 13–16.

Asa was upset because no one had remembered his birthday. He had awakened early that morning bright-eyed and jumped out of bed. He was ready to celebrate his birthday.

He got dressed and bounded down the stairs, taking them two at a time. He fully expected to see his family eagerly waiting for him so that they could sing "Happy Birthday" to him.

However, Asa was disappointed when he got downstairs. His mother had left him a note, telling him that she, his aunt, and his two brothers had gone shopping. Asa couldn't believe that the family had forgotten his birthday. They hadn't even invited him to go shopping with them. His mother's note said that the family had not awakened him because he was resting so peacefully when they checked in on him.

Asa trudged back upstairs and fell asleep. When he woke up an hour later, he went downstairs. He had dreamed that he heard voices downstairs. It sounded like someone was having a party. He rubbed his eyes and walked slowly downstairs, trying to recognize the voices he heard. The voices belonged to his friends, his family, and his brothers. When he reached the bottom stair, he couldn't believe his eyes. His house was filled with his family and friends. There, on the dining room table, were balloons and a birthday cake. Everyone turned around and yelled, "Surprise!"

13. Which of the following titles best represents this selection?
   A Families in the Winter
   B Asa's Birthday Surprise
   C A Long Summer Nap
   D Growing Older

14. What can you infer about Asa's family and friends?
   A They are boring.
   B They are selfish.
   C They are bitter.
   D They are fun-loving.

15. What can you conclude about Asa's family?
   A They enjoy playing tricks on him.
   B They forget their children's birthdays.
   C They keep him from getting any sleep.
   D They like to shop without Asa.

16. Which of the following words is a preposition?

> He had awakened early this morning and jumped out of bed.

A awakened

B out

C early

D bed

Use for 17–22.

The Snail and the Turtle

One day Mr. Snail and Mr. Turtle were talking at the park. They had a lot in common. They both had shells and they both moved very slowly. They frequently debated about which of them was the slowest. Mr. Turtle always took their arguments too seriously, while Mr. Snail always handled their disagreements in a good-natured manner. Mr. Snail insisted that no other creature on earth moved as slowly as he did. On the other hand, Mr. Turtle insisted that he was indeed the slowest creature of all.

The two decided to have a race. Mr. Turtle knew that their argument was silly, but he was so tired of Mr. Snail always bragging about how slow he was. Mr. Snail made being slow sound like the most wonderful attribute to have. Mr. Turtle was not as self-confident and was jealous of the friendly snail. They made arrangements to race the next day in the park.

On the day of the race, Mr. Turtle decided to take a nap so that he would be sure to win the challenge. When the race started, Mr. Turtle pulled ahead of Mr. Snail and hid in the bushes to take a nap. He slept for 10 hours! When he crossed the finish line, he had a smug expression on his face. He fully expected to see Mr. Snail already there. He was certain that he had won the race. However, Mr. Snail did not cross the finish line for another 14 hours! Mr. Snail proved that he was indeed the slowest creature on earth. Mr. Turtle congratulated Mr. Snail and said, "I'll never debate with you again." Mr. Turtle and Mr. Snail coexisted peacefully without debating . . . until the next day.

17. "The Snail and the Turtle" can best be described as a—

A tale.

B poem.

C news article.

D biography.

18. What is the setting of the selection?

A in a pond

B at a park

C on a sidewalk

D behind a barn

PROMOTING LITERACY

19. The conflict in the selection is solved with—

    A a third party.

    B a panel of judges.

    C a race.

    D a debate.

20. How are the snail and turtle alike?

    A They are sad.

    B They are slow.

    C They are singers.

    D They are joggers.

21. How are the snail and turtle different?

    A The snail was self-confident; the turtle was not.

    B The snail liked the park; the turtle did not.

    C The snail removed his shell; the turtle could not.

    D The snail was a sore loser; the turtle was a good sport.

22. You can best predict the turtle and snail will—

    A have ice cream.

    B move into the park.

    C visit mutual friends.

    D have another debate.

Read the sentences in the box. Decide the best way to write the underlined sentences. Circle the letter of the correct answer.

23.

> Malcolm is going to Rashad's house. They is going to work on a school project together.

    A They was going to work on a school project together.

    B They are going to work on a school project together.

    C They be going to work on a school project together.

    D Correct as written

24.

> Lisa was shopping for groceries. She had a coupon for two loafs of bread.

    A She had a coupon for two loaf of bread.

    B She had a coupon for a two-loaf bread.

    C She had a coupon for two loaves of bread.

    D Correct as written

25.

> Alonzo's father had prepared his favorite meal. <u>So to savor it, he ate slowly.</u>

A So to savor it, he ate very slow.

B So to savor it, he eats very slowly.

C So to savor it, he will eat slow.

D Correct as written

26.

> Lena's mom was not home. <u>She was at her womens softball tournament.</u>

A She was at her women's softball tournament.

B She was at her woman's softball tournament.

C She was at her womens' softball tournament.

D Correct as written

Read the selections and the questions that follow. Answer the questions in complete sentences.

Use for 27–29.

Juanita's Zoo Trip

Juanita was so excited. She was going to one of her favorite places with her family: the zoo. When they arrived, Juanita and her family went to see the elephants first. Juanita was amazed because they were huge. She was so anxious to see the other animals at the zoo that she ran ahead of her family to see the next animal exhibit. She ran up to the giraffes' pen. They were so tall. She turned around to speak to her family and saw that they were gone. Juanita panicked! Where was her family? She tried to remain calm as she retraced her steps back to the elephant exhibit. She breathed a sigh of relief when she saw her family. They were still looking at the elephants. She joined them and paid as much attention to them as she did to the animals at the zoo.

27. What is the main idea of the story?

_____
_____
_____
_____
_____
_____

28. What lesson do you think Juanita learned in the story? Support your answer using details from the story.

_____
_____
_____
_____
_____
_____

29. Fill in the story structure chart for the selection.

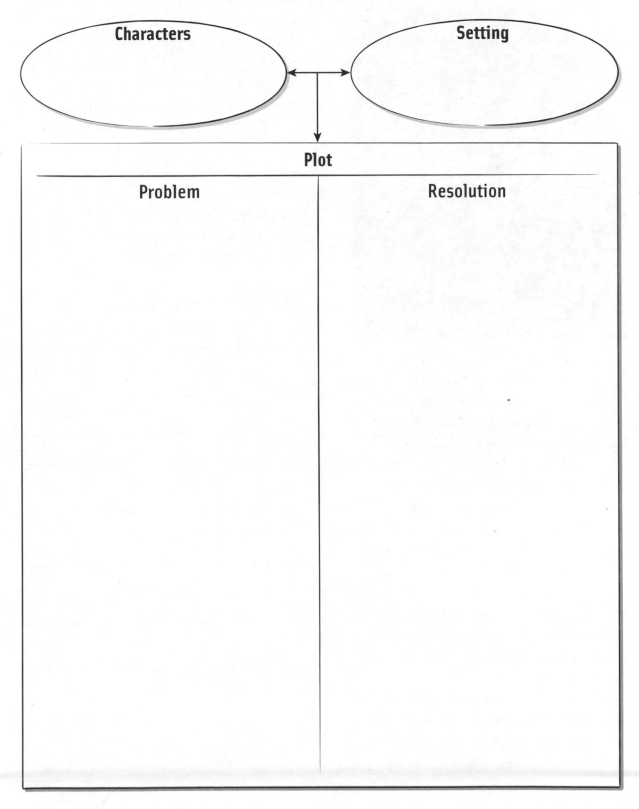

Characters

Setting

Plot

Problem	Resolution

PROMOTING LITERACY

Use for 30–32.

The Amazing Kangaroo

Kangaroos, found in Australia, are amazing animals. Male kangaroos are known as boomers. Female kangaroos are called flyers. Baby kangaroos are joeys. Kangaroos are mammal marsupials. This means that they are animals that carry their babies in their tummy pouches and feed them milk.

There are more than 40 different types of kangaroos. The largest is the red kangaroo. It is taller than the average male and weighs approximately 185 pounds, making it the largest marsupial in the world!

The kangaroo moves by hopping. It hops using its powerful hind legs. It also uses these back legs to protect itself by kicking its enemies. The kangaroo's long, thick tail balances its body when it moves. The kangaroo is very mobile and agile. It can hop at about 40 miles per hour. It can also jump over obstacles that are as high as 10 feet. However, the kangaroo's unusual shape makes it difficult for it to move backward.

The kangaroo rests in shady areas during the day and eats later in the evening. Its diet consists mainly of grass. Interestingly, the kangaroo can survive for months without water.

They are very interesting animals that are worthy of attention.

30. "The Amazing Kangaroo" is an example of general nonfiction. What is the difference between nonfiction and fiction based on this selection?

_____

_____

_____

31. What is the main idea of the selection?

_____

_____

_____

32. Why does the kangaroo most likely eat in the evening?

_____

_____

_____

Read each sentence. Write the meaning of the underlined word in each sentence.

33.

However, the kangaroo's unusual shape makes it difficult for it to move backward.

_____

34.

They are very interesting animals that are worthy of attention.

_____

35. List five important details about the kangaroo in the box.

Five Important Details About the Kangaroo

1.

2.

3.

4.

5.

Use for 36–37.

Spring Dreams

1 I sit in my classroom
2 Feeling a light spring breeze
3 I dream about having fun
4 Enjoying rainbows and sun
5 I smell the aroma of flowers
6 and refreshing rain showers
7 I dream about being free
8 when the dismissal bell rings at three

36. What type of writing is "Spring Dreams"? What tells you this? Use examples from the selection to support your answer.

_____

_____

_____

_____

_____

_____

_____

37. What do lines 3, 7, and 8 show?

_____

_____

_____

_____

_____

_____

Read each sentence. Rewrite the sentence using a proper noun for the underlined word.

38. Raul lives in a city, Texas.

_____

39. Lola speaks fluent another language.

_____

40. Lorenzo was born the day before a holiday.

_____

41. Martin lives on a street name.

_____

Read each sentence. Identify another meaning for the underlined word and use it in a sentence.

42. Isabella was blue because it was raining outside.

_____

43. The instructor used the answer key to grade the tests.

_____

44. Rewrite the paragraph. Use correct grammar, spelling, capitalization, and punctuation.

Karen is excited about thanksgiving day. her family members from Wisconsin are coming for a visit? They will eat a large tirkiy It will be a fun time for the hole family:

_____

_____

_____

_____

_____

_____

_____

_____

_____

_____

_____

_____

_____

_____

_____

_____

45. Choose one of the following types of writing and construct a well-organized essay. Write an introduction, several paragraphs, and a conclusion. You have 15 minutes to complete your essay.

- Fiction
- General nonfiction
- Biography
- Tale

_____

_____

_____

_____

_____

_____

_____

_____

_____

_____

_____

_____

_____

_____

_____

_____

_____

_____

Read each question and the answer choices that follow. Circle the letter of the correct answer.

1. What is the place value of 3 in 4,382,791?

  A millions

  B hundred thousands

  C ten thousands

  D thousands

2. Which is 346,294 rounded to the nearest ten thousand?

  A 300,000

  B 346,000

  C 346,300

  D 350,000

3.
$$\begin{array}{r} 718 \\ +\ 96 \\ \hline \end{array}$$

  A 804

  B 814

  C 824

  D 834

4.
$$\begin{array}{r} 2,124 \\ +\ 187 \\ \hline \end{array}$$

  A 1,937

  B 2,001

  C 2,201

  D 2,311

5.
$$\begin{array}{r} 1,043 \\ -\ 768 \\ \hline \end{array}$$

  A 265

  B 275

  C 285

  D 295

6.
$$\begin{array}{r} 23,451 \\ -\ 6,972 \\ \hline \end{array}$$

  A 16,479

  B 16,879

  C 17,479

  D 17,879

7. Peter bought a pair of shoes for $26.95 and a shirt for $12.86. How much did he spend in all?

  A $38.41

  B $38.81

  C $39.41

  D $39.81

8. Sandra had $8.73. She spent $3.89 on a new notebook. How much money did she have left?

  A $4.23

  B $4.84

  C $5.03

  D $5.24

9. 40 ounces = _____ cups

   A 3

   B 4

   C 5

   D 6

10. 8,000 milliliters = _____ liters

   A 8

   B 80

   C 800

   D 80,000

11. 9 yards = _____ feet

   A 0.9

   B 18

   C 20

   D 27

12. 7 pounds = _____ ounces

   A 14

   B 28

   C 70

   D 112

13. 400 centimeters = _____ meters

   A 0.4

   B 4

   C 40

   D 4,000

14. 22,000 grams = _____ kilograms

   A 2.2

   B 22

   C 220

   D 2,200

15. At which temperature would you need to wear a jacket outside?

   A 26°F

   B 62°F

   C 79°F

   D 83°F

16. $7 \times 10 =$

   A 0

   B 7

   C 35

   D 70

17. $9 \times 40 =$

   A 280

   B 320

   C 360

   D 380

18. $6 \times 400 =$

   A 24

   B 240

   C 2,400

   D 24,000

19. $718 \times 4 =$

    A 2,632

    B 2,672

    C 2,732

    D 2,872

20. $72 \div 9 =$

    A 6

    B 7

    C 8

    D 9

21. $540 \div 6 =$

    A 60

    B 70

    C 80

    D 90

22. $180 \div 1 =$

    A 0

    B 10

    C 90

    D 180

23. $62 \div 5 =$

    A 12 R1

    B 12 R2

    C 12 R3

    D 12 R4

24. $4,000 \div 100 =$

    A 4

    B 40

    C 400

    D 450

25. $468 \div 18 =$

    A 24

    B 25

    C 26

    D 27

26. $3,808 \div 34 =$

    A 92

    B 97

    C 107

    D 112

55. Graph each ordered pair.

(3, 3) (11, 3) (3, 11)

(1, 4) (15, 2) (11, 14)

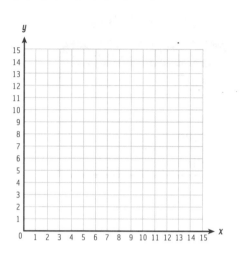

Draw a line on the grid connecting the first three pairs. What type of triangle is this?

_____

56. List all the possible outcomes of spinning both spinners at the same time.

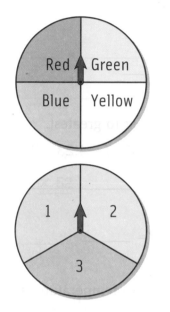

_____

_____

_____

_____

_____

_____

_____

_____

_____

_____

_____

_____

_____

_____

Read each question and the answer choices that follow. Circle the letter of the correct answer.

1. Grass is the first link in this meadow food chain. From what does the grass get energy?

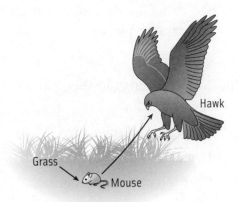

Grass

Mouse

Hawk

A   producers

B   decomposers

C   the sun

D   consumers

2. Which are the two types of bodies for invertebrates?

A   circular and elongated

B   circular and conifer

C   conifer and elongated

D   symmetrical and elongated

3. What plant structure absorbs water and nutrients from soil?

A   root

B   stem

C   leaf

D   cone

4. A seed will develop the roots, stem, and true leaves of the new plant when the seed—

A   terminates.

B   germinates.

C   becomes an aquifer.

D   becomes a conifer.

5. A **satellite** is an—

A   object in space that revolves around another object.

B   object in space that is stationary.

C   object in space that causes the water level on Earth to rise and fall.

D   object in space that causes precipitation on Earth.

6. **Gravitational pull** is—

   A the force that allows telescopes to see planets.

   B the force that allows the sun to give off light.

   C the force that one object exerts on another object.

   D the force that one object can turn into energy for another object.

7. The three main types of nutrients are—

   A vitamins, minerals, and carbohydrates.

   B carbohydrates, fats, and proteins.

   C vitamins, minerals, and fats.

   D unsaturated fats, saturated fats, and regular fats.

8. What is an ecosystem?

   A all of the interactions between living and nonliving things in an environment

   B all of the interactions between living things in an environment

   C all of the interactions between living things only in the pioneer stage

   D all of the interactions between living things only in succession

9. **Mechanical weathering** is the process in which—

   A sediments move downstream to form new structures.

   B sediments join together to create a new substance.

   C rocks join together into larger pieces.

   D rocks are broken down into smaller pieces.

10. Nerve endings in the skin are important for—

    A waste removal.

    B temperature control.

    C protection from germs.

    D sensing changes in the environment.

11. Hair color and skin color come from—

    A cells undergoing mitosis.

    B cell reproduction.

    C hair follicles.

    D melanin.

12. Which of the events on Miguel's list of events that can change Earth's landforms is most likely to cause a slow change to a landform?

avalanche
erosion
earthquake
volcano

A avalanche

B erosion

C earthquake

D volcano

13. Negatively charged particles in an atom are called—

A electrons.

B protons.

C atoms.

D magnets.

14. Which would cause Tim's socks to stick together after being taken out of the dryer?

A magnetic poles

B static electricity

C electrical circuits

D magnetic fields

15. Substances that allow a current to pass through them with the least amount of resistance are called—

A magnets.

B circuits.

C conductors.

D insulators.

16. **Inertia** is an object's tendency to—

A resist a change in motion.

B pull toward another object.

C push two objects toward each other.

D push two objects away from each other.

17. This is an example of what type of simple machine?

A wheel and axle

B wedge

C pulley

D lever

18. Which is the best description of a **depressant**?

A a chemical substance that slows down the function of the brain

B a chemical substance that kills disease-causing bacteria

C a chemical substance that speeds up the way the brain works

D a chemical substance that can only be prescribed by a doctor

19. Sarah has classified several animals. Which animal should she include with the animals in group B?

Group A	Group B
Vertebrates	Invertebrates
goat	earthworm
dog	octopus
turkey	spider
opossum	lobster
bear	

A frog

B hummingbird

C snake

D snail

20. Which is a part of an ocean ecosystem?

A saltwater

B fish

C plankton

D all of the above

21. Diseases such as polio and smallpox can be prevented by using—

A antibiotics.

B stimulants.

C vaccines.

D over-the-counter drugs.

22. Which is likely to cause the most erosion?

   A   a slowly moving river

   B   a pond

   C   a small creek

   D   a rapidly moving river

23. Building-block substances that rocks are made of are called—

   A   fossils.

   B   sediments.

   C   crystals.

   D   minerals.

24. Which is NOT a part of the water cycle?

   A   evaporation

   B   atmosphere

   C   maturation

   D   vapor

25. Heat can be transferred in three ways: conduction, convection, and radiation. Which picture shows heat transfer by convection?

   A

   B

   C

   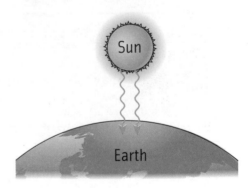

   D

   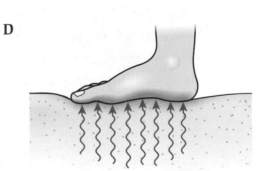

Read each question. Answer the questions in complete sentences.

26. Describe two ways that tobacco products can damage your health.

_____

_____

27. Describe the force that will be found between these two magnets when they are in the position shown. Use the terms *magnetic poles* and *magnetic fields* in your answer.

_____

_____

28. What is heat?

_____

_____

29. Describe how conductors, insulators, and resistors are related to each other. Give one example of a conductor and one example of an insulator.

_____

_____

_____

30. Explain how depressants and stimulants can negatively affect the body. Give one example of each.

_____

_____

_____

_____

_____

_____

_____

31. How are matter, mass, and volume related?

_____

_____

_____

_____

_____

_____

_____

_____

32. What are the three main gases found in air?

_____

_____

_____

_____

_____

_____

> Read each question and the answer choices that follow. Circle the letter of the correct answer.

1. Which of these forms the border between the United States and Mexico?

   A Sahara

   B Rio Grande

   C Rocky Mountains

   D Great Lakes

2. Which of these has the warmest temperatures in January?

   A Florida

   B Ohio

   C Michigan

   D Pennsylvania

3. The average weather conditions of a place or region is called the—

   A climate.

   B geography.

   C resources.

   D temperature.

4. All are precipitation EXCEPT—

   A hail.

   B rain.

   C snow.

   D earthquakes.

5. All are nonrenewable resources EXCEPT—

   A oil.

   B coal.

   C water.

   D gas.

6. Which imaginary line measures how far south a place is from the equator?

   A grid

   B Earth

   C longitude

   D latitude ·

7. Which of these rivers empties in Louisiana?

   A Hudson

   B Missouri

   C Mississippi

   D Buffalo

8. Which mountain system do the Northeast and Southeast share?

   A Appalachian Mountains

   B Rocky Mountains

   C Big Bear Mountain

   D Mount Rainier

9. Which group of Native Americans has lived in the Northeast for hundreds of years?

A   Cherokee

B   Natchez

C   Sioux

D   Iroquois

10. All are a part of the Interior Plains EXCEPT—

A   Nebraska.

B   Virginia.

C   Kansas.

D   Iowa.

11. In which Southwest state is the Grand Canyon located?

A   Arizona

B   Oklahoma

C   Texas

D   New Mexico

12. All were in the 1930s Dust Bowl EXCEPT—

A   North Dakota.

B   Kansas.

C   Nebraska.

D   Missouri.

13. Which river flows through the Central Valley?

A   Mississippi

B   San Joaquin

C   Colorado

D   Hudson

14. Irrigation made the Central Valley what type of leader?

A   political

B   industrial

C   agricultural

D   financial

15. Your state most likely has each of these EXCEPT—

A   a state dog.

B   a state flower.

C   a state bird.

D   a state motto.

16. What is the political center of your state called?

A   the state seal

B   the state capital

C   the state song

D   the state nickname

17. Which is the general name for the people who live in your town?

   A bankers

   B students

   C citizens

   D teachers

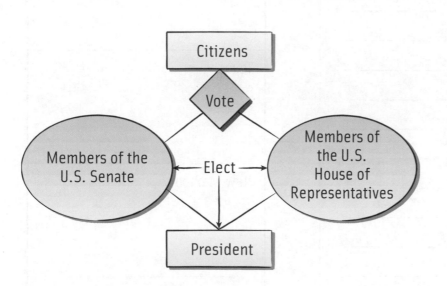

18. This diagram shows a—

   A democracy.

   B monarchy.

   C aristocracy.

   D dictatorship.

19. The process by which some people obtain American citizenship is—

   A immigration.

   B naturalization.

   C visualization.

   D legalization.

> **Read each question. Answer the questions in complete sentences.**

20. What is the significance of Nicodemus, Kansas?

_____

_____

_____

_____

_____

_____

_____

_____

_____

_____

_____

21. Name four crops that are grown in the Central Valley.

_____

_____

_____

_____

22. Fill in the chart, showing what products contribute to the Southwest's economy.

Southwest Resources
Arizona
Texas
New Mexico
Oklahoma

23. Name two groups of Native Americans associated with the Southwest.

_____

_____

24. Where are the wettest and driest places in the United States located? What are they?

_____

_____

_____

_____

25. Name two resources that contribute to the West's economy.

_____

_____

26. How are people resources? Give an example of how a person is a resource.

_____

_____

_____

_____

> **Read each selection and the questions that follow. Answer the questions in complete sentences.**

Use for 27–28.

The leaders of the different states got together to create this government. A government is kind of like a business. But it is owned by the people to work for the people. There is a book of rules that tells our government how it is supposed to do its work. It is called the United States Constitution.

The Constitution says that the government has three jobs. The first job is to make rules for the United States. These rules are called *laws*. The second job is to run the country. This means doing the things that the Constitution and laws of the United States say that the government should do. The third job has several parts: settling arguments when people disagree; deciding what a law means; and deciding whether people who are blamed for not obeying the law must be punished.

27. Name the three jobs of the government.

_____

_____

_____

_____

_____

28. How is the government like a business?

_____

_____

_____

_____

_____

Use for 29–30.

The first branch of the government is the legislative branch, which makes the laws. This branch is called Congress.

The second branch of the government is the executive branch. The leader of the executive branch is the president of the United States. The president makes sure that the government performs its jobs according to the laws that Congress makes. The president also commands the army, navy, and air force, and meets with leaders of other countries.

The third branch of the government is the judicial branch. It contains the courts. The courts decide how to punish people who do not obey the laws. The courts also settle arguments that people cannot settle themselves.

29. Fill in the chart with the three branches of government.

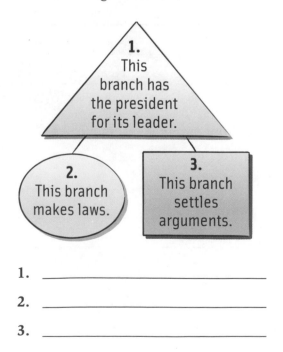

1. _____

2. _____

3. _____

30. How are laws related to the legislative branch and the judicial branch?

_____

_____

_____

_____

_____

_____

_____

_____

_____

_____

_____

_____

_____

_____

_____

_____

_____

_____

_____

_____

_____

**Read each selection in Part A and
answer the questions. Then read the
directions in Part B and write your essay.**

Part A: Short Answer

Use for 31–32.

The U.S. government collects taxes so it
can pay for things the country needs. For
example, taxes help to pay for highways
and bridges. U.S. taxes pay for uniforms,
ships, and airplanes for the army, navy,
and air force. Some of the taxes help
people who do not have much money to
buy things like food and medicine, and
to pay for a place to live. Taxes also help to
pay for doctors and scientists to discover
new medicines. These medicines can keep
people from getting sick and make them
better when they get sick. And, of course,
taxes pay the people who work for the
government—this includes the president
and the members of the Congress. (State
and local governments, like counties and
towns, also collect taxes. These taxes pay
for libraries, schools, teachers, and police
officers, for example.)

31. Why are taxes needed? How do they
affect you and your family? Give two
examples of how taxes are used.

_____

_____

_____

_____

_____

_____

_____

_____

_____

_____

_____

32. How do people who don't have
much money benefit from taxes?

_____

_____

_____

_____

_____

_____

_____

_____

_____

_____

Use for 33–34.

The Congress of the United States makes the country's laws that tell people what they can and also what they can't do. Some laws are made to protect people from certain crimes, such as stealing. Other laws make sure that the food that we eat is clean and healthy.

Congress is made up of two groups: the United States Senate and the United States House of Representatives. The people who live in the United States vote for the men and women who become a part of Congress. Voters must be at least 18 years old. Voting is part of a democracy. A democracy allows people to decide who will make laws in this country.

Members of the House of Representatives' term in office is two years. Members of the Senate, however, have a longer term in office—six years. At the end of their terms, there is an election in which they would have to win in order to stay a member of the House of Representatives or a senator.

Representatives and senators meet often to talk about the laws. Sometimes they talk about changing current laws, and sometimes they talk about making new ones. These discussions take place in Washington, D.C., in the Capitol.

33. How often are members of the House of Representatives and senators selected?

_____
_____
_____
_____
_____
_____
_____
_____
_____
_____
_____

34. How do laws help everyday citizens?

_____
_____
_____
_____
_____
_____
_____
_____
_____
_____
_____

SOCIAL STUDIES

Part B: Essay

> Write an essay using the information from the selections. You may also use your knowledge of social studies. Include an introduction, two supporting paragraphs, and a conclusion.

35. Support this statement in your essay:

The U.S. Constitution is an important document that helps the government make laws that take care of U.S. citizens.

_____

_____

_____

_____

_____

_____

_____

_____

_____

_____

_____

_____

_____

_____

_____

_____

_____

_____

Making the Grade: Everything Your 4th Grader Needs to Know

_____

_____

_____

_____

_____

_____

_____

_____

_____

_____

_____

_____

_____

_____

_____

_____

_____

_____

_____

_____

_____

_____

_____

_____

_____

Assessment Answers

PROMOTING LITERACY

1.	B	14.	D
2.	A	15.	A
3.	C	16.	B
4.	B	17.	A
5.	D	18.	B
6.	A	19.	B
7.	B	20.	B
8.	A	21.	A
9.	C	22.	D
10.	D	23.	B
11.	B	24.	C
12.	A	25.	D
13.	B	26.	A

27. The main idea of the selection is that Juanita became separated from her family during a trip to the zoo, until she retraced her steps to find them.

28. Answers will vary. Possible answer: Juanita learned that while she is anxious to see the various zoo animals, she should stay close to her family so that she does not lose sight of them again.

29. Characters: Juanita, her family; Setting: zoo; Problem: Juanita ran ahead of her family and lost sight of them; Resolution: She retraced her steps and found them.

30. The selection presents information about real people, places, things, and events—there isn't anything fictional in this story.

31. The main idea of the selection is that kangaroos are mammal marsupials that are large, powerful, and fast.

32. The kangaroo most likely eats in the evening because it is most comfortable eating in cooler temperatures.

33. Possible answers: awkward, challenging, hard, not easy, tough

34. Possible answers: awareness, focus, notice, observation, regard

35. Answers will vary. Possible answers: The kangaroo is found in Australia. The kangaroo is a mammal marsupial. The kangaroo travels by hopping. The kangaroo eats grass. The kangaroo can go for months without drinking water.

Scoring Rubric for Question 36:

4 POINTS
The student demonstrates a complete understanding of poetry by identifying the selection as poetry and accurately listing the features of a poem.

3 POINTS
The student demonstrates a nearly complete understanding of poetry by identifying the selection as a poem and accurately listing some features of a poem.

2 POINTS
The student demonstrates a partial understanding of poetry by identifying the selection as a poem and accurately listing a feature of a poem.

1 POINT
The student demonstrates little understanding of poetry by identifying the selection as a poem but not accurately listing the features of a poem.

0 POINTS
The student fails to demonstrate any understanding of poetry or its features.

37. Answers will vary. Possible answer: This student is fun-loving and restless. She is anxious for the school day to end so that she can go out and enjoy the nice spring weather.

38. Answers will vary. Possible answer: Raul lives in Houston, Texas.

39. Answers will vary. Possible answer: Lola speaks fluent Spanish.

40. Answers will vary. Possible answer: Lorenzo was born on the day before Thanksgiving.

41. Answers will vary. Possible answer: Martin lives on Elm Street.

42. Answers will vary. Possible answer: The sky was a beautiful shade of blue.

43. Answers will vary. Possible answer: Anaya used her key to open the door.

Scoring Rubric for Question 44:

4 POINTS
The student demonstrates a complete understanding of grammar, spelling, punctuation, and capitalization.

Example: Karen is excited about Thanksgiving Day. Her family members from Wisconsin are coming for a visit. They will eat a large turkey. It will be a fun time for the whole family.

3 POINTS
The student demonstrates a substantial understanding of grammar, spelling, punctuation, and capitalization, with a few errors.

2 POINTS
The student demonstrates adequate understanding of grammar, spelling, punctuation, and capitalization, with many significant errors.

1 POINT
The student demonstrates a limited understanding of grammar, spelling, punctuation,

Assessment Answers

and capitalization, only incorporating a few correct changes.

0 POINTS
The student demonstrates no understanding of grammar, spelling, punctuation, and capitalization.

Scoring Rubric for Question 45:

4 POINTS
The essay is well organized with a clear introduction, body, and conclusion. There are no errors in grammar, spelling, punctuation, or capitalization.

3 POINTS
The essay has an introduction, a body, and a conclusion. There are a few minor errors in grammar, spelling, punctuation, and capitalization.

2 POINTS
The essay lacks clear organization. There are significant errors in grammar, spelling, punctuation, and capitalization.

1 POINT
The essay lacks any organization. There are numerous errors in grammar, spelling, punctuation, and capitalization.

0 POINTS
The student demonstrates no understanding of how to organize an essay. There are so many errors in grammar, spelling, punctuation, and capitalization that the essay is unreadable.

MATH

1. B	14. B	27. A
2. D	15. A	28. A
3. B	16. D	29. B
4. D	17. C	30. A
5. B	18. C	31. C
6. A	19. D	32. C
7. D	20. C	33. B
8. B	21. D	34. B
9. C	22. D	35. B
10. A	23. B	36. C
11. D	24. B	37. D
12. D	25. C	38. C
13. B	26. D	39. B

40. 26,718; 26,817; 27,168; 27,618
41. 4,733
42. 828

43. Possible answers: 6:45, six forty-five, a quarter to seven
44. 4,472
45. 20
46. $\frac{1}{3}$
47. $\frac{1}{8}, \frac{1}{6}, \frac{1}{4}, \frac{1}{3}, \frac{1}{2}$
48. $\frac{2}{9}$
49. $5\frac{2}{3}$
50. $\frac{1}{2}$
51. 2.34, 2.43, 3.32, 4.23, 4.32
52. 3.67
53. range: 25; average: 84; mode: 86
54.

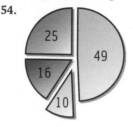

55. right triangle

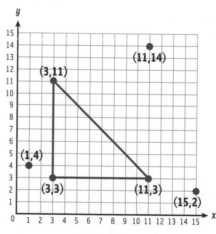

56. red and 1; red and 2; red and 3; green and 1; green and 2; green and 3; blue and 1; blue and 2; blue and 3; yellow and 1; yellow and 2; yellow and 3